MANAGING LANGUAGE IN *PIERS PLOWMAN*

Starting from a consideration of medieval definitions of the word as both *logos* and *verbum*, this reading of *Piers Plowman* shows that both scholastic and mystic attitudes to language are at play within the poem. Concepts of authority, authorship, interpretation and translation are explored as it becomes clear that these are inextricably linked, both in critical debates and in the text itself. It becomes increasingly apparent that the full potential of language can be realised only when we abandon the desire to express things unambiguously and allow ambiguity itself to be a power and a way of understanding. The rich fabric of Langland's text thus becomes something to enjoy and participate in, rather than battle with or seek to control. It also proves to be a meeting point for medieval and modern theories of text and reading, which are themselves enlivened by this complex and vivid poem.

Managing Language in 'Piers Plowman' focuses upon those sections of *Piers Plowman* which not only explore how, as Francis Bacon terms it, 'words manifestly force the understanding' but also illustrate how the confusions which language can create can be employed to lead towards different appreciations of understanding and away from the desire for 'innumerable controversies'. The quest for salvation within the poem provides a framework for Langland's illustration of how our reactions to language and knowledge interact to shape, if not actually dictate, the sort of understanding we achieve. Yet such speculative interests are constantly challenged by Wil's repeated question of how all this theology may help those caught up in the real world. So both he and the reader are brought back to realise that reading and writing are interpretative processes, carrying their own, intersecting spheres of responsibility. This realisation is supported by the circular nature of the poem, which denies its audience an end point, indicating that we must always seek to move on in appreciation and understanding, and in the application of that understanding. There can be no finite, all-encompassing reading or knowledge, but there is an invitation to continue or start again from a different place with an altered perspective – a chance to make new discoveries, or the same ones differently, and re-experience the process of the text.

G.A. RUDD lectures in English at the University of Liverpool.

Piers Plowman Studies

ISSN 0261–9849

Series Editor: James Simpson

Managing Language in
Piers Plowman

GILLIAN RUDD

D. S. BREWER

First published 1994
D. S. Brewer, Cambridge

ISBN 0 85991 392 9

D. S. Brewer is an imprint of Boydell & Brewer Ltd
PO Box 9, Woodbridge, Suffolk IP12 3DF, UK
and of Boydell & Brewer Inc.
PO Box 41026, Rochester, NY 14604-4126, USA

British Library Cataloguing-in-Publication Data
Rudd, Gillian
  Managing Language in "Piers Plowman". –
  (Piers Plowman Studies, ISSN 0261–9849; Vol.9)
  I. Title II. Series
  821.1
  ISBN 0–85991–392–9

Library of Congress Cataloging-in-Publication Data
Rudd, Gillian.
  Managing language in Piers Plowman / Gillian Rudd.
      p. cm. – (Piers Plowman studies, ISSN 0261–9849 ; 9)
  Includes bibliographical references and index.
  ISBN 0–85991–392–9 (hardback : acid-free paper)
  1. Langland, William, 1330?–1400? Piers the Plowman.
  2. Langland, William, 1330?–1400? – Knowledge – Language and
  languages. 3. Language and languages – Philosophy. 4. Knowledge,
  Theory of. 5. Philosophy, Medieval. 6. Ambiguity in literature.
  I. Title. II. Series.
  PR2017.L35R83 1994
  821.2'–dc20   93–40504

The paper used in this publication meets the minimum requirements
of American National Standard for Information Sciences –
Permanence of Paper for Printed Library Materials, ANSI Z39.48–1984

Printed in Great Britain by
St Edmundsbury Press Ltd, Bury St Edmunds, Suffolk

Contents

Part Four
MANAGING LANGUAGE

Acknowledgements

My thanks to Professor Alastair Minnis who has read this work in its several and various forms and provided comments and help constantly. For the less direct, but nonetheless welcome, influence of friends and colleagues at York and Liverpool I am also grateful and mention must also be made of Dr Avril Bruten, who first put me in the way of Wil's vision. Mr James Simpson has given assistance beyond the call of a series editor, which has been much appreciated; as has the patience of the Boydell & Brewer team who saw the results into print. The remaining errors and inadequacies are inevitably my own. Finally thanks to all my family, without whose unfailing support and humour this project would have foundered.

Abbreviations

AHDLMA	Archives d'histoire doctrinale et littéraire du moyen âge
arg.	argumentum
Bonaventure	*S. Bonaventurae Opera Omnia*. Quaracchi, 1882–1902
Bromyard, *SP*	John Bromyard (Johannes de Bromyard). *Summa Predicatium*. Nuremberg: Koberger, 1518
Catholicon	Balbus, Giovanni de, *Catholicon*. Mainz, 1460. Westmead Hants. Gregg International, 1971
CCSL	Corpus Christianorum, Series Latina. Turnholt: Brepols, 1954–
Henry of Ghent, *SQ*	Henry of Ghent. *Summa Questionum Ordinariarum*. Franciscan Institute Text Series 5. Paris, 1520; rpt. New York: St Bonaventure, 1953
Hilton, *Scale* 1	Walter Hilton *The Scale of Perfection*. Book I. Ed. Wykes, B.E. Michigan: Ann Arbor University Microfilms International, 1957, 1989
Hilton, *Scale* 2	An Edition from the Manuscripts of Book II of Walter Hilton's Scale of Perfection. Ed. Hussey, S.S. Ph.D. London, 1962
JEGP	Journal of English and Germanic Philology
PIMS	Pontifical Institute of Mediaeval Studies
PL	Patrologia Cursus Completus, Series Latina. Ed. Migne, J-P. Paris, 1844–64
q.	*quaestio*
resp.	*responsio*

Introduction

> Words still manifestly force the understanding, throw every-
> thing into confusion, and lead mankind into vain and innumer-
> able controversies and fallacies.[1]

'Managing Language in *Piers Plowman*' focuses upon those sections of the
poem which explore not only how 'words manifestly force the understanding' but also illustrate how the confusion which language can create
can be employed to lead mankind towards different appreciations of understanding and away from the desire for 'innumerable controversies'. In *Piers
Plowman* the quest for salvation provides a framework for Langland's illustration of how our reactions to language and knowledge interact to shape, if
not actually dictate, the sort of understanding we achieve. It is in Passus
VIII–XIV that Langland illustrates 'the vain and innumerable controversies
and fallacies' which do indeed throw Wil into confusion and often the
readers with him, as a succession of personifications provide a plethora of
answers to the question of what Dowel is or entails. It is, therefore, upon
this section of the text, comprising the third and fourth of Wil's visions, that
the following reading of the *Piers Plowman* B-Text concentrates.

The way one seeks to understand things, and the language one uses to do
so, are determined to a large extent by the type of knowledge one is seeking.
Two major, but widely different attitudes, are reflected in *Piers Plowman*,
both of which were recognised and defined by followers of each school of
thought. A brief summary of the two is provided by the *Summa Theologica*,
ascribed to Alexander of Hales and completed by his pupils in 1245:

> . . . alius est modus scientiae, qui est secundum comprehensionem veri-
> tatis per humanam rationem; alius est modus scientiae secundum affec-
> tum pietatis per divinam traditionem. – Primus modus definitivus debet

Unless otherwise indicated in the notes, all B-Text references and quotations are taken from
A.V.C. Schmidt, ed., *The Vision of Piers Plowman* (London, 1978); all those from the C-Text are
from D. Pearsall, ed., *Piers Plowman by William Langland, an edition of the C-Text*, York
Medieval Texts, second series (London, 1981).

1 Francis Bacon, *Novum Organum*, Book 1, ed. and tr. Basil Montague, *The Works of Francis
Bacon Lord Chancellor of England: A New Edition*, 19 (London, 1831), 36.

esse, divisivus, collectivus; et talis modus debet esse in humanis scientiis quia apprehensio veritatis secundum humanam rationem explicatur per divisiones, definitiones et ratiocinationes. – Secundus modus debet esse praeceptivus, exemplificativus, exhortativus, revelativus, orativus, quia ii modi competunt affectui pietatis.

(. . . one is the method of science which operates through the understanding of the truth of human reason, while another operates through the inculcation of a pious disposition [*affectus pietatis*] by means of divine instruction. The first mode must be by definition, analysis and deduction; such a mode must exist in human branches of knowledge because the apprehension of truth in accordance with human reasoning is unfolded through analysis, definitions and logical arguments. The second method must be by way of precept, example, exhortation, revelation and prayer, because those methods are appropriate to a pious disposition.)[2]

If the approach chosen sees as its end the type of knowledge which enable its followers to define things in precise terms, the form of language, or discourse, favoured will reflect these priorities by relying on processes of deduction and definition to make points and drive home arguments. If, however, an alternative appreciation of knowledge is selected, one whose practitioners aim to achieve a state of understanding which reaches beyond the bounds of language and definition, then the discourse used will tend to be more emotive and figurative, making use of the affective power of words to evoke a sense of understanding and using a higher proportion of images to describe the sensation of understanding, rather than seeking to define it in precise terms. For the purposes of this reading of *Piers Plowman* the first way has been termed 'deductive', the second 'affective'. The attitudes towards knowledge and language associated with each discourse are explained and discussed in Part One.

The fact that knowledge, language and authority are interlinked is illustrated at an early stage in *Piers Plowman* when Wil voices the central concern of the poem in its initial form:

Teche me to no tresor, but tel me this ilke –
How I may save my soule, that seint art yholden. (B.I.83–84)

The formulation of Wil's plea to Holi Chirche may be seen to include all three major elements of managing language which are in play in this sudy of the text. The idea of authority is evident in the phrase 'that seint art yholden': Wil does not ask how he can save his soul until he knows that the woman he addresses commands respect and authority. Holi Chirche is considered to be a suitable figure to ask because she is regarded as a saint, a

2 Alexander of Hales, *Summa Theologica*, Quaestio 1, cap. 4, art. 1, resp. 2, Vol. 1 (Quaracchi, 1924), 8b. The translation is based on that found in A.J. Minnis and A.B. Scott, eds., *Medieval Literary Theory and Criticism c.110–c.1375; The Commentary Tradition* (Oxford, 1988), p. 214.

position which has been conferred upon her – 'yholden' is passive. This assumes that the ways such prestige is conferred is reliable – an assumption which is challenged when Lady Mede is encountered, since her social standing and the respect she commands are revealed to be the result of corruption. Furthermore, the request to be told – 'tel me this ilke' – assumes that the kind of knowledge Wil seeks here can be told and learnt intellectually. This attitude governs the deductive approach to knowledge through reason, but it is undermined by the affective approach, which encourages its followers to experience understanding individually, and put more trust in such direct apprehensions than in scholarly definitions. Finally, the demand to be taught raises questions of how best any kind of knowledge may be passed on, and indeed whether it is preferable to attempt to pass it on or to put others in the way of gaining it for themselves. Discussion of communicating knowledge leads into the realms of interpretation, a practice which involves knowledge, language and also some form of authority, since without these there is no reason to call any particular reading an interpretation rather than a misunderstanding.

This study of the interaction of knowledge and language in *Piers Plowman* has shown that both the deductive and affective discourses are present in the text and that they are constantly undermined, not only by each other but also by the emphasis in the poem on where the ordinary people who have responsibilities in the world and have very little direct access to learning, may find reliable guidance on how to live in order to merit salvation. When looking at the definitions of Dowel, Dobet and Dobest in Passus VIII–XIV in particular, the opportunities for misguidance, unintentional or otherwise, become strikingly apparent, especially as represented by the figures of the Doctor of Divinity and Haukyn. Both these figures reveal how easily the learning they have acquired can be misinterpreted and misapplied, mainly because they over-emphasize one aspect of their knowledge at the expense of the others. The need for moderation and modification in the light of alternative views is thus presented in terms of how such misplaced emphasis adversely affects the way one lives. Recognition of this need for constant modification and re-evaluation leads to a realisation of how unsure language itself is. Words are not the thing itself but must be interpreted, and that process of interpretation is fraught with difficulties. The idea of interpretation is most evident in the Pardon scene, where the introduction of a text within the poem gives Langland the opportunity to present a variety of reactions to a text which is assumed to be utterly authoritative because it comes from Truth, but can be properly understood and enacted only by the supposedly uneducated person of the ploughman.

However, as well as demonstrating that a concern with the ambiguous nature of language is fundamental to the poem, this study has also shown that attitudes towards texts which twentieth-century readers tend to regard as modern, are not only well suited to reading medieval literature but also are not as far removed from some medieval conceptions as may be supposed. Undoubtedly one of the most evident similarities between the medieval and a branch of the modern is a lack of concern for discovering what the writer might have meant. Preference is given to what the readers themselves may find in and bring to the text. As Beryl Smalley has pointed out, the reader took 'less interest in the mind of the author and more in the author's product; he put his own meaning into it. The text was more alive than its author to him'.[3] Given this, any approach to a text which emphasizes the interaction between the text and the reader, rather than the author's intention, may be used with impunity for exploring medieval works. The fact that there are precious few biographical facts about Langland is an additional incentive for making use of such criticism.

Since this reading of *Piers Plowman* concentrates on the language and discourses in the text rather than on the possible biographical, social or political aspects of the poem, it has not seemed out of place to make use of such theorists as Foucault, Barthes and de Man when their writings have provided useful insights into the text.[4] Indeed, although this could in no way be termed a post-structuralist or deconstructionist analysis of *Piers Plowman*, it demonstrates that the descriptions of reading and the text put forward by some post-structuralists, can be illuminating, especially when medieval critical thought is taken into account. In the light of this, George Steiner's description of the difference between deconstruction and traditional criticism, given in *Real Presences*, is particularly interesting. He defines the issue as quite simply that of the meaning of meaning as it is re-insured by the postulate of the existence of God:

> "In the beginning was the word". There was no such beginning, says deconstruction; only the play of sounds and markers amid the mutations of time.[5]

For Steiner, deconstruction is a view of literature at the furthest remove from any view based on a belief in the Divine Word. To make the contrast clearer he uses the image of the Ark of the Covenant, guarantee of both God and *logos*.

---

[3] B. Smalley, *A Study of the Bible in the Middle Ages*, 3rd edn (Oxford, 1982), p. vii.

[4] James Simpson's approach to the text in *'Piers Plowman', An introduction to the B-Text* (London and New York, 1990) is more orientated towards the institutions of Langland's day. It is interesting to note, therefore, that one of his major conclusions is that 'the meaning of the poem lies not so much in one kind of reading or another, but in the movement between them'. He also makes use of notions of discourse adapted from, but based on, those put forward by Foucault. This position is clearly not far removed from my own.

[5] G. Steiner, *Real Presences* (London and Boston, 1989), p. 120.

Deconstruction dances in front of the Ark. This dance is at once playful . . .
and, in its subtler practioners (Paul de Man, for example), instinct with
sadness. For the dancers know that the Ark is empty.[6]

However, the distinction is not as clear-cut as Steiner implies since whether
the Ark is full or empty makes no difference, for in either case the area in
which the human *verbum* exists is in the serious play of the dance in front of
the Ark. In the creed of deconstruction (according to Steiner) there can be
only play because there is no finally determined meaning or Truth; in the
creed of the *logos* there is play because, although there is an arch-signifier, or
ultimate Truth, it is beyond human expression. The result for the dancers is
the same. The difference lies not between deconstruction and religious belief, but between both these attitudes and those which seek to enter the ark
and define its contents.

This leads to one further point about *Piers Plowman*. Like many Middle
English texts (e.g. *Pearl* and *Sir Gawain and the Green Knight*) it does not
come to a final end, but instead returns the reader to the text. This trick of
denying the audience a final full stop is in accordance with the view that
one must always seek to move on in understanding, or in application of that
understanding. Even in Ruysbroek, where the image is that of a ladder, one
does not stop when one reaches the seventh, topmost, rung, but must
always be going up and down.[7] The message is surely that stasis is death, or
at least an invitation to corruption. This is demonstrated in *Piers Plowman*
where the several attempts to establish ideal societies are undermined when
it appears that the ideal has been achieved. Every attempt at a new, reformed community may seem to succeed for a while, but the moment it
stops trying to move towards perfection, it must fall, must be undermined
by either the laziness of wasters and the cold blast of famine, or by the
decadence of its members, who finally allow flattery to corrupt them. Unity
itself crumbles in the poem because its inhabitants do not remember that
appearances can deceive, especially the appearances of friars, and they do
not test the flatterer's ability with language when he speaks graciously
(B.XX.331–357). Yet the attempts must still be made, for as long as one is
searching one may be getting nearer the truth, nearer to knowledge and
understanding, or at least staving off corruption and stagnation. The same
principle applies to the desire to rely solely on either the deductive or the
affective route to knowledge. Neither route can offer permanently reliable
guidance which will be applicable to all people at all times, for people and
circumstances change. This is also the reason why there can be no single,

6 G. Steiner, *Real Presences*, p. 122.
7 Jan van Ruysbroek, *The Seven Steps of the Ladder of Spiritual Love*, tr. F. Sherwood Taylor
(London, 1943), p. 61.

concrete, unchanging definition of Dowel, only a description which reflects the type of knowledge and discourse dominant at the time.

Discourse, according to Foucault, is the place where power and knowledge join together. He also points out that while discourse transmits power, it also 'undermines and exposes it, renders it fragile and makes it possible to thwart it'.[8] This dual ability is one which David Lawton specifically attributes to allegory:

> Allegory deals in power, knowledge, authority; equally it can challenge or negate them. It constructs ideology, and can deconstruct it.[9]

Piers Plowman is surely to be regarded as a text in which the processes of transmission, production and simultaneous testing and subversion are enacted. It is an exposition of the play between the discourses of learning (*scientia*) and wisdom (*sapientia*), of the interaction between knowledge and understanding and an exploration of how power and authority can be gained, bestowed and undermined; and because it is all this, it is also a demonstration of the creative power of language. Above all it is a vivid example of how the impossibility of finding a form of language which expresses any form of comprehension fully and unambigiously can provide the basis for a rich and demanding text. For Langland's poem illustrates that there is only the attempt, which fails. Yet for *Piers Plowman* the recognition of this failure is not regarded as the end of the attempt, but an invitation to try again from a different perspective and a chance to make new discoveries and experience a wider understanding.

---

[8] M. Foucault, *The History of Sexuality, Volume One*, tr. R. Hurley (Holdsworth, 1979), pp. 100 and 101.
[9] D. Lawton, 'The Subject of *Piers Plowman*', *The Yearbook of Langland Studies*, 1 (1987), p. 25.

Part One

LANGUAGE, KNOWLEDGE
AND AUTHORITY

The Apostle tells us that in the beginning was the Word. He gives us no assurance as to the end.[1]

[1] George Steiner, 'The Retreat from the Word', *Language and Silence: Essays on Language, Literature and the Inhuman* (1970; rpt. New York: 1977), p. 12.

1

Language and the *Logos*

The opening of St John's Gospel provides an almost overwhelming claim for the immense power of language. The Word is creator, mediator, redeemer and co-eternal with the Supreme Godhead. With such a manifesto at its heart Christianity, and following that much of western thought, was bound to become powerfully logocentric, and therefore to give words and language a privileged position in society. The symmetry at the heart of this perception of language is expressed with calm logic by St Bonaventure (1221–74) in his *Breviloquium*:

> ut sicut genus humanum in esse exierat per Verbum increatum et in culpam ceciderat deserendo Verbum inspiratum; sic a culpa resurgeret per Verbum incarnatum.
>
> (Just as mankind came into being through the uncreated Word and fell into sin by abandoning the inspired Word, so it should rise from sin through the incarnate Word.)[2]

Bonaventure thus places the Word at the heart of every stage of mankind's history and, by implication, at the heart of every individual's spiritual progress also. In doing so he stresses the eternal, uncreated nature of the Word which John declares with his opening statement *In principio erat Verbum*. It is the Word which exists from the beginning; it is the Word with which John starts, and with which every writer, especially a Christian writer, must come to terms.

The *Glossa Ordinaria* and Nicholas of Lyra's Literal and Moral Postills (completed 1331) all stress the principle of divinity which John asserts. As the *Glossa Ordinaria* says, John's first sentence refutes any possibility of Christ's life having begun with the nativity:

---

[2] St Bonaventure, *Breviloquium*, IV, 1, conclusio. *S. Bonaventura Opera Omnia*, V (Quaracchi, 1891), 242a. Tr. E.E. Nemmers, *Breviloquium* (St Louis and London, USA, 1946), p. 111.

> Contra eos qui propter temporalem Christi natiuitatem dicebant Christum non semper fuisse, incipit de aeternitate verbi dicens: In principio erat verbum.
>
> (Against those who, concerning Christ's birth on earth, said that Christ had not always existed, he begins, declaring the eternity of the word: In the beginning was the Word.)[3]

From this we progress through the co-existence of Word and God to the concept of the creative word, an aspect Bonaventure's summary omits. This concept takes the word beyond a purely passive role as a medium for simply communicating or reflecting people's views, to being an active, creative power. Indeed, John goes on to present the Word as the life-giving force:

> Omnia per ipsum facta sunt: & sine ipso est nihil. Quod factum est in ipso, vita erat: & vita erat lux hominum.
>
> (All things were made through Him: and without Him was nothing made. What was made in Him was life: and the life was the light of man.)

Such powerful statements, asserting the origin of the Word and its co-existence with the Godhead, not only give no reassurance as to the consequences of the creative power of language, but also raise disturbing questions as the implication seems to be that God as *Logos* was directly responsible for the evil which manifestly exists in the world: a conclusion apparently contrary to the nature of God as Supreme Good. This paradox is resolved by a very specific reading of the word '*nihil*', according to which it is interpreted as meaning 'things which count as nothing'. The *Glossa Ordinaria* presents it like this:

> . . . dixit de natura filij, de operatione ipsius supponit omnia per ipsum facta sunt. omnia id est quicquid est siue in substantia: siue in aliqua naturali proprietate. Ecce auctor bonorum. Et sine ipso factum est nihil: quia non ab eo est quod non est naturaliter, sed quod est peruersio naturae: vt malum siue idolum. Ecce non est auctor malorum.
>
> (. . . he spoke of the nature of the son, of the works of the same he added that all things were made through him. All things, that is whatever exists either in substance or in other natural properties. Behold the author of good. And without him was made nothing: because what does not come from him is not natural, but is perverse to nature: such as evil or idols. Behold he is not the author of evil things.)[4]

---

[3] Quotations for the *Glossa Ordinaria* are taken from *Sacra bibla cum glossa ordinaria et expositione lyre litterali et morali*, 7 vols (n.p., pr. J. Petri and J. Froben; 1508), vol. 5, f. 185v. All references to the *Glossa Ordinaria* and Nicholas of Lyra's Postilla and Moral gloss are to this edition.

[4] *Glossa Ordinaria*, vol. 5, f. 185v.

The implication here is that all things were created according to the good laws of nature and that any evil is a subsequent turning away from the original intention of the creator. The *Glossa* later includes a quotation from Augustine as further elucidation, which simultaneously declares the uncreated nature of the Word and its innate good:

> Non est creatura per quem omnis creatura facta est. Malum non est factum per ipsum: nec ipsum idolum: qua nihil sunt, nulla sua natura subsistunt.
>
> (It is not through a created [being] that all created things are made. Evil is not made by him: nor idols: insofar as they are nothing, they do not exist in any way in his nature.)[5]

Evil, or, more accurately, the possibility of evil is thus regarded as a facet of a created being, a sign of its lack of divinity. As it is not a positive attribute of divinity it can be declared to be nothing.

Nicholas of Lyra's Literal Postill refutes this line of reasoning and takes the much more straightforward approach of reading the phrase as simple emphatic repetition of the previous declaration of universal creation:

> Et sine ipse factum est nihil. quia est spirituales creaturae sunt a deo sicut ab efficiente.
>
> (And without him nothing was made, that is the spiritual creatures are from God just as from an efficient [power].)[6]

Both corporal and spiritual things are created by the same power; there is no distinction. Nor does Nicholas see the need of the Manichean notion of two primary causes, one good, one evil, to explain the occurrence of evil. In fact his refutation of this theory implies a belief in synderesis – an innate inclination in all things for the good – which finally results in a depiction of the devil as not entirely evil:

> Alij autem dixerunt quod per nihil intelligitur diabolus: quem dicunt esse sine verbo factum. Sed hoc patet esse falsum: quia diabolus non est natura malus. Si enim malum esset integrum: seipsum destruerit. & ideo natura ipsius bona est. & ideo facta est a verbo, a quo omnia bona procedunt.
>
> (But others have said that by 'nothing' must be understood the devil: whom, they say, was made without the word. But this is obviously false: because the devil is not evil by nature. For if he were utterly evil he would have destroyed himself, and therefore his nature is good, and therefore was made by the word, from which all good things come.)[7]

---

[5] *Ibid.*
[6] Nicholas of Lyra, *Glossa*, vol. 5, f. 186r.
[7] *Ibid.*

Evil is seen here as a deliberate turning away from the good for which all creation was originally intended; it is not itself a separate entity, nor the creation of another Prime Mover which created evil just as God created good. It is not the devil's nature that is evil, but his choice of how he uses and develops it. The creative powers of the Word are undiminished and the innate good of all creation asserted, but at the same time the existence of evil has been acknowledged.

Yet this assertion of the power of words, of language, also admits the possibility of wrongful creation, or abuse of creation, and with that comes great responsibility. For the potential of creating evil at the same time as good, even inadvertently, seems to lay the onus on writers, who also create through words, to ensure that the right use of their creations is correctly understood. Yet this demands a certain control of both the creation and any who may encounter it, which may not be possible. If the creations of the Divine Word cannot be safeguarded from misuse, how much more open to abuse and misinterpretation are the far lesser creations of human words. All writers must be aware that their words may have a different, even opposite, effect from the one they intended, and, unlike the Divine Word, they cannot redeem the consequences of any falling away from the original intention.

George Steiner refers to 'the god-rivalling, therefore potentially sacrilegious character of the poet'.[8] There is, of course, one crucial difference between the poet's language and the original creating Word; the poet works with a limited, mortal language, which by its nature can never attain a true expression, let alone an imitation, of the divine. Nevertheless, religious writers strive to give some intimation of that divine language in their work, particularly when they are dealing with such topics as spiritual enlightenment or the way to achieve salvation. The continuing difficulty is how to express an unlimited Word or *Logos* by means of a limited word, and avoid misconstructions which could lead to wrong readings. This knotty problem and the concomitant issue of the writers' responsibility, which both originate in the opening of St John's Gospel, are dealt with more particularly in the definitions of *Logos* and *verbum* found in Giovanni de Balbus' *Catholicon*, the great Medieval Latin dictionary, which was completed by 1286.

It is perhaps odd to find a Greek word listed in a Latin dictionary, especially where there appears to be a clear Latin equivalent, yet the Catholicon lists both *Logos* and *verbum*, thereby indicating that there are two distinct concepts at work here: the notion of the divine, ontological *logos*, usually termed in Modern English 'the Word', and the more everyday perception of language as an essentially human construct, listed by Balbus under *verbum*. The two are linked, but the difference is crucial as it intimates a broad division into two discourses.

---

[8] G. Steiner, 'Silence and the Poet', *Language and Silence*, p. 39.

Logos

The entry under *logos* is short and seems to be primarily a restatement of the opening of St John's Gospel. It reads:

> Logos id est sermo vel racio secundum Hugitio. vel secundum Jeronem in epistula ad Paulinum. In principio inquit erat verbum et verbum erat apud deum et deus erat verbumque. logos grece multa significat. Nam et verbum est, et racio et supputacio, et causa uniuscuiusque rei per quam sunt singula que subsistunt. que universa recte intellegimus in Christo, quare videlicet Christus dicitur verbum capitulumque ad patris dicentis manifestacionem. causa capitulum ad reorum creationem. Racio capitulum ad creatorum ordinacionem. Suppotacio capitulum ad ordinatorum distinctiones.

> (Logos, that is speech or reason according to Hugitio [of Pisa]. Or according to Jerome in his letter to Paulinus: In the beginning, he says, was the word and the word was with god and god was the word. Logos in Greek means many things. For it is word, and reason, and reckoning and the origin of those things for which there are individuals which act as substitutes, through which we rightly understand the universals in Christ, namely because Christ is called the word and head in order to make manifest the words of the father. [He is] the head of causes for the creation of things; the head reason for ordering creation; the head reckoning for distinguishing the orders [of things].)[9]

Here, although the first definitions of *logos* are as the human faculties of speech or reason, we are immediately moved on to the definition of *logos* as divine, and given a more detailed exposition of its meaning. Jerome not only emphasises its divine nature, but also makes it clear that the Greek term includes more concepts than its apparent equivalent in Latin. It is more than just *verbum*, it is *racio* and *supputacio* as well. The importance of the inclusion of *racio* in this definition will become apparent when the figure of Reson is discussed; here it is the aspects of understanding and assessing or ordering that concern us. The Word is more than speech, it is revealed as a power for translating and rendering all things comprehensible – *ad patris dicentis manifestacionem*. Just as Christ is the mediator between man and God, so language too is a mediator, either between man and man in the form of speech or between God and man in the form of understanding.

The inclusion of the ability to understand as a facet of the Word is not unique to Balbus. It is evident also in the glosses on the opening of St John where the verse *Quod factum est in ipso, vita erat: et vita erat lux hominum* is expanded in Nicholas of Lyra's Moral Postill as follows:

> Quod factum est in ipso, vita erat. Nam omnis creatura in verbo pre-existit intellegibiliter. Intelligere vero est vivere: & intellectio vita.

---

[9] Balbus, *Catholicon*, unfol. s.v. 'logos' (Mainz, 1460; facsimile rpt. Aldershot, 1971).

(What was made in him was life. For all creation existed intelligibly before in the word. Indeed to understand is to live: and understanding is life.)[10]

He goes on to declare that the understanding, or intellect, is the light of man. So, by bringing aspects of understanding and comprehension into his defintion of *logos*, Balbus has included connotations of a life-giving force, for, as Nicholas states, 'to understand is to live'. When we follow the lead of this entry and turn to Jerome's letter to Paulinus, we find that the notion of understanding is a key concept and, further, a caution that understanding is not the equivalent of learning.

In this letter (which had acquired a certain familiarity through being included in the "Paris Bible" and later adopted as a Prologue for the Wycliffite Bible) Jerome contrasts the advanced training and learning of the Pharisees with the simple understanding of the untutored 'churls', Peter and John, suggesting that they achieved a level of understanding which baffled the Pharisees, despite all their learning. Furthermore, he implies that the opening of St John's Gospel contains a complete understanding of all that the Greek word *logos* signifies.

> The pharysews ben stonyed in þe doctryne of þe lorde & wondren in peture & Ioon . how þey cunnen þe lawe: siþ lettre3 þey lerned not what euer forsoþe to oþer men excersise . & eche day þinkyng in þe lawe was wont to 3euen: þat to hem þe holy gost tolde. & After þat it is (I)wryten; þey werun goddis tau3t men . þat is able men to li3tly ben (I) tau3t of god.[11]

Jerome's position is clear: even the most unlearned man may come to a true understanding of the *logos* if his disposition is such that he can be taught directly by the spirit. John was one such, and so his description of the Word contains a greater understanding of the concept than may be found in many more learned works. Once again the elements of understanding, communication, reason and order, are all contained in the concept of the Divine Word.

Yet post-lapsarian man is incapable of direct understanding of Truth. Even John was denied full unveiled vision as the repeated, acknowledged lacunae of Revelations demonstrate. To understand may be to live, and this light of understanding may be the light of man, but it is a light which shines in darkness. As Bonaventure puts it, after the Fall

---

[10] Nicholas of Lyra, *Moraliter*, f. 186r.

[11] *The Epistle of Seynt Jerome*, a Middle English translation of Jerome's *Epistula ad Paulinam*, printed as a 'Prologus' to the Wyclifite Bible in *MS Bodley 959 Genesis-Baruch 3.20 in the Earlier Version of the Wyclifite Bible*, vol. 1, ed. Conrad Lindberg (Stockholm, 1959), 28.

. . . ineptus erat ad divinam virtutem imitandam, ad lucem cognoscen-
dum. ad bonitatem diligendam.

(. . . man was unsuited for imitating divine virtue, for learning of its light, for
loving its goodness.)[12]

Moreover, since mankind was prevented by its carnal nature from aspiring
to direct knowledge of the *logos*, the *logos* had to descend to human level: *ad
eripiendum hominem de hoc statu Verbum caro factum est* (in order to rescue
man from this state 'The Word was made flesh').[13]

In order for the Word to be comprehensible, or even approachable, by
man it must take on a 'veil of flesh'. The Incarnate Word is not only a
redemptive force but also a mediating one, a meeting point of two different
languages – the pure, divine *logos* and the human *verbum*. It is thus involved
in an act of translation, a carrying-over from one state to another of understanding through language and meaning. This process necessarily involves
some degree of approximation, since man is incapable of understanding the
Divine Word in its transparent state, and so any exact translation which
encompassed all that the *logos* signified would be equally incomprehensible. As Tzevtan Todorov points out in his *Introduction to Poetics*

. . . the invisibility of language exists only as a limit (to which we come
closest, probably, in the case of a purely utilitarian, functional discourse); a
limit which it is necessary to conceive but which we must not attempt to
grasp in the pure state. Try as we will to consider words as the simple
garment of the ideal body, Pierce tells us that this garment can never be
completely shed, but only exchanged for another that is more diaphanous.
Language cannot vanish completely, becoming a pure metaphor of
meaning.[14]

In other words, we must have the ideal of a transparent language which
describes and communicates exactly, but we must also recognise that this is
an ideal and so is unachievable. Rather than passing on its matter wholly
and precisely, language subtly alters what it describes by interposing a layer
between matter (or signified) and perceiver. This means that any description is to some extent an approximation or estimate of the object described.

This position is supported, in terms of Christian theology, by the dogma
that it is only man who speaks, who has need of language.[15] The angels,
who have direct apprehension of God, do not speak (unless to man), they

---

12 Bonaventura, *Breviloquium*, IV, 1, p. 241b; tr. p. 110.
13 *Ibid.*
14 Tzevtan Todorov, *Introduction to Poetics*, tr. R. Howard (Brighton, 1981), p. 22.
15 Zygmunt Baranski's article, 'Dante's Biblical Linguistics', *Lectura Dantis* (Fall 1989), pp.
105–43, is of interest here, especially pp. 107–110. He points out that Dante regarded
language as a gift unique to humans which is evidence of God's love for mankind, but is
necessary only on earth. The ability to speak is a sign of rationality, linked to the exercise

intuit. The point of the garment, however diaphanous, is that it gives some indication of the shape it clothes; once that is no longer required the garment, language, disappears. This in turn leaves us with the notion of language as essentially human and it is this view of language as a man-made construct that is found in definitions of *verbum*.

Verbum

The concept of language as a human construct – *verbum* – is far less complex than that of *logos* since it is regarded as a tool whose function can be analysed and understood, rather than as a force. For St Augustine language is one of the many man-made institutions which surround us, and which have come about in order to serve a precise purpose – that of communication. As such it has clear limitations, the most fundamental being that language works as a form of contract, which is reliable only if both sides maintain the agreement:

> Namque omnia, quae ideo valent inter homines, quia placuit inter eos, ut valeant, instituta hominum sunt. . . . Sed quia multis modis simile aliquid alicui potest esse, non constant talia signa inter homines nisi consensus accedat.
>
> (For all practices which have value among men because men agree among themselves that they are valuable, are human institutions. . . . But since one thing may resemble another in a great variety of ways, signs are not valid among men except by common consent.)[16]

This essentially human aspect of language is reflected in the entry for *verbum* in the *Catholicon*, which begins with an etymology relating *verbum* firmly to the terrestrial, leaving reference to the divine word until later in the entry:

> verbum a uerbero . . . derivitur hoc uerbum . . . sermo. quare in eius perlacione uerberatur aer. vnde et quedam pars oracionis per excellenciam dicitur uerbum quare frequencius in eius perlacione uerberatur aer quam in perlacione alterius partis.
>
> (verbum. this verbum . . ., speech, is derived from 'to vibrate'. For the air is vibrated by carrying it. And from this each part of speech is called a 'word' by excellent reasoning because the air vibrated more frequently in carrying them than in carrying other parts.)[17]

Underlying this presentation of words and speech is the notion of a

---

of free will, which Dante expands in the *Commedia* to draw a comparison between loss, or abuse, of language and sin.

[16] Augustine *De Doctrina Christiana*, 2; xxv, *CCSL*, vol. 32, p. 38. Tr. D.W. Robertson, *On Christian Doctrine* (1958; rpt. Indianapolis, 1980), p. 38.

[17] *Catholicon*, s.v. 'verbum'.

fundamental synderesis of language: the intention is to convey people's thoughts accurately:

> Et scia quid secundum Augustinem uerba ideo sunt instituta non ut per ea homines inuicem fallant sed per ea in alterius noticiam cogitaciones suas ferant. Verbis ergo uti ad fallaciam non ad quod sunt instituta peccatum est sicut dixi in mendacius.
>
> (And know that according to Augustine words were established not so that men could deceive enemies through them but so that by them they could convey their thoughts to others' notice. Therefore to use words for deception, not for what they were established, is a sin just as I have said under 'lying'.)[18]

Thus we are provided with a straightforward explanation of human language both as physical phenomenon and as social contract. Yet although, unlike *logos*, *verbum* itself may be easily comprehensible, it is not therefore uncomplicated, for the explanations and definitions of *verbum* all work on the assumption that the basic purpose of language is to provide, as far as possible, an honest and true reflection of the speakers' intentions. So even when language is considered without reference to the divine origin of words there is still a responsibility for truth. Without the 'common consent' of Augustine, that words should signify agreed concepts and be used accordingly, the result is a chaos of (mis)understandings and deceptions.

Once the possibilities of misunderstanding or deliberate abuse of language are admitted we move into a different sphere of reference, one in which words can no longer be regarded as reliable, albeit approximate, but instead become slippery and uncertain. Mary Carruthers terms this sphere that of an

> analysis of words as ambiguous tools of thought, capable not only of revealing a true cognition but also of generating a corruption of misunderstanding[19]

– and it is this region that Langland selects as the arena of his poem. The difficulty he portrays in *Piers Plowman* is that of finding any secure form of guidance, or even speech, in a world where possibilities of wrong interpretations abound. Langland alerts us to these complexities of language and interpretation very early on in the poem when he provides a dramatised instance of miscomprehension in the meeting of Holi Chirche and Wil.

---

[18] *Ibid.*
[19] Mary Carruthers, *The Search for St. Truth: A Study of Meaning in Piers Plowman* (Evanston, 1973), p. 4.

When Wil and Holi Chirche meet in Passus I there is no indication that there will be a difficulty created by their use of language. Wil asks for an interpretation of the Tower and the Field of Folk, and is provided with one which he seems to understand perfectly. However, as their conversation progresses, it becomes apparent that in fact the two are not using language in the same way: they are not intending to mislead each other, they just have different ideas of the aims of the language they use and what the 'contract' is. It becomes increasingly clear that Holi Chirche is concentrating on the elements which link language with the divine whereas Wil continues to consider language as a human contract with essentially temporal referents. Their choices are appropriate to their characters, but not exclusive; Holi Churche initially uses the *verbum* discourse and the discourse of the *logos* is not debarred humans. If speakers or writers aim to express Divine concepts and their understanding of them, they could adopt a discourse which attempts to shake off the worldly associations of the man-made contract and seeks to speak of notions in as transparent a way as possible. To work in such a discourse is to seek to use language to push against and try to pass beyond the limits of factual knowledge and exploit the creative powers of words to enter into and express a higher form of understanding. Once the two discourses are put side by side the possibilities for incomprehension become abundantly clear, for where *verbum* aims to overcome the ambiguities rife in language and make all clear cut, *logos* seeks to exploit these ambiguities, to retain the link with the Incarnate Word and so give some intimation of a cognisance beyond the powers of mortal words; even, perhaps, to hint at the 'god-rivalling' power of language.

All this is exemplified in the conversation between Holi Chirche and Wil which revolves around various ways of interpreting the word 'tresor'. Initially they both use 'tresor' in the same way as the 'moneie of this molde that men so faste holdeth' (B.I.44). Plainly these are the worldly goods which belong to the temporal sphere and which must be rendered unto Caesar as part of the contract between ruler and ruled (B.I.46–57). This is the meaning still in use at B.I.70 where Holi Chirche cautions against putting one's trust in wealth – 'That trusten on his tresour bitrayed arn sonnest.' However, a new interpretation of the word is introduced with Holi Chirche's redefinition of 'tresor' as 'Treuthe', which she then works through in the speech which follows (B.I.85–137). The links between treasure and government are still there, but now it is an acknowledgment of Truth as the way things ought to be, which is rendered to the ruler (Christ) by those he governs (his followers) and it is the understanding of Truth which is then given as payment, just as previously it was the ruler's duty to pay his workers fairly and look after them:

> – For rightfully Reson sholde rule yow alle,
> And Kynde Wit be wardeyn youre welthe to kepe,

> And tutour of youre tresor, and take it yow at nede,
> For housbondrie and he holden togidres.   (B.I.54–57)

Holi Chirche has thus switched discourses. She is now using a language in which the notion of treasure has been cleansed of its money-grubbing associations and has come to stand for the highest spiritual good. She is seeking to exploit the possibilities which a view of language as linked to the Divine offers. This, then, is the redeemed language of the *logos*, no longer troubled by venial connotations, but concerned primarily with communicating the Divine dimensions of terrestrial concepts. For Wil, however, 'tresor' is still a temporal term, which has no place in spiritual concerns. He is still using the human discourse of *verbum* and has not realised that by redefining 'tresor' Holi Chirche has signalled a change of discourse and a concomitant redefinition of the language contract. In Wil's discourse 'tresor' and 'soule' have no meeting place:

> Tecche me to no tresor, but tel me this ilke –
> How I may save my soule . . .   (B.I.83–84)

Each of them is using and responding to the word in an entirely truthful way, but in totally different discourses: Augustine's contract can no longer operate and the result is incomprehension. Mary Carruthers says of this passage,

> It becomes quite clear, in fact, that Wil and Holy Church are speaking two quite different languages, though they are using the same lexicon. And unless they can agree upon the significance of the word, come to understand the exact reference of the verbal sign, it is useless as a cognitive tool.[20]

It is surely correct to say that they will continue to misunderstand each other until Wil recognises that there is an alternative lexicon, or discourse, at work. However, to imply that the aim is to use words as cognitive tools runs the risk of missing the point of what Holi Churche is doing here. For it is possible to regard this passage as the first, subtle introduction of the *via negativa* in which the very uselessness of words is exploited, as their inability to express the divine paradoxically creates an apprehension of it. Even so the most expert practitioners pass beyond the use of language into a direct apprehension of the Godhead.

However, even if this is a hint at an approach to understanding which is suggested again at later points in the text, it is a hint which Wil fails utterly to pick up. Even after Holi Chirche's explanatory speech he is incapable of understanding 'tresor' as anything other than worldly riches. He is aware that his understanding does not match Holi Chirche's meaning, however,

---

[20] Carruthers, p. 6.

and asks for help, but in terms which reveal that he cannot free his conception of 'tresor' from earthly connections:

> 'Yet have I no kynde knowynge', quod I, 'ye mote kenne me bettre
> By what craft in my cors it comseth, and where.'   (B.I.138–39)

He is rebuked and given another long explanation, but there is no indication that he has understood Holi Chirche's second speech any better than the first. Indeed, his attempt to learn her discourse comes to nothing and is set aside as the concept of 'tresor', its meanings and uses, is explored in a different genre as Langland moves from debate to personification and the episode of the court scenes. Here 'tresor' is personified in the shape of Lady Meed, and the previous conversation between Wil and Holi Chirche is replayed in figurative terms in Lady Meed's trial.

The meeting of Wil and Holi Chirche thus serves as an illustration of the distance between what may be termed the language of the *logos*, the redeemed language used by Holi Chirche, and the language of *verbum*, the human construct used by Wil. We would expect a figure representing the Church to be able to use the discourse of the *logos*, but it is significant that Wil does not at first detect the change, and even when he does, he is incapable of following suit and changing discourse likewise. This theme of lack of understanding between users of different discourses recurs throughout the poem: the Pardon scene; the meeting with Scripture; the banquet with the Doctor of Divinity, to name but a few. The majority of such confrontations or meetings occur between a church and a lay figure in which the representative of the Church assumes that their position and education bring them closer to the discourse of *logos* than the layman, who is relegated to the language of *verbum*. In fact there is no guarantee that a figure connected with the Church is actually capable of using the discourse of *logos*, as the priest's inability to understand the Pardon in Passus VII shows. Nor are the unlettered automatically excluded from the redeemed language, as Jerome's letter to Paulinus points out. However, by first using the episode of Holi Chirche and Wil to dramatize the possible lack of communication between *logos* and *verbum*, and then, later in the poem, setting up the position between educated cleric and religious perceptive layman, Langland is able to demonstrate that the assumption that a Church representative will necessarily be a reliable or useful guide in matters of religious understanding does not hold true. It is often the uneducated figure who is more receptive to the discourse of the *logos* while the learned cleric continues to use the deductive discourse of *verbum*.

Given the prevalence of the theme of lack of communication between *logos* and *verbum*, the appearance of Christ in Passus XVIII, where Christ comes to the joust in Piers' form, is striking in its difference. This episode is an enactment of the idea of words as mediators which has an analogue in St

14

Bonaventure's explanation of the need for the Incarnation as the only way the *logos* could become approachable by men. Just as the *logos* must be transformed into man in order to become comprehensible, so Christ the Word must be transformed into a personification in order to take part in the action of the poem: he must be translated into a suitable discourse. Yet the joust as such never takes place; instead the poem shifts from the allegorical mode of the tournament into an account of the Crucifixion and Resurrection (B.XVIII.28 following). It is tempting to see this passus as an occasion where two discourses mingle and become mutually comprehensible, but this is not the case. While the story of the Crucifixion is being retold the jousting metaphor is abandoned, for although Pilate takes his seat as an umpire, the action of the poem turns into a simple relation of the trial of Christ, complete with mockery, crown of thorns and the actual crucifixion, rather than a combat with Death played out in the terms of a medieval joust. When the tournament metaphor finally returns in B.XVIII.96 it has become a part of the redeemed discourse in that there is no expectation of a description of a joust. There is no longer any need for an allegorical tournament because the concept has been redefined by its collocation, just as Holi Chirche's use of 'tresor' redefined the meaning of that word. Thus it is possible for Pees to say simply 'For Jesus justede wel, joye bigynneth dawe' (B.XVIII.180). The 'joust' is assumed to have taken place; there is no need for a detailed explanation of its meaning.

However, when Langland once again uses the figure of Christ the knight and returns to the metaphor of the tournament in the new vision of Passus XIX, the concept of a champion is worked through and with it the use of the concepts of knight, king and conqueror.

> Quod Conscience, and kneled tho, 'Thise arn Piers armes –
> Hise colours and his cote armure; ac he that cometh so blody
> Is Crist with his cros, conquerour of Cristene.'
> . . .
> 'Thow knowest wel,' quod Conscience, 'and thow konne reson,
> That knyght, kyng, conquerour may be o persone.
> To be called a knyght is fair, for men shul knele to hym;
> To be called a kyng is fairer, for he may knyghtes make;
> Ac to be conquerour called, that cometh of special grace,
> And of hardynesse of herte and of hendenesse –
> To make lordes of laddes, of lond that he wynneth,
> And fre men foule thralles, that folwen noght hise lawes.
>
> (B.XIX.12–33)

Here we are dealing with the concept of Redeeming Word incarnate in the text and abiding by the terms of the prevalent dicourse. In contrast the previous passage in Passus XVIII illustrated how the *logos* could transform the discourse of *verbum* into a language which approaches that of *logos*. It is an instance of the power of the *logos* to redefine language similar to Holi Chirche's redefinition of 'tresor' in Passus I.

Passus XVIII and XIX thus present two different, but equally correct, ways of using the concepts of Christ-the-knight and the tournament. Each takes the commonplace notion of what a champion is and changes it by placing it in a new discourse. This is more than a simple trick of enriching the language, it is a tool for understanding. As Rita Copeland has pointed out, this is troping in the literal sense of 'turning':

> But troping is only part of a matrix of a rhetorical concern with the way that language creates meanings by turning – 'troping' in its literal sense – and appropriating signifiers from one context to another, forcing a revaluation of understood meanings through new figurations.[21]

Such translation and revaluation can clearly be enriching, adding not only to the variety of language, but also to the depth or breadth of understanding. However, as Paul de Man has cautioned, such benefits do not come free of drawbacks. He refers to tropes as 'smugglers', pointing out that this act of carrying a figure from one discourse to another necessarily carries risks of carrying over connotations as well, which may be seen by any individual reader but be unintended by the author:

> Tropes are not just travellers, they tend to be smugglers and probably smugglers of stolen goods at that.[22]

Both attitudes to troping rely on the fact that the knowledge which exists in the readers' minds before they read the text, or work, in which the troping takes place will affect their reaction to the troping within the text. This tacitly allows the readers an active as well as a passive role in the text as they bring to it elements other than those consciously presented to them by the writer. So the crucial element of knowledge is introduced into the matrix of speech and understanding.

---

[21] Rita Copeland, 'Rhetoric and Vernacular Translation in the Middle Ages', *Studies in the Age of Chaucer*, 9 (1987), 41–75.

[22] Paul de Man, 'The Epistemology of Metaphor', *Critical Inquiry*, 5 (1978), 19.

2

Aspects of Knowledge

The type of knowledge brought to a text, together with the assumption about the use of language and the type of understanding or interpretation one hopes or expects to gain, must affect the way that text is received. As Todorov puts it,

> Every work is rewritten by its reader, who imposes upon it a new grid of interpretation for which he is not generally responsible, but which comes to him from his culture, from his time, in short from another discourse; all comprehension is the encounter of two discourses: a dialogue.[1]

Such encounters between discourses occur repeatedly in *Piers Plowman*, not just in Wil's meetings and questionings of various figures, but also in the juxtaposition of different modes of language which expand and explore how one arrives at any form of comprehension or knowledge (as the discussion of B.XVIII and B.XIX in chapter 1 demonstrated).

The interpretation of any discourse is affected by the previous knowledge which the reader brings to bear, and also on the mode of expression of that knowledge, as Todorov points out. Hence, not only may the different discourses of *verbum* and *logos* meet and interact, but different discourses of knowledge may also be in use. Comprehension can thus be seen to be the result of the interaction of language, knowledge and interpretation, and therefore the three are inextricably linked. This is shown to be the case in *Piers Plowman* where it is because of a lack of knowledge that Wil fails to recognise Holi Chirche's shift of discourse and so interprets her words inappropriately. Even when he realises his mistake his ignorance prevents him from using the same lexicon and so leaves him with an imperfect

---

[1] Todorov, *Poetics*, p. xxx. The interaction or play between discourses in *Piers Plowman* has led to Bakhtin's term 'dialogic discourse' being applied to the poem by, for example, David Lawton, in his article 'The Subject of *Piers Plowman*', *Yearbook of Langland Studies*, 1 (1987), pp. 1–30, which is discussed at the end of this chapter.

understanding of what she has said, as his plea for 'kynde knowynge' and more instruction reveals:

> 'Yet have I no kynde knowynge,' quod I, 'ye mote kenne me bettre
> By what craft in my cors it comseth, and where.'   (B.I.138–39)

Holi Chirche complies, but we suspect that Wil is still little the wiser as he abandons his request for knowledge of truth and instead begs for some way to recognise the false. Given Augustine's definition of evil or falsehood as the absence of good or truth, this new request is indicative of Wil's restricted ability to understand Holi Chirche, for one must have some apprehension of truth in order to know what falsity is, as well as *vice-versa*. Had he been able to recognise and understand the term 'tresor' in Holi Chirche's language Wil would have been closer to the 'kynde knowynge' he seeks and so in a position to go on to explore what the true and the false are from a position of basic knowledge. As it is he still looks for meanings in his own, earth-bound, terms and so when he realises that he cannot understand what he is being told he turns to a concept which is more within his sphere of comprehension, since it is very much part of his world – falsehood. This, of course, is not necessarily a failure on Wil's part. It is, however, an indication of the limitations of Holi Chirche's discourse, for it is clear that one must be in a position of understanding and be possessed of some degree of knowledge before being able to explore the connotations of her words. Wil's decision to abandon a search for truth in Holi Chirche's terms in favour of more earthly and immediately comprehensible concepts is an instance of how *Piers Plowman* emphasises the importance of understanding things in terms of the every-day world inhabited by the majority of human society.

So, comprehension depends on interpretation; but interpretation in turn is fundamentally affected by our previous conception of what the language we are attempting to understand is aiming to communicate. As Steiner points out, the Apostle's words give us a beginning, but no security as to the end. This is partly because we ourselves fix the end of language by selecting the type of understanding and knowledge we wish to attain. The encounter between Wil and Holi Chirche has shown how a genuine attempt at understanding may be thwarted by a wrong interpretation occurring without either party intending to mislead the other. If we are to avoid such dead-ends we must be aware of the type of comprehension we seek and of the form of language appropriate to it. In order to achieve this we need to look at the forms of cognition open to us and their different discourses.

The relevance for *Piers Plowman* of the Augustinian division of the soul into cognitive and affective aspects (*intellectus* and *affectus*) has been the object of much discussion, notably J.S. Wittig's comprehensive article '*Piers Plowman* B, Passus IX–XII: Elements in the Design of the Inward Journey'.

There is a well established link between this division and a second pair of entities, *scientia* (knowledge or learning) and *sapientia* (wisdom), which have likewise received much attention.[2] The temptation is to regard these pairs as convenient equivalents of binary opposites so that *intellectus* is seen as solely appropriate to *scientia* and *affectus* to *sapientia*. If the third pair of terms offered in this reading is added to the equation, it would appear fitting to align the language of *logos* with *affectus* and *sapientia*, and that of *verbum* with *intellectus* and *scientia*. Such temptation must be resisted, however, as, although such alignment does occur, it is not automatic, indeed Langland seems to have been interested in blurring the boundaries. Thus, when Holi Chirche speaks to Wil using the discourse of *logos* she is appealing to his *intellectus* rather than his *affectus* and uses an argumentative framework associated with *scientia*. As these terms will figure largely in the discussion of *Piers Plowman* that follows it seems useful to include here a fairly brief survey of their various derivations and connotations, more particularly as the interpretations offered here may shed light on this reading of the text as a whole.

The basic contrast between *sapientia* and *scientia* is obvious from the roots of the two words. *Scientia* comes from a verb (*scio*) and so is associated with active acquisition of knowledge and learning. One enacts a verb, one deduces knowledge and may put it into practice; what one learns tends to be abstract, a theory, which can be understood fully, or proved, only when applied. In contrast *sapientia* comes from a noun – *sapor* (taste) – which summons up the world of the senses and trusts to the reality of experience rather than theory. It is perhaps this more affective aspect of *sapientia* that means it is often regarded as the higher of the two. Augustine declares that we progress to wisdom through knowledge, *'tendimus per scientiam ad sapientiam'*,[3] while Balbus, after initially describing it as the knowledge of human and divine things (*est sapientia rerum diuinarum et humanarum cogniscio*), finally places it firmly in the regions of contemplation of the divine:

> Sic ergo distingui potest inter illa tria. Scilicet scienciam intellectum et sapientiam. Sciencia ualet ad rectam ad ministracionem rerum temporalium et ad bonam inter malos conversacionem. Intelligentia ad creatoris et creaturarum invisibilium speculaciones sapientia vero ad solius eterne ueritatis contemplacionem et delectacionem.

---

2 James Simpson deals with these two forms of knowledge and their particular relation to *Piers Plowman* in his article 'From Reason to Affective Knowledge: Modes of Thought and Poetic Form in *Piers Plowman*', *Medium Aevum*, 55 (1986), pp. 1–23 where he demonstrates that the poem's form mirrors a shift in modes of thought which takes place in the text. A.J. Minnis also makes use of the divide between *scientia* and *sapientia* in his two articles dealing with medieval theories of imagination (see Bibliography).

3 Augustine, *De Trinitate*, XIII: xix; 24, *CCSL*, 16.

(Thus, therefore, it is possible to distinguish between those three, namely knowledge, intellect and wisdom. Knowledge pertains to the right, to the administration of temporal things and to turning to good among evil. Intelligence [pertains] to creatures and speculation about invisible creatures; but wisdom to the contemplation and delight of eternal truths alone.)[4]

Yet although *scientia* is defined as temporal knowledge only, it is not an indiscriminate amoral cognition but carries with it an understanding of the difference between good and evil and a preference for good. This is a point which Augustine emphasises in book twelve of *De Trinitate* where he quotes, and then comments on, Job 28:28:

Verum scripturarum sanctarum multiplicem copiam scrutatus inuenio scriptum esse in libro Iob eodem uiro loquenta: 'Ecce pietas est sapientia; abstinere autem a malis scientia est'. In hac differentia intellegendum est ad contemplationem sapientiam, ad actionem scientiam pertinere.

(But in examining the manifold riches of the sacred Scriptures, I find it written in the book of Job, where that same holy man is speaking: 'Behold, piety is wisdom, but to abstain from evil is knowledge'. In this distinction it is to be understood that wisdom pertains to contemplation, knowledge to action.)[5]

Wisdom may be regarded as the higher form of understanding, but knowledge is not to be dismissed. There is some point in being able to abstain from evil, especially in a life of action – a pertinent point for a poem which includes a figure who calls himself the 'Actif Man' and is replaced in the later version by the more explicit Activa Vita.

The contrasting etymologies of *scientia* and *sapientia* give some indication of the language used when discussing or describing their actions and effects. The knowledge of *scientia* is acquired through rational exploration of a topic and the careful deduction of one thing from another to give a final, proven result. In so doing this approach uses the terminology of debate and rational, logical progression to communicate its findings to others. One knows something when one can describe it and explain it to another who does not necessarily have any prior knowledge of the subject, or when one can give a good reason for knowing something to be the case. As the *Catholicon* puts it:

Scio . . . sapere scientiam habere uel cognoscere. et est proprie scire reddere racionem quam noueris. Nosse uero tantum que audieris.

(Scio . . . to know, to have or to recognise knowledge and properly 'to know' is to give an account of what you may know. Indeed to know as much as you have heard.)

4   Balbus, *Catholicon*, s.v. 'sapientia'.
5   Augustine, *De Trinitate*, XII: xiv; 22. The translation used here is taken from *The Trinity*, tr. S. McKenna, *The Fathers of the Church*, 45 vols (Washington, 1963).

The last phrase of this entry is particularly interesting as it indicates that this kind of knowledge is a type which may be learned indirectly and theoretically; one hears it rather than experiences it. This is a marked contrast to the more evocative language used in the entry for *sapio*, where the second meaning is as follows:

Item sapere id est habere sapiencias. et hic significatio tracti est ex prima sicut per saporem cibos discernimus. sic per sapientiam res. et sicut gustus aptus est ad discrecionem saporis ciborum, sic et sapiencia ad discernendas causas rerum.

(Again, sapere is 'to have wisdom', and this meaning is derived from the first [definition – as 'taste'] just as we distinguish food through taste, so [we distinguish] things through wisdom; and just as taste is apt for discovering the tastes of foods, even so is wisdom for discovering the causes of things.)

Here we are presented with the notion of wisdom as something which acts as immediately as taste, which requires no reasoning ability for it to work and yet is fundamental to the understanding of the world around us. This affective power of wisdom, which may by-pass the intellect while yet retaining one aspect of the rational – the ability to discriminate, which recalls the inclusion of *racio* in the definition of *logos* – is central to the descriptions and treatises which deal with the ways to achieve wisdom or enlightenment. These works do not necessarily rely on rational argument or deductive reasoning as much as on the ability to inspire their readers with a sense of what the desired end consists of and feels like. The vocabulary of *sapientia* is figural and emotive; its favourite mode is figurative or descriptive, either by parable or by recording an experience. Its proof is not the proof of argument, tried in debate, but of direct experience, which the author tries to re-create or invoke.

Given such different descriptions of knowledge, it comes as no surprise that the two schools have contrasting modes or forms of language. The deductive school of thought prefers methods of debate which rely heavily on the powers of reason and take account of arguments both for and against the views they wish to impress on their audience. This attitude results in the impressive and dense form of the various *summae* in which the statement to be discussed is presented, the objections to it put foward, the reponses to the points given and only then is the final opinion reached. An alternative style of debate and discovery favoured by the deductive route to knowledge was the dialogue form which was used by Augustine in his *De Magistro* and St Gregory in his *Dialogues* and first seen in *Piers Plowman* in the exchange between Holi Chirche and Wil. The beauty of this mode is its form: a pupil asks questions of gradually increasing complexity and is answered at length by a teacher figure. The argument can thus progress through carefully worked out stages and come to an unchallenged conclusion when the pupil or interrogator agrees with the teacher. Even if the two speakers are on the same intellectual level, the fact that one tends to question and the other answer until agreement is reached, means that the effect of the format is much the same as where the two characters are pupil and teacher. This style of discourse is less dense than that of the *summae* as the intermittent questions and the fact that there are two characters, however shadowy, make the text more accessible to a listener or reader and so easier to follow. As with the *summae* format, the emphasis is on logical progression and rational argument, with the constant, underlying assumption that all questions have a comprehensible answer, which can be provided by a superior intellect or eventually arrived at by exercise of one's own rational powers.

Sapientia's alternative, emotive approach does not place such emphasis on a rational progression. Instead these texts aim to capture the state of understanding as closely as they can and proceed by means of parable, allegory and figurative language; this preference often leads them to be termed 'mystic'. There can still be a notion of progression from one view or state to the next, but this progress is often contained within the framework of an overall image such as the ladder of *The Scale of Perfection* of Walter Hilton (d.1396), which is ascended and descended as Hilton describes the levels of contemplation. The use of cloud images in the late fourteenth-century treatise *The Cloud of Unknowing*, in which contemplatives are urged to place the cloud of forgetting between them and the world and possibly to enter briefly into the cloud of unknowing itself, is a similar use of an image in order to communicate an idea of progress in the chosen method of acquiring understanding. Alternatively there is the detailed use of allegory as exploited in the twelfth century by Richard of St Victor (d.1173) in his *Benjamin Minor*, where the sons of Jacob are interpreted as progressively enlightened stages on the journey to wisdom.

Different as these two approaches and modes of argument are writers frequently made use of both discourses and outlooks in varying degrees. The twenty-second article of Henry of Ghent's *Summa Questionum Ordinararium* is a case in point. He is discussing whether or not God is knowable to man, and, if so, to what extent. He presents first Augustine's opinion, that the intellect is capable of attaining a direct apprehension of truth without requiring the mediation of temporal things, and then Hugh's exegesis of Jacob's ladder. Hugh states that the angels have no need of the ladder as they fly on the wings of contemplation, but man is incapable of such easy passage and so must use the rungs of created things in order to reach a perception of God. It is at this point that Henry (d.1293) presents his own understanding of the matter:

> . . . homo naturaliter ordinatur ad duplicem cognitionem intellectualem, quarum vna est ad quam ex puris naturalibus studio & inuestigatione potest attingere: & talis cognitio procedit de deo & de creaturis, quantum philosophia se potest extendere. Alia vero est, ad quam non potest

attingere nisi dono luminis alicuius supernaturalis gratiae vel gloriae aduita, & vtraque via potest fieri homini notum deum esse: & hoc est quod solet dici. quod deum esse, potest dupliciter homini esse notum. Vno modo via naturalis rationis. Alio modo via supernaturalis reuelationis.

(. . . man is naturally appointed with twofold intellectual perception, of which one is that which he is able to achieve purely by natural study and investigation: and such knowledge proceeds from God and from created things, as far as philosophy can stretch itself. But there is the other, which he cannot achieve unless aided by the gift of some supernatural light of grace or glory, and man is able to know God by both paths: and this is what is usually said, that man may know in two ways what God is. One way is the path of natural reason. The other way is the path of supernatural revelation.)[6]

Each of the two routes lead to a form of truth, and may result in an enlightened understanding, but they are distinct approaches with separate spheres of reference and make different demands upon their practioners.

If one wishes to proceed by the way of deduction one favours the use of definitions and a gradual progress through the steps of thought and understanding often based on empirical knowledge of the surrounding world. This route requires no previous knowledge or intimation of the desired end, since the actual process of debate will provide all the necessary information, as the arguments both for and against the issue are put forward and discussed. Naturally one needs some skill in debate in order to assess the sides of the argument, but such skills would be acquired over a period of time as one saw how arguments were dismissed and learnt the tricks of the trade. Moreover, this system would also provide the pupils with a teacher or guide figure who would point out the 'correct' conclusion until they were able to assess the arguments on their own. The important factor is that such guidance comes from an external source, the book or teacher (in *Piers Plowman*, Holi Chirche or the friars are among such figures) rather than from an internal faculty or innate knowledge. If, however, one favours the other path, then one seeks the gift of divine illumination by grace and the main effort is directed towards achieving a state in which the reception of this grace is possible. Like the parables which Christ refused to explain to those who listened, this second approach is directed towards those who are in a state in which the words will make sense without the explanations of the deductive route. It is a case of 'he who has ears let him hear' (Matthew 13:9). The defence given in Matthew 13:10–13 for the use of parables is relevant where it is said that parables are used so that only those who have enough comprehension of the matter in hand to interpret the parable at least in part will understand its point, whereas those without such information or

---

6 Henry of Ghent, *Summa Questionum Ordinariarum*, article XXII, q.v. Franciscan Institute Text Series, 5 (Paris, 1520; facsimile rpt. New York, 1953), f. 134.

sympathy will find it meaningless. Understanding figurative speech or parables demands a prior knowledge, hence the emphasis on the experience and description of the states of enlightenment which appear in the mystic texts as they write about the approach to their form of understanding or wisdom. Hence, too, the use of figurative or emotive language rather than definition and deduction.

Clearly those seeking knowledge of any kind need to be aware of the choice offered by these two approaches and to elect to follow one or the other according to what they wish to know and how they wish to know it. The same is true of those who pass on knowledge, or teach how knowledge may be attained. Indeed there is a twofold process at work here for not only must a teacher fit the discourse to the type of knowledge being taught, but also suit the language to the seeker. There is a general recognition of the dangers of teaching one who is not correctly prepared, for lack of proper preparation can lead to misunderstanding and so to error. This awareness of the possibility of miscomprehension due to inappropriate training or preparation is seen most clearly in the opening of *The Cloud of Unknowyng* where the author describes very clearly the type of people who ought to read his work:

> I charge þee & I beseche þee, wiþ as moche power & vertewe as þe bonde of charite is sufficient to suffre, whatsoeuer þou be þat þis book schalt haue in possession, . . . þat in as moche as in þee is by wille & auisement, neiþer þou rede it, ne write it, ne speke it, ne ȝit suffre it be red, wretyn, or spokyn, of any or to any, bot ȝif it be of soche one or to soche one þat haþ (bi þi supposing) in a trewe wille by an hole entent, purposed him to be a parfite folower of Criste, not only in actyue leuyng, bot in þe souereinnest pointe of contemplatife leuing þe whiche is possible by grace for to be comen to in þis present liif of a parfite soule ȝit abiding in þis deedly body.[7]

Those who are not so disposed are not dismissed as evil or ignorant – on the contrary, the author acknowledges that they may 'be ful good men of actiue leuyng' – but nevertheless 'þis mater acordeþ noþing to hem'. The point is that, however well disposed or good-living one is, if one is not prepared in the manner required for the type of knowledge offered one will be at best unaffected, at worst utterly misled and inclined to misconstrue the text.

Langland presents repeated instances of how such confusion is possible in the many moments of confusion which arise from Wil expecting to be taught in one way and actually being offered knowledge in another. The majority of these instances occur during his search for Dowel, in which he meets various intellectual faculties from whom he demands, and receives,

---

7 'Þe Cloud of Unknowyng', in *The Cloud of Unknowyng and Related Treatises*, ed. P. Hodgson, Analecta Cartusiana 3 (Salzburg and Exeter, 1982), p. 1.

definitions of Dowel, Dobet and Dobest. Yet Wil is repeatedly baffled by the information he receives from such figures as Wit and Thoght, because it does not seem to tell him what he wants to know. He seeks definitions of Dowel in an attempt to understand it more fully, yet he never receives a definition which satisfies him, or leaves him sure of what Dowel is. At first this may seem puzzling since Wil has chosen the course he wishes to pursue, and seems to be going the right way about acquiring the skills to go with it as he seeks guidance from such figures as Thoght, Wit, Clergie and Studie. Furthermore, since he starts his quest lacking in knowledge he is surely right in selecting the form of learning which requires no prior knowledge, viz. the deductive approach and indeed his ability to engage in debate and judge the quality of the arguments put forward increases throughout the poem. Given his apparently correct procedure, it is reasonable to expect that he should find what he is seeking in some degree. Yet his encounters with the deductive faculties are always in part unsatisfactory. The reason for the repeated failure to find a satisfactory answer to his questions becomes evident when the reader realises that the problem is that the knowledge Wil seeks through debate and deduction is in fact the affective understanding which is usually communicated through figurative and emotive language, not exacting argument. This affective element of Wil's quest has been evident from early in the poem when Holi Chirche linked knowledge, Truth and love (B.I.142ff) and not only declared that love of the Lord is innate (B.I.142–43) but also is a cure for all sin (148–49) and the gateway to heaven (201–05). The importance of love and the knowledge that leads to it echo throughout the poem and are clearly re-asserted in Kynde's reply to Wil's question 'what craft be best to lerne?' when he is told 'lerne to love' (B.XX.207–8). The gradual accumulation of the affective elements in the text is in keeping with the character of Wil himself in that, as Mary Carruthers points out, he himself is part of the emotive approach to understanding as *sapientia*:

> . . . Will is not only the dreamer-narrator of the poem; he also personifies the will, the Will behind the whole poem. And the will is not a rational faculty, but an appetitive one, to use the scholastic term. It is moved by veneration or disapprobation.[8]

Were this the only aspect of Wil it would be clear that Langland's dreamer ought to seek knowledge only through the more emotive discourse of the approach which leads to the wisdom of *sapientia*. However, the will is also the faculty of choice and, as has been illustrated above, choice is an important element of the rational approach since it involves weighing up arguments and types of thought and deciding which is the most convincing. So

---

[8] Carruthers, p. 93 and see ch. 4 passim.

Wil is not entirely out of his sphere when he seeks knowledge through the deductive route, but it becomes increasingly obvious that although the option of rational exploration is open to him, it is not as satisfactory as the attitude which aims to surpass the bounds of reason.

It is Dame Studie who recognises that Wil would gain greater benefit from being instructed in a different way from that which he has been offered since Passus VIII, thus reviving an option which was first presented to Wil by Holi Chirche.[9] She herself is incapable of directly returning him to this path; she can only encourage him to change course, yet she is aware of an aspect of this matter of choosing the correct path that has so far been overlooked, as her tirade to Wit reveals:

> She was wonderly wroth that Wit me thus taughte,
> And al starying Dame Studie sterneliche seide.
> 'Wel artow wis,' quod she to Wit, 'any wisdomes to telle
> To flatereres or to fooles that frenetike ben of wittes!' –
> And blamed hym and banned hym and bad hym be stille.
>
> (B.X.3–7)

She is berating Wit for not selecting the appropriate form of teaching for Wil, so implying that not all the responsibility for choosing an appropriate route to knowledge lies solely with the seeker. The teacher has a responsibility too. The recognition of this fact brings us to a third area of discourse which links with those of language and knowledge, that of authority.

[9] Cf. Carruthers, p. 89.

3

The Authority Of Writing

Dame Studie points out that part of a teacher's responsibility is to be aware of the type of language and form of knowledge best suited to the pupil. This is, of course, a commonplace of rhetorical teaching, and was firmly reiterated in that popular medieval defence of preacher's rhetoric, the fourth book of Augustine's *De Doctrina Christiana*. Underlying Dame Studie's statement is the assumption that a teacher is automatically in a position of authority and may be regarded as a fit person to make such decisions. Clearly this assumption has its appeal for the learner, as it implies that it is possible, albeit perhaps difficult, to find someone who is fitted by training and position to provide reliable guidance. Once such a figure is found the learner's own difficulties are largely resolved as all decisions and queries can be safely referred, or deferred, to the teacher. This desire for a guru-figure, or figures, or even a definitive text to follow, is manifested in *Piers Plowman* in Wil's constant search for a secure guide. Thus Langland presents us with Holi Chirche, the King, Reson, Conscience and the various other personifications – and, of course, Piers Plowman himself.

However, as the explorations of the areas of language and knowledge have indicated, the learner or listener, too, has a responsibility to assess the credentials of those who purport to teach. It is no easy matter, for not only can the learners be deceived by appearances into perceiving authority where none exists, but they can also be misled by general opinion, force of habit or a desire to hide their own ignorance, which prevent them from questioning or examining the authority before them and proving its worth. The matter is summed up well by Roger Bacon in his *Opus Majus* of 1267 under the heading *Causa erroris*:

Quatuor vero sunt maxima comprehendendae veritatis offendicula, quae omnem quemcumque sapientem impediunt, et vix aliquem permittunt ad verum titulum sapientiae pervenire, videlicet fragilis et indignae auctori-tatis exemplum, consuetudinis diuturnitas, vulgi sensus imperiti et pro-priae ignorantiae occultatio cum ostentatione sapientiae apparentis.

(Now there are four chief obstacles in grasping the truth, which hinder every

27

man, however learned, and scarcely allow anyone to win a clear title to learning, namely, the example of fragile and unworthy authority, influence of custom, popular prejudice, and concealment of our own ignorance accompanied by an ostentatious display of our knowledge.)[1]

Gaining knowledge is not the problem here; the difficulty is being certain that the knowledge one gains and the sources one turns to are reliable and worthy of respect. One also has to be careful not to let an inflated self-esteem hamper the search, or bias an opinion. Bacon's words seem to query every aspect of every type of knowledge and authority or authority-figure, for all our estimates of knowlege are open to influence from custom if nothing else. However, Bacon is not challenging the established authority of church and saints, nor, it transpires, the authority of those who are manif-estly worthy of being regarded as authorities because of their wisdom. On the contrary, the authority he is dealing with is precisely

> quam sine Dei auxilio violenter usurpaverunt multi in hoc mundo, nec ex merito sapientiae, sed ex propria praesumptione et desiderio famae, et quam vulgus imperitum multis concessit in pernicionem propriam judicio Dei justo. . . . de sophisticis enim auctoritatibus, multitudinis insensatae loquor, quae aequivocae sunt auctoritatis sicut oculus lapideus aut de-pictus nomen habet oculi, non virtutem.

> (that authority, which without divine consent many in this world have unlaw-fully seized, not from the merit of their wisdom but from presumption and desire of fame – an authority which the ignorant throng concedes to many to its own destruction by the just judgement of God. . . . for I am speaking of the sophistical authorities of the irrational multitude, men who are authorities in an equivocal sense, even as the eye carved in stone or painted on canvass has the name but not the quality of an eye.)[2]

The aim of the learner or listener must be to be able to distinguish the name from the quality, since it is the quality, not the name, which makes a person worthy of being regarded as an authority.

From Bacon's description it is apparent that authority can come from three main sources: divine consent, merit of wisdom and also, though per-haps spuriously and mistakenly, from popular acclaim. These sources give rise to different kinds of authority which have distinct spheres of reference. In order to be able to assess the relative merits of different forms of auth-ority and if a particular source is in fact authoritative at any given moment, it is necessary to have a basic grounding in these various types and the differences and similarities between them.

---

[1] Roger Bacon, *Opus Majus*, Book I:1, ed. J.H. Bridges (Frankfurt/Main, 1964), 1, 2. Tr. R. Belle Burke (1928; rpt. New York, 1962), p. 4 (adapted).
[2] Bacon, I:1, 4; tr. Burke, p. 5.

Once again reference to the *Catholicon* will help to define the various possible meanings of 'author'. Balbus divides the term *auctor* into three main types, each with its individual etymology and variant spelling, and gives brief examples of people who might be termed authors according to these separate definitions. The first definition is of *auctor*, which is traced through *augeo* to mean 'increaser' and from that, 'leader'. Following this derivation all emperors and rulers could be termed *auctores* because they extend or enrich the state. By extension God may also be termed our *auctor*, as He is our leader and enricher:

> Et secundum primum significacionem imperatores propre dicuntur auc-tores ab augendo rempublicam. Saepe eciam deus dicitur noster auctor i.e. noster dux. noster augmentator.

> (And following the first meaning generals are rightly termed 'auctores' from enlarging the state. Often, even God is called our 'auctor' that is, our leader, our increaser.)[3]

According to this definition, there is little problem about whether or not a person in a position of power deserves the title of author, as the right to the title rests solely on the fact of holding the position. Anyone who guides, rules or enriches others may be regarded as an authority, and command suitable respect. It is only when Bacon's warning about the ignorant throng conceding leadership to those who do not deserve it is taken into account that this definition of *auctor* becomes open to question. However, although a bad ruler or leader may be an unworthy authority, there is no doubt that anyone who wields power and commands obedience has a certain power which may be equated with some form of authority. The extent to which this can be undermined by the ruler's unworthiness will be explored in more detail in a later section, wherein the vision of the King and his court is discussed. For the time being it is necessary only to recognise that power and authority, while distinct, are nevertheless linked.

The second definition Balbus offers is one which is equivalent to the Greek *autentim* – 'authority'. When it is used in this way it is to be spelt without the 'c', i.e. *autor*, and loses the direct link with ruling evident in the first definition. However, the common element of seeking for direction or guidance remains, since the examples Balbus cites for this definition are Plato, Aristotle and Priscian, all of whom were respected as 'philosophers and discoverers of the arts', as Balbus calls them. In other words, they produced works which became authoritative texts in their own right, and as such were regarded as valuable repositories of knowledge. These texts were demonstrably true and so were reliable sources to which one could turn for information or instruction:

3 *Catholicon*, s.v. 'auctor'.

29

Secundum uero secundam significacionem. philosophi et inuentores ar-
cium ut plato aristotiles priscianus et quilibet excellens persona debent
dici autores.

(Indeed, following the second meaning, philosophers and discoverers of the arts
such as Plato, Aristotle, Priscian and whoever is of excellent character ought to be
called authors.)

The last phrase is of special interest here, for it introduces the idea of
reputation as a qualifying element for *auctores*; an aspect which was omitted
altogether from the first definition. There is a suggestion that, for Balbus,
whereas a ruler is to be judged purely in terms of how good a governor he
is, a philosopher must be seen to be living up to the standards he sets in his
works. This is an issue which is of crucial importance when the character
and standing of theologians and teachers of spiritual knowledge are considered, and has a bearing on Langland's portrayal of the friars, especially
the Doctor of Divinity.

Finally, Balbus comes to a definition of *autor*, derived from the Greek verb
auieo, whose Latin equivalent Balbus gives as *ligo* – 'to tie or bind together'.
This leads to an interpretation which is nearer to the twentieth-century
usage: that of composer of a work, whether of fact or fiction. Simply the act
of writing qualifies one for the title *autor* according to this definition, and
there is no implication that the compositions must contain an element of
instruction or knowledge, as those of the philosophers do. The form of the
words is enough to give the work an intrinsic value, for, as he says, 'Virgil
and Lucan and even Ovid and other poets ought to be called authors'
because they 'string their songs together in feet and metres':

Secundum uero terciam uergilius et lucanus et eciam ouidius et ceteri
poeti debent dici autores qui ligauerunt carmina sua pedibus et metris.

(Indeed following the third [meaning] Virgil and Lucan and even Ovid and the
other poets who strung their songs together with feet and metres, ought to be
called authors.)

The inclusion of the other, unnamed, poets is vital as it means the claim to
be an author rests solely on the fact that one has written. Had Balbus cited
only Virgil, Lucan and Ovid without this extension into 'the other poets',
this would not be the case, as all three of these named writers were regarded as *auctores*. However, as the entry stands any claim to higher or
more reliable knowledge or insight has disappeared and with it the need to
be of 'excellent character'. This, then, is the simplest and most inclusive
definition of an author, as the mere existence of a text qualifies its writer for
the title.

This subtle shift of emphasis from the person to the text is also evident in
the concept of *auctoritates* as quotations from highly regarded writers or
texts which, when cited or quoted, invest the user with a certain aura of

authority. These quotations achieved their prestige either through having intrinsic worth because they are profound sayings, clearly true and worthy of imitation, or through being authentic, that is, the original words of an expert in the field to which the quotation applies. These criteria are discussed in more detail by Alastair Minnis in his *Medieval Theory of Authorship*,[4] but even from this brief overview it is possible to see how the ideas of authority and where it comes from overlap with attitudes towards language and knowledge. For, just as the character of a writer can invest his works with authority, so an authoritative text can convey prestige to its writer or citer. It is, to some degree, a two-way process, but it is not one which is secure from corruption or abuse.

Corruption of both text and position can arise from several sources. First of all one can misunderstand the knowledge or text one applies, so that, although the original was correct, the later use is erroneous; it this which the *Cloud* author hopes to guard against in his introduction by limiting the readership of his work to those already pre-disposed to understanding it as he intended. Secondly, there is the corruption which comes about through quoting only part of the original, leaving out the rest either through ignorance or because it would disprove the argument. Langland presents us with an instance of this in Lady Mede's citation of Proverbs 22:9 to 'prove' her claim at B.III.334–335a:

> 'That thei that yyven yiftes the victorie wynneth,
> And muche worshipe have therwith, as Holy Writ telleth –
> *Honorem adquiret qui dat munera &c.'*

Conscience's reply reveals how Mede abuses her *auctoritas* by not completing it:

> '. . . if ye seche Sapience eft, fynde shul ye that folweth,
> A ful teneful text to hem that taketh mede:
> And that is *Animam autem aufert accipientium* &c.
> And that is the tail of the text of that tale ye shewed –
> That theigh we wynne worshipe and with mede have victorie,
> The soule that the soude taketh by so muche is bounde.'
>
> (B.III.347–353)

Any prestige Lady Mede acquired through being able to cite texts to support her case is rapidly diminished as our perception of the type of 'worshipe' attained changes radically when the missing half of the quotation is supplied. It is true that respected schoolmen used half-quotations in their set debates and some even went on to destroy their own previous arguments by completing the quotation in a response to the orig-

---

4   A.J. Minnis, *Medieval Theories of Authorship*, 2nd edn (Aldershot, 1988) see esp. pp. 10–12.

inal premiss and so refuting it.[5] Yet the fact that theologians employed such tactics does not make this use of *auctoritates* any less dangerous. Outside the sheltered climate of the academic debate, the possibility of deliberate corruption like that intended by Lady Mede remains; as does the possibility of one less learned and well prepared than Conscience being deceived by it.

Finally, there is the corruption which comes about through the 'four chief obstacles to truth' described by Roger Bacon above, which is essentially the result of an inability to apprehend the truth. As he points out, the difficulty is to rid oneself of the assumptions and premisses which prevent an unbiased assessment of the authenticity of a speaker, author or text. This is not to say that the readers must themselves have a direct apprehension of truth: were that the case it would be both unnecessary and impossible to learn, since one would have acquired the knowledge one sought before beginning to learn it. What is necessary is the ability to recognise when someone else has the right sort of understanding or knowledge and is passing it on in an appropriate manner. In other words, one must dissociate as far as possible from the pressures and expectations of the 'ignorant throng' in order to arrive at a reliable assessment of the work or author being examined. Once again it is a two-way process, for an ability to perceive some apprehension of truth in another, or in a text, proves that the listeners or readers are capable of assessing the information before them and so are properly prepared to learn more, or apply the knowledge they already have in a responsible way. Equally, this perceived truth provides the authenticity which validates both writer (or speaker) and text.

The degree of anxiety surrounding the recognition of the possibility of these various forms of corruption or misunderstanding is evident in the discussions of the 'detractor', a figure closely linked, through contrast, to that of the author.

Put briefly, a detractor is one who misleads others through words, whether wittingly or unwittingly. This concept was clearly of interest to Langland, since, as Judson Boyce Allen has shown, all the quotations which appear in the B-Text version of Passus VII as additions to the A-Text have in common the theme of the detractor. Allen goes on to point out that the priest of the pardon scene, as an educated man, is in a position to use words as weapons and attempts to do so when he belittles Piers, thus proving himself to be an example of such a detractor.[6] These observations affirm Allen's view that Langland is more concerned with the way information is passed on rather than with the information itself. In other words, *Piers Plowman* does not challenge Church dogma, but it does query the way it is

---

5 See Minnis, *Authorship*, Ch. 6.
6 Judson Boyce Allen, 'Langland's Reading and Writing, *Detractor* and the Pardon Passus', *Speculum*, 59 (1984), 342–62.

transmitted. However, his claim that Langland regards the Christian as safe from such detractions is not borne out by the text, since *Piers Plowman* as a whole is concerned with the ways in which it is possible to misunderstand or be misled in matters of faith. Nevertheless Allen is clearly right in regarding the priest of Passus VII as a detractor, and indeed the implications of his article can be extended to all the figures in the poem who reveal a similar ability with words, in particular the friars and the doctor of divinity, who will be discussed in detail at a later stage. These figures, like the priest, are undermined by the fact that they can be seen as types of detractor.

The figure of the detractor was clearly one which caused concern, as the following entry from William of Mons' *Distinctiones* reveals:

> Detractorum tria sunt genera, sic conititur ex illo versu: Nec fecit proximo suo malum etc. Quidam enim invenit et concipit detractionem habens materiam vel occasionem detrahendi vel non habens mendacium fingit aliquod in proximum quod crudelius est. . . . Quidam autem audit et refert detractionem. Tercius tamen refert. Primus materia invenit, secundus eam auget et multiplicat, tertius authoritatem detrahendi prestat, et ita eam coroborat. Si enim deesset auditor, et detractor.
>
> (There are three kinds of detractor, as is borne out by this verse: do not do harm to your neighbour etc. For one invents and creates the detraction, having the means or occasion for drawing it out, or even not having [such means], conceives a sort of wrong against his neighbour, which is more serious. . . . But another hears and passes on the detraction. The third only passes it on. The first invents the material, the second increases it and multiplies it, the third preserves the authority by drawing it out and so corroborates it. For if the hearer did not exist, neither would the detractor.)[7]

The shift in emphasis is remarkable: suddenly the responsibility no longer rests solely with the speaker, for the listener too is involved. William has brought the role of the audience to the fore and, by recognising the part simple repetition plays in lending authority to a detraction, has undermined the attitude which laid all the blame at the feet of the speakers. The hearer must be able to judge the soundness of the opinions he passes on or elaborates, or run the risk of being an unwitting detractor: 'myn auctor seyth' is not a valid excuse. In order to be able to assess the value of a speech one must be equipped with at least some means of telling whether or not the idea or the speaker is suspect. This does not require a detailed knowledge of the matter of the discourse, but it does require either a complete trust in the integrity and authority of the speaker, or the ability on the listeners' part to judge his words. Seen in this context, Wil's insistent demands to be made to understand, and his constant calls for explanations and knowledge, are

---

7 Willelmus de Montibus, *Distinctiones*, Oxford, Bodleian Library, MS. Bodley 419, f. 27r, quoted in Allen, p. 354, note 25.

revealed as attempts to provide against becoming involved in the detraction process, however innocently.

William was not alone in his recognition that detraction does not necessarily spring from malicious intent. Robert of Basevorn's near paranoia about quoting texts exactly goes beyond a desire to prevent such deliberate misuse as Mede's, reflecting his awareness that detractions, or misleading interpretations and mistakes, can be perpetuated unwittingly – gaining authority and prestige as they are handed down. He insists upon precise quotation of Biblical texts; even changing the tense or person in order to maintain grammatical correctness is wrong. To his mind any change made to the text could occasion error because the audience might fail to recognise the quotation and so misinterpret it. Furthermore he cautions against using an unusual translation, as this, too, could lead to misunderstanding as a result of simple ignorance or unfamiliarity:

> Immo, vitiosum reputatur si quis in themate letteram accipit translationis alterius quam communiter usitatae.
>
> (Indeed, it is considered incorrect if one puts in his theme a quotation from another translation than the one commonly used.)[8]

Regardless of whether or not one accepts this 'consideration' its simple existence indicates how much importance was attached to the pure word and its power. It was essential that those given the power of wielding the word could be trusted to understand it properly and be relied upon not to pass on suspect or misleading notions. Inevitably the problem of the reliability of human authority arises, about which St Bonaventure expressed his reservations in the *Breviloquium*:

> . . . non est certa auctoritas eius qui potest fallere vel falli; nullus autem est, qui falli non possit et fallere nesciat, nisi Deus et Spiritus Sanctus:
>
> (. . . the authority of him who is able to deceive and be deceived is not assured, and there is no-one who is not able to deceive and be deceived, except God and the Holy Spirit:)[9]

In the light of the exchange between Wil and Holi Chirche one could add that even where the speaker is clearly a representative of God, the possibility of unintentional misunderstandings exists. The alternative is to ignore

---

[8] Robert of Basevorn, *Forma Praedicandi*, ch. XVI, p. 251; tr. p. 134. The Latin text is printed in Th-M. Charland, *Artes Praedicandi*, Publications de l'Institut d'Etudes Médiévales d'Ottawa (Paris and Ottawa, 1936), pp. 231–323. This translation is taken from 'Robert of Basevorn's *Forma Praedicandi* (c.1322)', tr. L. Krul, in *Three Medieval Rhetorical Arts*, ed. J.J. Murphy (Berkeley, Los Angeles and London, 1971), pp. 115–201.

[9] Bonaventure, *Breviloquium*, Prologus 5: De modo procedendi ipsius sacra scripturae, p. 207a, tr. pp. 15–16. See also Minnis-Scott, p. 319.

the mediator altogether and judge the message itself. In terms of Christian doctrine this attitude had good precedent in the prophecies and the gift of the Paraclete of speaking in tongues. Here the speaker became simply the amanuensis and the onus of understanding rested with the listener, although in a far less worrying way than that put forward by William of Mons. In this case a distinction had to be made between the author and originator of a work, a distinction drawn by Henry of Ghent with elaborate meticulousness, verging on obscurity:

> Ille non dicitur auctor operis qui exemplar ostendit ad quod faciendum est; sed qui opus ad exemplar describit. Sicut patet in artificiali imaginis descriptione: & in scientiis philosophorum, de quibus Apostolus Roma: Deus illis revelavit quarum ipsi tunc auctores dicuntur: quia revelata descripserunt.
>
> (He is not called the author of a work who displays the exemplar in order to have it made [copied]: but he who transcribes the work to the exemplar. As is plain in the artificial description of an image and in the knowledge of philosphers, about which the Apostle said in Romans: 'God revealed to them those things of which they were then called the authors' because they transcribed what had been revealed.)[10]

This passage forms part of the first quaestio of Article IX which is devoted to author and effector, or producer, of theology (*De auctore seu effectore theologica*). The article is divided into three parts which reveal Henry's concern with the related areas of author (*auctor* – originator), scholar and learning (*doctor*), and listener or receiver of knowledge (*auditor*). In the first *quaestio*, where he deals with the *auctor* and his authority, Henry states that the authority of knowledge rests on the originator of that knowledge (if the source is suspect so is the learning which comes from it). So there are two aspects to be taken into consideration concerning authority: who the author is and what his authoritative standing:

> Et quia ab auctore suo scientia ipsa habet auctoritatem: ideo circa hoc queruntur duo
> Primum de auctore huius scientie
>   Secundum de eius auctoritate
>
> (And because knowledge itself takes authority from its author /originator then there are two [areas] to be investigated in this matter. First, concerning the author of this knowledge. Second, concerning his authority.)[11]

The vital thing is knowing who the original author of any work is, which in turn demands a recognition of the difference between the original author of a work and its writer or recorder. Henry investigates this issue by debating whether one can confidently say that the Old and New Testaments were

---

10 Henry of Ghent, *SQ* IX, q. ii, arg. 2, f. 71rH.
11 Henry of Ghent, *SQ*, IX, f. 70r.

written by the same author, which leads him on to the even more problematic area of the distinction between author and writer. This distinction is clearly fundamental to any creed of divinely inspired writing and of great relevance to the debate on the authority vested in language which arises from discussions about authorship, authority and the Divine Word. It is when Henry's steps of argument in his ninth *quaestio* have brought him to the point where ideas of authority and attitudes towards language meet that the above quotation occurs, whose remarkable density requires some effort to unravel.

Possibly the best way to approach this issue of author versus writer is through the instance Henry himself supplies: that of the biblical writers being credited with the authorship of the books that appear under their names, whereas in fact they were acting as amanuenses for God's word. In the previous section of the quotation Henry is drawing a parallel between divinely inspired writers, who make the divine word available to the world, and the scribe, who provides an exemplar of a work, which may then be copied by others, but which he himself did not invent. The nub of the matter is that readers will attribute the work to the writer, i.e. the scribe of Henry's parallel, without pausing to ensure that he is actually the conceiver of the words, or ideas, recorded. This results in accepting all that is written as being exactly as intended by the originator, and proving any interpretations from the words available, with a confidence in the accuracy of those words that may well be misplaced. In an age of manually transcribed books there was naturally great awareness of the room for scribal error and even deliberate alteration. Given this it was impossible to attribute every word of any work to an author without proviso and when it came to resting a case on the prestige of the author it was crucial to be sure who he was and not confuse him with the scribe. It is this point of the uncertainty and tension surrounding the issue of authorship that Henry wants to make clear before he tackles the difficulties that surround the effect a medium may have on its message, which he goes on to in the third *quaestio* of this same article.

The debate about the effects of medium on message were usually conducted in terms of human media, i.e. recorders of faith or preachers. Robert of Basevorn puts the problem of the character of the preacher with simple clarity when he points out that by becoming a preacher a man takes on a duty to improve others. This duty carries with it an obligation to live up to the expectations of his position:

> Et causa est quia injungit se in officium cujus finis per se est facere alios bonos. Et in hoc est magna et maxima praesumptio quod ipse in actus hierarchios se initiat et divinos, potestans se publice quasi divinum et deiformem cum simpliciter sit deformis.

(And this is because he enjoins upon himself a duty whose end in itself is to make others good. In this there is a great, even a very great, presumption that he is initiated into hierarchial acts, yes divine acts, and publicly shows himself to be, as it were, divine and godlike, although actually deformed.)[12]

This was the hinge of the whole topic of the bad preacher, since if one accepted Robert's position it rendered such figures as Solomon and David bad preachers whose teachings ought to be regarded with great suspicion. Yet they were also favourite sources of *auctoritates*, despite the fact that their periods of lapse were as well known as their times of exemplary living. In the cases of Solomon and David this difficulty was surmounted by declaring that they wrote as penitents, no longer in a state of sin, and so could be used as *auctores* with a clear conscience; not all instances could be solved so easily. As far as the present issue of medium is concerned the point is that any medium restricts the message being conveyed by it, which means that to assert that anything found in the Bible is God's authoritative, definitive dictum is to be culpably blind to the possibilities of corruption by the human intermediary. Henry of Ghent presents this case in Article IX quaestio iii, where he is careful to use the term *fides* – faith, not knowledge:

> Fides qui fit ab aliquo principio per medium, fit secundum exigentiam medii. . . . Ista scientia fides non adhibetur propter dei auctoritatem: nisi mediata testimonio hominum: quare cum homines decipi & decipere possunt: non est huic scientie credendum ex auctoritate dei: cum sit mediante talium testimonio.
>
> (Faith which is handed on by some originator through a medium is handed on according to the limitations of the medium. . . . This faith is not to be quoted as knowledge in the place of God's authority; except as mediated by the witness of men: whence, since men are able to be deceived and to deceive, this knowledge must not be believed [to be] from the authority of God, since it is mediated by such witnesses.)[13]

Again there is a tacit admission of the difference between *scientia*, which is knowable by human reason, and *sapientia* or, as here, faith, which is not.

The similarity in terminology between Henry and St Bonaventure (*'decipi & decipere'*; *'fallere vel falli'*) reveals a shared preoccupation with the opportunities for deception, intentional or otherwise, which indicates that the difficulties surrounding the issues of authority and media were closely linked. Each has to confront the impossibility of total freedom from corruption, either in the source or in the interpretation and subsequent repetitions. The problems became particularly vexed when the information being transmitted was theological. It did not matter if a scholastic discussion of

---

12 Robert of Basevorn, ch. IV, p. 241, tr. p. 123.
13 Henry of Ghent, *SQ*, IX, q. iii, arg. 1, f. 72rO.

theology (or indeed any other subject) was couched in esoteric language, as it could be assumed that such discourse would be addressed to a suitably qualified coterie. However, if a theologian, or one assumed to possess religious knowledge, was asked for information by one seeking to understand matters of faith in order to lead his life according to the tenets of the Church, then it would be culpable to reply in terms obviously incomprehensible to the questioner.

It would seem, then, that authority and authenticity are closely linked. The only kinds of author who do not rely on their words being invested with an autonomous respect are the ones who rule – Balbus' first sense of *auctor*. The other kinds of author all enter into a two-way process whereby what they say is respected because they say it, and they are respected because of what they say. If what an *auctor* says or writes is discovered to be wrong his claim to authority must be dismissed or at least diminished. Given this process the vehicle of the *auctor*'s words becomes very important, for it is the final testing ground of any claim to authority. At the same time the text itself can be assessed in terms of intrinsic worth to see if it expresses truth regardless of the standing of its author. So the text is striving for authenticity on two fronts. On the one it aims to reproduce its writer's intention as closely as possible, while the authors in turn are striving to express a form of comprehension or cognition which is as close to the truth of the matter as they perceive it as they can make it. On the other front the text is aiming to attain an intrinsic worth which would endow it with an autonomous authority, independent of its author's standing. As M.-D. Chenu puts it, 'L'opinion de l'«auteur» est *authentique,* et ses dites sont en effet appelés *authentica.*' (The opinion of the 'author' is authentic and his words are in effect called authorities [*authentica*].)[14]

The opinion of the writer may be authoritative, but it is the words which are perceived as being authentic. Hence it is the text which actually carries and expresses the authority, and as such it can become more prestigious than the writer. This is especially true of the Bible, which contains the Word of God, but which is written and so mediated by human authors, all of whom will necessarily fail in their attempt for pure authenticity to a greater or less degree. It is the text which is the ultimate authority, for even if the writers have fallen short they have nevertheless attempted to express their intention, albeit imperfectly, and it is possible that a later reader may be able to arrive at some perception or understanding of what lies behind the text as a result of the writers' attempts at authenticity.

The fact that the Bible is the ultimate, unquestionable authority is demonstrated in *Piers Plowman* in Passus XVIII where the Four Daughters

---

[14] M-D. Chenu, '*Auctor, Actor, Autor*' (Paris, 1927), p. 83.

of God are recounting and debating the events of the Easter weekend and discussing their meanings and ramifications. These four are presenting different interpretations and understandings of the Crucifixion, each of which reflects the conclusions one could arrive at through reading the events in different ways. Truth gives precedence to the actual events, Mercy to the events as evidence of the mercy of God, Rightwisnesse to the events as proof of the operation of divine justice and Pees regards the eventual outcome as a sign of the promise of final peace. Their debate is broken into by the entrance of the character Book, the Bible personified and a representation of the Living Word.

The meeting of Truth, Mercy, Pees and Rightwisnesse is less of a coming together of four necessary attributes than a demonstration of how they operate in different spheres. In their respective areas these attributes are authoritative; what they say cannot be denied or challenged, except by reference to a different sphere of knowledge. Thus, when Truth meets Mercy in B.XVIII.121 they ask each other the meaning of the sudden darkness which attends the death of Christ. Truth wants to go and find out what it all means; she is 'wendynge to wite what this wonder meneth.' (B.XVIII.126). The implication is that for Truth, knowledge is something which can be sought, found, defined and clarified. This is similar to the representation of Truth in a Tower in the Prologue; in each case the image is of a concrete object which it may be difficult to arrive at, but nevertheless can be perceived as a firm entity. However, in this case the strange events of Passus XVIII lie beyond Truth's usual sphere of action for they are a 'wonder', something she cannot define, yet which she feels impelled to go and explore in order to understand. Mercy, in contrast, knows that 'murthe it bitokneth' (126) and recounts in brief the birth and life of Christ – the manifestation of God's mercy and the sequence of events which lead up to and makes sense of the miracles they are now discussing. Truth is unable to believe Mercy because she knows for a fact that those who are damned are bound for eternity, and can cite an authority to prove it:

> For that is ones in helle, out cometh it nevere;
> Job the prophete patriark repreveth thi sawes:
> *Quia in inferno nulla est redempcio.* (B.XVIII.148–49a)

This is the sort of knowledge Truth deals in – it remains consistent regardless of circumstance. In contrast Mercy bases her knowledge on experience and proves it by force of analogy with scorpion's venom, the poison of which can be cured only by the power of the dead beast:

> 'Thorugh experience,' quod heo, 'I hope thei shul be saved.
> For venym fordooth venym – and that I preve by reson.
> For of alle venymes foulest is the scorpion;

May no medicyne amende the place ther he styngeth,
Til he be deed and do therto – the yvel he destruyeth,
The first venymouste, thorugh vertu of hymselve.   (B.XVIII.151–56)

In spite of Mercy's argument and proof the difference is not resolved. Instead Truth defers to Rightwisnesse, who, as the embodiment of justice, will know more than either Truth or Mercy about whether or not the damned can be saved. Mercy acknowledges this, but at the same time prefers to defer to Pees, who will know the meaning of the light over hell because Love will have told her. By choosing Pees and, through her, Love, as her auctor, Mercy retains her link with knowledge as something felt rather than defined – with *sapientia* rather than *scientia*.

The encounter between Rightwisnesse and Pees that follows is similar to that between Truth and Mercy, as Rightwisnesse presents a conclusion based on knowledge deduced from the basic principles of justice whereas Pees has received her understanding of events directly from communication with Love. Like Truth, Rightwisnesse is incapable of accepting the type of knowledge Love possesses, regarding it as madness. Also, like Truth, she cites the facts of the sequence of events following the expulsion from the garden of Eden, and declares that God's judgment is eternal (XVIII.187–202). Furthermore, she declares that this fact is recorded by Truth as well as herself:

> . . . I, Rightwisnesse, recorde thus with Truthe
> That hir peyne be perpetuel and no preiere hem helpe.
>
> (B.XVIII.198–99)

Both Rightwisnesse and Truth base their judgment of the situation on precedent. In response Pees merely asserts that she will pray that there may be an end to their sufferings and points out that without some knowledge of grief mankind could not know happiness. There is no real argument here, only a stalemate, for Rightwisnesse and Pees, like Truth and Mercy, are approaching the matter from different directions, as Langland indicated by having them come from the north, south, east and west respectively. Nor is there any indication of a hierarchy which would provide a clue as to which of the four to follow, for they are sisters and so equal. It is at this point of stasis that Book enters upon the scene.

Book is immediately recognisable as a figure of authority. Described as a 'beaupeere', he has two 'brode eighen' to see all things and which, as representations of the Old and New Testaments, indicate that he includes the workings of the absolute truth and justice of God as well as His mercy and love. Furthermore, he is a 'bold man of speche' who opens his address with the assertive and apt oath of 'By Goddes body!'. He attests the truth of the description of events given by Mercy and Pees and goes beyond them to forecast what will happen in the future. His is the authentic and final word on the matter, which is immediately shown to be true as the poem moves on to the Harrowing of Hell. In a way, then, Book is the synthesis of the four approaches personified by the Four Daughters of God, and he is certainly the origin of their views as each could cite him as authority. He is not challenged, yet he does not actually enter into the debate and resolve it either. In fact he does not interact with the other four figures at all. Unlike them he is given no introduction and, after delivering his speech, he takes no further part in events and so fades from the scene. Paradoxically, this appearance of the ultimate authority seems to have been of no help whatsoever.

Yet perhaps this should not surprise us, for the authority of the Bible has never been disputed. It is not the events described by the four sisters which are under debate, but their meaning, their effects and how they ought to be reacted to or acted upon. The difficulty is not discovering the truth of the matter, but of how to understand it. The problem is that all four daughters are right in what they say, and all have the backing of the ultimate, definitive Text, the final authority. Yet the very fact that all of them are right indicates that any approach to a full understanding of this particular text must include all the aspects represented here by the meeting of the Four Daughters. It is only when all four are gathered together, only at a crossroads of approaches which is also an interchange of ideas, that Book can appear as a personification, a full entity, rather than be merely cited or referred to in sections. By including a representation of the Book as a living word which contains within it the plurality of truths presented by the Four Daughters of God, Langland re-asserts that *Piers Plowman* is a text which explores the areas of interpretation and the interaction of discourses and approaches to knowledge. It is not a text in search of an ultimate, transcendent Truth or arch-signifier which will give meaning to everything else, for the existence of such an Arch-Signifier is evident in the belief in Christ, the incarnate *logos*. Belief in the Word is a founding principle of the poem which was acknowledged from the very beginning of the text where Truth is represented by a castle. The status of Truth and Book, which are both aspects of the same Arch-signifier, is thus guaranteed by the *logos* and so Book's entrance as the source of all interpretation represented by the Four Daughters is a reiteration of the poem's fundamental faith and a reminder that it is ideas of interpretation, not ideas of truth, which are explored in *Piers Plowman*.

In order to read *Piers Plowman* as such an exploration we must be aware of the various forms of authority, their strengths and weaknesses. The same is true of the areas of language and knowledge which this introduction has outlined. Regarded in the light of these investigations it becomes clear that plurality and interaction are crucial elements of the poem. It is an appreciation of this which leads David Lawton to comment:

The question is rather, I think, whether singleness of truth is ever truly visible in the world constituted by human language, or in a text where the final passus shows the Unity of established Christendom as radically plural and unstable. This is to insist not that there is no "single Truth", but that the singleness of truth is what is most at stake in Langland's use of language. For *Piers Plowman* is a dialogic not a monologic poem.[15]

Lawton declares that he is using 'dialogic' in the same sense as Bakhtin, that is, 'dialogic' describes a text in which the reader is led to a conclusion by entering into a dialogue with the text, assessing the various versions put forward by it and deciding in favour of one of them. Usually the readers are directed to their conclusion by indications within the text as to which view is to be preferred, but there is no guarantee that different readers will come to the same conclusion about what the text is saying, nor, indeed, that one reader will always reach the same point after each reading. A dialogic text demands that its readers are actively involved in the process of reading, whereas a monologic one presents its case to the audience, making it clear which opinion is supported, which rejected, and requiring only a passive, auditory role from its readers.[16] In Bakhtin's terminology the dialogue referred to takes place between reader and text only. However, Todorov's use is more relevant to *Piers Plowman* for it is clear from such passages as the meeting of the Four Daughters of God that there are dialogues between the various characters and discourses within the poem as well as between the text and its audience. For, just as we as readers bring to bear on the poem 'a grid of interpretation' which is formed by a combination of our culture, education and individual circumstances, so, in *Piers Plowman*, we are brought to act as witnesses to a similar process enacted in Wil's journey through the text. For Wil is an interpreter of the events in the poem as well as an enactor of them. He can thus be regarded as a figure of a reader who brings to the events he witnesses his own 'grid of interpretation'. His 'grid' becomes our 'literary perspective', to use another of Todorov's terms, for it is supplied by the poem and offered as a possible viewpoint for the reader. This literary perspective is more stable than any individual reader's reaction to the text during any given reading. Drawing an analogy between written and plastic art, Todorov notes that various standpoints may be represented within the work which represent the view of the spectator or reader and may also explicitly acknowledge the presence of this reader, so that, to use his own example, a figure in an icon may be turned towards the spectator when in fact the action of the picture would demand that this figure look at another figure in the scene. As spectators we are thus presented with a position the text expects us to take towards it, which we

---

[15] D. Lawton, 'The Subject of *Piers Plowman*', *Yearbook of Langland Studies*, 1 (1987), p. 3.
[16] See Lawton, p. 3 and note.

recognise and adopt either unawares, or with the knowledge that we are taking on a role as we do so – that of 'reader'. These literary perspectives, offered or perhaps almost imposed by the text, are static and unaffected by the individual emotions or conditions which each reader brings to the text and which will affect their reaction to it, if not actually their critical response. Todorov concludes,

> literary perspectives do not concern the reader's real perception, which always remains variable and depends on factors external to the work, but a perception presented within the work, although in a specific mode.[17]

The interaction between the various discourses and determining factors that Langland provides in *Piers Plowman*, including Wil's interpretation of his visions and any assessment of them we may make based on information provided by the rest of the poem (for the reader does not always agree with Wil's conclusions, his assessment of the Pardon scene being a case in point) make up such a literary perspective. It is, therefore, the literary perspectives and the dialogues between the discourses of knowledge, language and authority and how they are used, which form the centre of interest for this particular reading of *Piers Plowman*.

When faced with this plethora of alternative discourses, attitudes to knowledge and the pervading question of authority, the reader, like the seeker after knowledge, is thrown back onto their own ability to discriminate and judge the information presented to them. In this process of seeking understanding and acquiring information the role of reason is central, at least initially.

---

[17] Todorov, *Poetics*, p. 33.

4

Langland's Reson and his Heritage

It has already become clear that reason has an important part to play in any approach to understanding and in definitions of language, witness the inclusion of reason as *racio* in the *Catholicon* entry for *logos*. The aspect of reason that the *Catholicon* is drawing on here is the Platonic one of reason as the controlling principle underlying the order of the universe, or of creation, hence its close relation to *logos*. This aspect of the term endorses J.A. Alford's persuasive presentation of the reading of Reson in *Piers Plowman* as a principle, and clearly any discussion of Reson must take account of this view.[1] Yet one must not lose sight of the fact that Reson is also a representation of the rational faculty in its fullest form i.e., as Alford puts it, 'clearly not the "reason" of any particular individual' (p. 210), no more, one might add, than any of the personifications in *Piers Plowman* can be restricted to being embodiments of the attributes of any one person. It is precisely this entirety which distinguishes a personification from a representative.[2] If one is called upon to represent either a group or a concept the question of what actually 'being' a king, say, or Reson or Wil actually entails is raised: how is such an entity composed? In contrast, an entity which is called into being in order to take part in the action *as* the concept (king, Reson or Wil) has no such problems. It *is* a king, Reson or Wil in all its variety and it is for others, the readers, other characters or audience, to understand how this entity's actions and words are integral to the thing they personify. An example might be the figure of Lyere in *Piers Plowman*, who leaps away from the disintegrating court of Passus IV and into a multiplicity of existences, involving a change in gender as well as appearance. The moment such a creation ceases to act as the embodiment of its concept, it also ceases to be a full personification; it leaves the stage, is

---

[1] J.A. Alford, 'The Idea of Reason in *Piers Plowman*', *Medieval English Studies Presented to George Kane*, eds E.D. Kennedy, R. Waldron and J.S. Wittig (Woodbridge, Suffolk, 1988), pp. 199–215.

[2] Edward Burns provides one of the best accounts of the subtleties of personification and allegory when he discusses the use of personae in *Character: Acting and Being on the Modern Stage* (London: Macmillan, 1990), see especially pp. 1–3 and 40–64.

redefined (or redefines itself as Piers does at the end of Passus VII), or simply ceases to exist. In the case of Reson, therefore, it is possible, indeed necessary, to regard him as not only principle, but also faculty. Reason itself is a concept which attracted, and still attracts, much debate. For some it was the attribute which divided mankind from the animals and enabled humans to have some apprehension of the Divine; for others it did indeed assist in gaining such apprehension, but had to be left behind if the pinnacle of understanding was to be achieved; others again were more interested in the aspect of reason as the ordering and judgemental faculty. In all cases reason attracted some degree of respect, but with this respect could come reservations. Langland had a rich heritage to explore and exploit.

Whenever a figure of Reason enters a text, whether as personified faculty or as governing principle, that figure and her/his opinions command serious consideration, if not unquestioning obedience. This is true not only of the majority of readings of the figure in *Piers Plowman* (even those which hint that reason is eventually left behind in the text; James Simpson's 'From Reason to Affective Knowledge . . .' being one such piece) but also in other medieval works, such as *Le Pèlerinage de la Vie Humaine* and, most notably *Le Roman de la Rose*.[3] In this last the character has attracted much discussion over the centuries from the quarrel over the text engaged in by Christine de Pizan and Jean Gerson on the one hand and the Col brothers on the other, to John Fleming's work today.[4] Such reaction to a personification of reason reflects the critics' high estimation of the intellectual and rational faculties often to the disparagement of the emotional and affective. This prejudice is

---

3 The title *The Romance of the Rose* is used to indicate reference to both the original French poem and the Middle English translation attributed to Chaucer. When reference is to the French only the French title will be used, or its shortened form *Roman*; the modern English translation used is that of C. Dahlberg (see Bibliography). If only the English version is intended the Middle English title will be used in its shortened form, *Romaunt*.

The translation of Guillaume de Deguileville's *Le Pèlerinage de la vie humaine* that has been used is the anonymous, late fourteenth- or early fifteenth-century text entitled *The Pilgrimage of the Lyf of the Manhode*, ed. Avril Henry EETS o.s. 288 (London, 1985). As Henry's introduction makes clear, this translation is based on the 1330–31 version of Deguileville's text, whereas Lydgate's more widely known translation and expansion of the text is taken from the second French version. Lydgate's text was therefore deemed to be too far removed from the 1330–31 poem and too late a translation to be of direct relevance here. The text given by Henry is not only closer to the version likely to have been available to Langland, but also gives us some idea of how the *Pèlerinage* was read in the late fourteenth or early fifteenth century.

4 The letters and some discussion of the progress of the debate over the *Roman* may be found in J. Baird and J. Kane, eds., *'La Querelle de la Rose': Letters and Documents*, North Carolina Studies in Romance Languages and Literatures, 119 (Chapel Hill, 1978) and also in E. Hicks, ed., *Le débat sur 'Le Roman de la Rose'*, Bibliothèque de XVe Siècle, 43 (Paris, 1977). For a major twentieth-century discussion of the figure of reason see J. Fleming, *Reason and the Lover* (New Jersey, 1984).

also evident in certain medieval estimations of reason, but when exploring presentations of reason, it is worth bearing in mind that the affective approach also commanded respect and that there seems to have been less desire to observe strict demarcation between the rational and affective.

The Romance of the Rose contains a character, or characterization, of reason similar to that in Langland. She is given implicit authority by entering the action of the poem, in both Guillaume Lorris' section and in Jean de Meun's continuation, from a tower, a metaphor for external authority which is also found in *Piers Plowman*, where Holi Chirche comes to the dreamer from the castle (B.I.4). This detail is retained in the translation attributed to Chaucer:[5]

> A long while stod I in that stat,
> Til that me saugh so mad and mat
> The lady of the highe ward,
> Which from hir tour lokide thiderward.
> Resoun men clepe that lady,
> Which from hir tour delyverly
> Com doun to me, withouten mor.
>
> (*The Romaunt of the Rose*, 3189–3195)

This description is closely echoed later, when again she comes down 'out of hir tour' (4619–4622). This is clearly a figure to be respected. Her vantage position in the tower gives her a detached overview of the action of the poem and allows her to descend to advise the lover at suitable moments. Furthermore, the initial description of her includes a brief resumé of her lineage, which is impeccable:

> For certeyn, but if the letter ly,
> God hymsilf, that is so high,
> Made hir aftir his ymage,
> And yaff hir sith sich avauntage
> That she hath myght and seignorie
> To kepe men from all folye.
> Whoso wole trowe hir lore,
> Ne may offenden nevermore.   (3209–3216)

With such an introduction John Fleming's assertion that 'Lady Reason's dazzling credentials assure us that we can believe her, indeed that we must believe her'[6] appears to be fully justified. However, there is a crucial clause in the last passage quoted above, which states that Reason has the power to keep men from folly *if they will pay attention to what she says* (3215). In other words Reason can provide the wherewithal to make an informed decision,

---

[5] Geoffrey Chaucer, attrib., *The Romaunt of the Rose*, in *The Riverside Chaucer*, ed. L.D. Benson (Oxford, 1988), pp. 686–767.

[6] J. Fleming, *Reason and the Lover* (New Jersey, 1984), p. 64.

but, as in Langland, she does no more than that, the final choice depending on the individual's will.

It could be said, then, that Langland's Reson has a precursor in the Reason of *The Romance of the Rose* which may well have influenced Langland, either directly or through the tradition shared with *Le Pèlerinage*. In each case Reason is a respected judge of earthly matters and a great fount of knowledge. Jean de Meun's Reason discourses on a wide number of topics, ranging from the different types of love and friendship to an explanation of youth and age and the proper use of wealth. Indeed it was her ability to discuss all things in a remarkably detached and pragmatic manner that became one of the main points of dispute in the debate about the poem, which began in around 1400 with Christine de Pizan attacking Jean de Meun's figure of Reason, and the Col brothers defending it.

It was Reason's advice that it is better to deceive than be deceived that particularly disturbed Christine de Pizan. The difficulty sprang from the fact that Reason has been given such an impressive introduction:

> Et encore ne me puis taire de ce, dont trop suis mal content: que l'office de Raison, laquelle il mesmes dit fille de Dieu, doye mectre avant telle parole et par maniere de proverbe comme je ay notee en ycellui chapitre, la ou elle dit a l'Amant que «en la guerre amoureuse . . . vault mieulx decevoir que deceuz estre». Et vrayement je oze dire que la Raison maistre Jehan de Meun renia son Pere a cellui mot, car trop donna autre doctrine. Et que mieulx vaulsist l'un que l'autre, s'ensuivriot que tous deux feussent bons: qui ne peut estre. Et je tiens par oppinion contraire que mains est mal, a realement parler, estre deceu que decevoir.

> (Further I cannot be silent about a subject that so displeases me: that the function of Reason, whom he even calls the daughter of God, should be to propound such a dictum as the one I found in the chapter where Reason says to the Lover, "In the amorous war, . . . it is better to deceive than to be deceived". And truly, Master Jean de Meun, I dare say that Reason denied her heavenly father in that teaching, for He taught an utterly different doctrine. If you hold one of these two to be better than the other, it would follow that both are good, and this cannot be. I hold a contrary opinion: it is far less evil, clearly, to be deceived than to deceive.)[7]

The problem here is that Christine de Pizan is treating Reason as a moral guide, rather than the assessing faculty she really is in Meun's text. Reason is the daughter of God only insofar as she allows mankind to weigh up alternatives and from that basis make an informed choice, unlike the other animals who act according to instinct only. The distinction is made by Boethius in Book Five of *The Consolation of Philosophy*. Chaucer's rendering reads:

---

[7]   E. Hicks, ed., *Le Débat sur le Roman de la Rose* (Paris, 1977), pp. 14–15.

By this resoun, thanne, ther comen many maner knowynges to dyverse and differynge substaunces. For the wit of the body, the whiche wit is naked and despoiled of alle oothre knowynges – thilke wit cometh to beestis that ne mowen nat moeven hemself her and ther, as oistres and muscles and oothir swich schelle-fyssche of the see that clyven and ben norisschid to roches. But the ymaginacioun cometh to remuable bestis, that semen to han talent to fleen or to desiren any thing. But resoun is al oonly to the lynage of mankynde, ryght as intelligence is oonly the devyne nature. . . .

Semblable thing is it, that the resoun of mankynde ne weneth nat that the devyne intelligence byholdeth or knoweth thingis to comen, but ryght as the resoun of mankynde knoweth hem.[8]

It is intelligence which has the touch of the divine and hence the moral overtones; reason is merely the attribute which distinguishes mankind from the rest of the sentient world. As such it is the faculty which gathers and processes knowledge, but not the one which gives this knowledge a definitive moral value. Instead reason will tell you which is the preferred course of action in view of the prevailing conditions. Hence, to apply this principle to *The Romance of the Rose*, in the war of love it is better to deceive than to be deceived, in purely practical terms, for this increases one's chance of winning the desired object. It is only against the larger canvass of general moral behaviour that it becomes better to be deceived, and Jean's Reason is not acting against such a background; she is advising a particular lover in a particular situation.

Interestingly, even in such particular and restricted circumstances Reason is not regarded as the definitive authority for the Lover. It has already been stressed that reason cannot force the Lover to follow her advice, since that must be the Lover's own choice. It further transpires that Reason is not even the only possible source of advice, as there is the alternative proffered by Friend. Friend's claim to authority rests on his personal experience of the matter in hand, as he himself has been a lover in his time (*Romaunt* 3371–3377; *Roman* 3123–3145). The Lover is thus given the option of following the theoretically-based advice of Reason or the empirically-based suggestions of Friend. This means that the Lover can choose to ignore Reason and so to deny her authoritative standing, deciding that Reason can have no jurisdiction in matters of love and courtship. This is indeed what happens, as the Lover elects to follow Friend's advice and supposed example, rather than heed the dictates of Reason. However, although the Lover decides to ignore Reason, the reader does not have to follow suit. On the contrary, the reader is free to realise that Friend is necessarily biased and that Reason speaks no more than the truth when she tells the Lover that he would be better

---

[8] Chaucer, *Boece*, Book V, prosa 5, p. 465.

advised to avoid the God of Love and devote himself to the other types of love she describes than to become involved in the deceptions and madness attendant on his love for the Rose (*Roman* 2996–3097 and 4229ff). Equally, however, the reader is able to recognise that it is the mark of a true lover to turn away from reason, even after he has been forced to acknowledge the truth of Reason's forecasts, as happens in lines 4147–4150:

> Bien le m'avait Raison noté;
> Tenir m'en puis pour rassoté
> Quant des lors d'amer ne recrui
> E le conseil Raison ne crui.
>
> (Reason warned me well of this situation. I may count myself as bereft of reason when from that time I neither renounced love nor trusted Reason's advice.)[9]

Instead the Lover chooses the more emotional and emotive path offered by Friend, which appears not only more attractive, since it encourages him to continue in his love for the Rose, which he has already declared he has no intention of renouncing (7220), but is also the advice of an authority he considers more appropriate to his situation (10003–06):

> Ainsine Amis m'a conforté,
> En cui conseil grant confort ai;
> E m'est avis, au meins de fait,
> Qu'il set plus que Raison ne fait.
>
> (Thus Friend comforted me. I took great comfort from his counsel, and it seemed to me, indeed, that he knew at least more than Reason did.)[10]

Naturally, Friend's advice has the added advantage of being what the Lover wants to hear, but nevertheless the Lover does not question that the value of experience is to be taken at least as seriously as the force of rational argument.

The moment when the Lover decides to follow Friend rather than Reason is clearly the moment of choice, but in fact by the time this point is reached the Lover has already queried Reason's position as the voice of authority by accusing her of using lewd language (*Roman* 6901ff), which he regards as ill-suited to a woman of high status. Reason's defence is that both the objects she names and the names themselves are in themselves neither good nor evil, but have been made so by association, which has nothing to do with her. Her argument must be given due weight, but so must the Lover's, for, if nothing else, the fact that Reason uses these words shows that she is in the wrong setting. The language she uses does not fit the situation she is in,

---

9 *The Romance of the Rose*, tr. C. Dahlberg (Hanover and London, 1986), 4148–50, p. 92.
10 Dahlberg, 10003, p. 179.

or is addressing, and this inappropriateness undermines her position, despite the fact that what she says is perfectly true. The Lover seizes on this displacement to dismiss Reason for the time being, just as later he uses the fact that she has no empirical knowledge as an excuse to reject her advice in favour of Friend's.

The Lover's decisions and actions are not necessarily the best possible and are open to dispute by readers, but the simple fact that Reason can be dismissed as irrelevant indicates how authority can be affected by the predisposition of the audience and by the setting in which it operates. Regardless of the high esteem and capacity for judgement Reason can be assumed to possess, she can be rejected when the setting is not one in which the rational, deductive skills are prized. Friend's first-hand experience seems to be more appropriate to a matter of love than Reason's level-headed advice to steer clear of all dealings with the God of Love.

Le Pèlerinage de la Vie Humaine reinforces the ambiguous nature of what at first appears to be a thoroughly trustworthy figure of reason. Here again Resoun enters the main action of the text from a tower, descending from it to give the Pilgrim advice on how best to treat the wounded:

> And þerfore I am descended and come to advise you, þat þer be in yow no rudeshipe, ne crueltee, ne felnesse: but beth pitous to yowre woundede folk, and merciable, and softe. Treteth hem alle sweteliche, and þanne shal yowre oynement stonde in stede.[11]

Soon after this Resoun is presented as giving dictates to God's representative, here Moses, on how to behave:

> Now vndirstonde þis lessoun, for it is to þe worth a gret sermoun. þouh þou seme horned withoute, lat þin herte be al naked withinne; and be merciable withinne, whateuere þow be withoute.[12]

So it is clear that the faculty of reason is established as the one responsible for discerning proper action and behaviour and dictating how mankind ought to treat fellow mortals. However, it is also the faculty which distinguishes mankind from the other beasts. The Resoun of the *Pèlerinage* sets this out in the clearest terms:

> I am Resoun bi whom ye been [discerned] from oþere bestes and ounliche as longe as ye shule have me ye shule be men. And whom ye wole go withoute me ye shul wel mown avaunte yow ye be but as doumbe bestes and as coltes þat be cloþed. Withoute me ye shul neuere have wurshipe,

---

[11] *The Pilgrimage of the Lyf of the Manhode*, ed. Avril Henry, EETS o.s. 288 (London, 1985), pp. 8–9.

[12] *Pilgrimage*, p. 9.

be ye neuere so gret lordes. If ye [wole] make jugementes, silogismes oþer arguments withoute me, shul ye neuere have conclusioun þat ne shal come to confusioun.[13]

This speech consists of an uncontested flow of thought which progresses from the assertion of reason as mankind's defining asset to the ability to argue and use syllogisms. The movement is from an ability to consider to an ability to use the mind to argue and arrive at definite conclusions. This is a progression which is similar to that recommended in the search for *scientia*, for knowledge as facts, something solid which can be known, defined – a 'conclusioun'.

So far this representation of reason is similar to that of *The Romance of the Rose*, a similarity acknowledged within the text by a direct reference where the Pilgrim is told that fleshly love drives out reason 'and þat withoute glose ye mowen se in þe romaunce of þe Rose' (497). The limitations of this Resoun becomes clear when the Pilgrim turns to her for explanation of the transformation of bread into flesh which Moses has just performed. She confesses herself confused and blind and incapable of offering any interpretation:

> Heere lakketh me myn vnderstondinge and my wit al outerliche: I am blynd, I see nothing, I haue lost al my sighte. I was neuere so abashed in al my live.[14]

She recognises this as something beyond her sphere and so, baffled, returns to her tower. Even in the second part of the *Pèlerinage*, where Resoun displays her ability to lead the Pilgrim back from the distractions of the body proffered by Rude Entendement, she tells the Pilgrim that Grace Dieu, not herself, is the only reliable guide he needs. She adds that although she is willing to accompany him on his journey, he will not always be able to see her because of mists and clouds. Nevertheless, even if not immediately apparent, she will be there:

> . . . but algates if þou hast neede of me, seche me aboute þee, for if þou seeche me bisiliche, þou shalt fynde me rediliche.[15]

He will be able to find her if he makes an effort, but it is made clear that he will be entering a realm that is not her accustomed habitat.

So, Resoun in the *Pèlerinage* is presented as a figure who has the ability to differentiate between good and evil and to overcome the worldly temptations which can distract the Pilgrim form his journey. She commands

---

[13] *Pilgrimage*, p. 12.
[14] *Pilgrimage*, p. 20.
[15] *Pilgrimage*, p. 84.

respect and has a degree of authority evident in the Pilgrim's deference towards her and also symbolically in her residence in the tower. However, she defers to Grace Dieu in her turn and is incapable of understanding the Eucharist, so can be only a companion for the Pilgrim on the later stages of his journey, not a guide. She is not an infallible authority for every occasion, just as Reason in *The Romance of the Rose* is not always the most appropriate advisor for the Lover. Both the texts admit of limitations in the jurisdiction of Reason, yet both also present her as the undisputed final judge of earthly, intellectual matters, indispensable for proper government of either state or individual. This interpretation of reason is also found in *Piers Plowman*, but there are vital discrepancies.

As the above brief survey has shown, the power of reason was regarded as essential if one was to be able to discriminate, judge, rule or bring order to the world and so achieve some measure of understanding of it – in other words to act rationally in the fullest sense of the term. Since the approach to knowledge as *scientia* relies on the processes of deduction and definition to arrive at a final, clear conclusion and since these in turn rely upon discriminating judgement and choice, it is not surprising to find a definition of wisdom and the role of the wise which is closely linked to reason. Indeed knowledge of this type is termed the highest perfection of the faculty of reason. The definition comes from Aquinas, but he arrives at this correlation of wisdom and rationality by referring to Aristotle's notion of the role of the wise:

> Sicut dicit Philosophus in principio *Metaphysicae*, sapientis est ordinare. Cuius ratio est, quia sapientia est potissima perfecto rationis, cuius proprium est cognoscere ordinem. Nam et si vires sensitivae cognoscere res alquas absolute, ordinem tamen unius rei ad alium est solius intellectus aut rationis.
>
> (The Philosopher teaches at the beginning of the *Metaphysics* that the proper task of the wise is to bring order into affairs. The explanation for this is to be sought in the fact that wisdom is the highest perfection of reason, and it is reason which brings things to order. In fact, although it is possible to know some things directly by experience, only the intellect or reason can know the order which relates one thing to another.)[16]

The underlying assumption is that one does not know a thing properly until one can define it and put it in its appropriate place in the order of things. As this assumption is common to a notion of wisdom which regards the 'proper task of the wise' as being to bring order into affairs and to a definition of

---

[16] Aquinas, *Commentum in X libros ethicorum ad Nicomachum*, I lect, i., in *Aquinas, Select Political Writings*, ed. A.P. D'Entrèves, tr. J.G. Dawson (Oxford, 1959), pp. 188 and 189.

reason as the ordering faculty, it is natural that the perfection of reason should become the route to wisdom.

The high regard given to reason is stated even more firmly in Aquinas' *De Regimine Principum*. It is not surprising to find the ability to order and govern highly placed in a work which deals with methods of rule, but Aquinas actually equates Reason with the Divine:

> Nam sicut universa creatura corporea et omnes spirituales virtutes sub divino regimine continentur, sic et corporis membra et ceterae vires animae a ratione reguntur, et sic quodammodo se habet ratio in homine, sicut Deus in mundo.
>
> (Just as the divine control is exercised over all created bodies and over all spiritual powers, so does the control of reason extend over the members of the body and the other faculties of the soul: so, in a certain sense, reason is to man what God is to the universe.)[17]

Once again the emphasis is firmly on controlling and ordering the world. It is this which makes it natural that Reson should become one of the governing triumvirate in the first part of Langland's poem, sharing the power with Conscience and the King.

Reson's position as part of this ruling elite is asserted first by Conscience in Passus III:

> I, Conscience, knowe this, for Kynde Wit it me taughte –
> That Reson shal regne and reaumes governe . . . (B.III.284–85)

The appeal to the authority of common sense and innate knowledge personified in Kynde Wit shows that there is no question about Reson's right to rule; it is an obvious tenet of common sense which requires no exploration or further discussion. This assumption is thus identical with that found in Aquinas: Reson's authority and right to be part of the governing process come from an acceptance of order and definition as high priorities of understanding. For, although Langland is presenting us with a view of how a society ought to be run, he is not painting a political picture only. It is also an illustration of how the members of the 'commune' ought to govern themselves, giving ruling places to their conscience, common sense, and reason in regulating their actions and their world.

Indeed Reson's standing is so high that Conscience refuses to act without his assistance:

> 'Nay, by Crist!' quod Conscience, 'congeye me rather!
> But Reson rede me thereto, rather wol I deye.' (B.IV.4–5)

---

17 Aquinas, *De Regimine Principum*, XII, in *Aquinas, Select Political Writings*, pp. 66 and 67.

The King, in his turn, admits that it is Reson not Conscience who will

> ... rule my reaume and rede me the beste
> Of Mede and of mo othere, what man shal hire wedde,
> And acounte with thee, Conscience, so me Crist helpe,
> How thow lernest the peple, the lered and the lewed! (B.IV.9–12)

The message is clear: when it comes to matters of judgement the appropriate faculty should be used.

Themes of restraint and judgement run through the description of Reson; his attendants all emphasise his standing as a virtue which knows when and how to act. Furthermore this certainty comes from constant assessment of each situation and what it demands rather than from blindly applying a set of rules. Hence he rides upon a horse whose name, "Suffre-til-I-se-my-tyme", indicates that patience is an integral part of right reasoning, and whose harness, 'witty-wordes', demonstrates that this is a patience tempered with learning. The bridle is designed to keep his head low, an obvious reference to the humility which prevents hasty and wrongful judgements. Altogether this is a representation of a dispassionate and careful faculty.

However, although Reson's capacity as a judge is not in doubt, he has no aspect of mercy or clemency. He declares twice that he will have no pity until the society he is governing has radically reformed and become a type of Utopia:

> 'Reed me noght' quod Reson, 'no ruthe to have
> Til lordes and ladies loven all truthe
> And haten alle harlotrie, to heren or mouthen it.' (B.IV.113–15)

An assertion he repeats twenty lines later: 'by the Rode! I shal no ruthe have/ While Mede hath the maistrie in this moot-halle' (B.IV.134–35). This portrayal of Reson as being without any mitigating or softening qualities fits in with the discussions of reason's qualities and limitations found in Book Two of Walter Hilton's *Scale of Perfection*. When describing the processes by which the soul approaches God, Hilton draws a sharp distinction between the sort of knowledge attained by the soul and that achieved by reason. He describes how the soul, enlightened by love, attains an apprehension of God which is of an entirely different order from the knowledge a theologian achieves through the operation of reason alone:

He [the soul] seeþ Him not what He is. for þat may no creature done in heuen ne in erþe; nor he seeþ Him not (as) He is, for þat siȝt is oonly in þe blis of heuen. Bot he seeþ Him þat He is: an vnchaungeable beynge, a souereyn miȝt, souereyn soþfastnes, souereyn goodnes, a blissid lif, an endeles blis. þis seeþ þe soule, & mikel more þat comiþ withal; not blyndely & nakedly & vnsauourly, as doþ a clerke þat seeþ Him bi his clergi

only þurgh miȝt of his naked resoun, bot he seeþ Him in vndirstandynge
þat is counfortid & liȝtned bi þe gifte of þe Holy Gost . . .[18]

Nor is it in the realms of spiritual apprehension alone that 'naked reason' is
regarded as limited:

It is ful harde & a grete maistrie to a man þat stondiþ only in wirkynge of
his owne resoun for to kepen pacience, holy rest & softnes in herte, &
charite to his euen-cristen if þei disesen him vnskilfully & don him
wronge, þat he ne schal sumwhat don ageyn to hem þurghe stirynge of ire
or of malencoly, eiþer in spekynges or in wirkynge or in boþe.[19]

Clearly, to be a perfect paragon of reason would be a severe disadvantage
for anyone seeking spiritual improvement. Yet in a way such rigidity is both
admirable and necessary, especially when considering the role Langland's
Reson is called upon to play. For the Reson of these early passus is a judge
who is all the more reliable for not being open to bribes, nor being swayed
by arguments for clemency which so nearly persuade the King.

However, there is an apparent contradiction here, for by strengthening
his statements by swearing 'by the Rode' and 'By Him that raughte on the
Rood' Reson is placing his actions in stark contrast to the central precepts of
forgiveness, clemency, self-sacrifice and redemption which suffuse the Incarnation and Crucifixion. His words thus undercut his deeds. Nevertheless
Reson cannot be dismissed as simply erroneous; he represents the rigorous
codes of a judgement which differentiates right from wrong in absolute
terms and acts accordingly. By so doing Reson is doing no more, and no
less, than acting true to character. As the *Cloud* author puts it,

Reson is a myȝt þorou þe whiche we departe þe iuel fro þe good, þe iuel
fro þe worse, þe good fro þe betir, þe worse fro þe worste, þe betir fro þe
best. Before er man synned, myȝt reson haue done al þis by kynde. Bot
now it is so blendid wiþ þe original synne þat it may not kon worche þis
werk bot ȝif it be illuminid by grace.[20]

Reason's function is thus one of discrimination only. The *Cloud* author is
quick to point out that, having decided which alternative is the good one,
whether or not one chooses to act upon that choice depends on the operation of the will:

---

[18] Walter Hilton, *The Scale of Perfection*, Book 2, ch. 32, ed. S.S Hussey, 'An edition from the
manuscripts of Book 2 of Walter Hilton's *Scale of Perfection*', unpublished Ph.D. thesis,
University of London, 1962, p. 137. I am grateful to Prof. Hussey for letting me see and
use a copy of this thesis.
[19] Hilton, *Scale*, Book 2, ch. 38, p. 170.
[20] *Cloud*, ch. 64, p. 65.

Wille is a my3t þorou whiche we chese good, after þat it be determined
wiþ reson . . .

It is the aspects of determining, ordering and controlling that we meet in
Langland's Reson. However, Reson does not act on his own. As suggested
by the *Cloud* author, other faculties are required to work with Reson in order
for a right decision to be made and be carried out. Hence Reson refuses to
act without Conscience, just as Conscience refuses to judge without Reson
(B.IV.4–5; 192–93).

The point is that ruling a kingdom, or oneself, involves more than merely
ordering a society or character; it also involves aspects of spiritual guidance
and choice. So, although Reson begins by preaching to the realm in Passus
V and tells each person how they ought to be acting, which is a matter of
judgement, he does not have the qualifications to complete the role of a
priest and confessor. His place as preacher is taken by Repentaunce – a
character more fitted to include the aspects of mercy and understanding
which Reson lacks but which are necessary for a confessor. For although
Reson can lay down the precepts he cannot stir the people to follow them –
he is an assessing and detached figure who works in an intellectual and
dispassionate sphere, and as such is not equipped to elicit emotional responses from his audience. It requires the more affective power of Repentaunce to work from Reson's principles and change the role of preacher into
that of confessor, prior to the confession of the seven deadly sins.

This shift from Reson to Repentaunce indicates that Langland is employing Reson as a figure who, by his very nature, is primarily concerned with
temporal matters, judging and assessing them in order to arrive at a logical
conclusion which will bear examination, or even simply allow for the order
necessary for any system of government. It is a role Reson maintains
throughout the poem, whether he is being cited as a judge as in B.XI.131 or
seen as the governing force in the natural world in Passus XI 335ff. The final
impression is of a faculty which is vital but which has a strongly defined
sphere of jurisdiction. This is perhaps stated most explicitly in B.XIX where
reason is listed as one of the gifts the Magi bring to Christ:

> That o kyng cam with Reson, covered under sense.
> The second kyng siththe soothliche offrede
> Rightwisnesse under reed gold, Resones felawe.
> Gold is likned to Leautee that laste shal evere,
> And Reson to richels – to right and to truthe.
> . . .
> Ertheliche honeste thynges was offred thus at ones
> Thorugh thre kynne kynges knelynge to Jesu. (B.XIX.86–95)

The gift of incense, connected with truth and rightness, is called the gift of
reason and presented with the gift of loyalty and justice combined in the

notion of 'leautee'. Most important, though, is the fact that all three gifts are explicitly called things of earthly value – 'Ertheliche honeste thynges' – and presented to Christ at the time He becomes man. The implication must be that these virtues are vital in earthly terms but may cease to have such importance when earthly things are left behind.

So the figure of Reson in *Piers Plowman* has wide, if not complete, knowledge of temporal matters and is able to assess the facts of any given situation and provide a judgement that can be relied upon to be unbiased and informed, as long as the matter in hand falls within the bounds of reason's jurisdiction. However, there is no compulsion to follow the dictates of reason alone; it is an essential feature of all the characterizations of reason referred to above that the action of the will is required to put their advice into action. Nevertheless, reason is essential, both as the principle which maintains the ideal of order and the faculty which divides mankind from the beasts. Moreover, it also begins an approach to the divine because it is connected with the intellect. Although this aspect of reason is not explicitly represented in *Piers Plowman* it is nonetheless indicated by the attitudes expressed towards Reson by such figures as Conscience and Ymaginatif. It is therefore worth considering briefly the function of reason as a basis for an approach to knowledge which demands the ability to define and deduce.

5

Reson and Ymaginatif

Although reason's discriminating and assessing powers are highly valued, it is the link with the *logos* that gives reason its high standing as it enables mankind to rise above pre-occupation with earthly matters and involvement with temporal things only, to the contemplation of things spiritual. It is this Neo-Platonic view that Alan of Lille (1125/30–1203) presents in his *Distinctiones* when he calls reason '*vis animae qua anima movetur ad contemplationem coelestium*', the power of the soul by which the soul is moved to the contemplation of heavenly things.[1] This interpretation of reason frees it from its seemingly necessary involvement with earthly matters which dominates the discussions and representations of reason encountered in Aquinas, *The Romance of the Rose* and *Le Pèlerinage de la Vie Humaine*. However, this presentation of reason must be modified when John Trevisa's view is taken into consideration.

In the translation of Bartholomaeus Anglicus's *De Proprietatibus Rerum*, which John Trevisa completed in 1398, we find reason as the fourth property of the soul, closely aligned with the fifth, intellect:

> Þe ferþe is *racio* 'resoun', þat demeþ betwene gode and euel and soþ and fals. Þe fifþe is *intellectus* 'vnderstondynge and inwit', þerby he knowiþ materles and bodiles þinges as God and angelis and oþir siche. . . . *racio* and *intellectus*, beþ in þe soule, in þat he may be departid from þe body and abide departid as an aungel.[2]

Reason is still associated with the power to distinguish and discriminate, as before, but here it is also one of the powers which enables the soul to continue to exist after the death of the earthly body.

Yet, although Trevisa awards reason this higher place in the order of things, he nevertheless retains the association of reason with temporal

---

[1] Alan of Lille, *Distinctiones*, quoted in Fleming, *Reason and the Lover*, p. 31.
[2] John Trevisa, *On the Properties of Things*, Vol. 1, Book 3, ch. 6, ed. M.C. Seymour (Oxford, 1975), p. 95.

matters. Reason is only one of two virtues which work closely together and it is the other half of this duo, intellect, that has jurisdiction of the higher things:

> In þat he haþ twey maner aspect, for he biholdeþ þe ouer þinges and so he is iclepid *intellectus*, and beholdiþ þe neþer þinges and so he is iclepid *racio*.[3]

This fine distinction between intellect and reason allows Trevisa to recognise that an ability to differentiate good from evil and truth from falsehood is essential if man is to reach a contemplation of more intangible things, while also allowing him to maintain the view that reason is a fundamentally mortal faculty. Since reason only achieved its high position after mankind's fall from the original state of affairs in which the good was known by intuition – kynde – reason can be a fallen or temporal virtue at best; as such it must be associated primarily with earthly things. For in order to fulfil its role as judge reason must be impartial, dispassionate and be able to give due weight to everything. However, this very ability links reason incontrovertibly with temporal matters since once a level of spiritual contemplation is reached the affairs of this world, over which reason presides, become negligible. Hence a faculty such as reason, which operates by weighing up relative worth in earthly terms and for practical uses, becomes superfluous when one attains a more spiritual perspective; or, indeed, when one leaves this world for the next.

The recognition of the limitations of reason leads to the realisation that reason must be superseded if wisdom as *sapientia* is to be achieved. This is reflected in the *Benjamin Minor* of Richard of St Victor (d.1173) where Rachel is the representative of reason from whom 'springeþ riȝt knowynges & cleer vnderstondyng';[4] yet she must die after the birth of Benjamin, who stands for contemplation. This is explained by stating that in superseding reason contemplation simultaneously reveals how limited it is:

> Benjamin itaque nascente, Rachel moritur, quia mens ad contemplationem rapta, quantus sit humanus rationis defectus experitur.
>
> (And so when Benjamin is born, Rachel dies, because the mind, having been carried away to contemplation, experiences how great the failure of human reason is.)[5]

---

3 Trevisa, p. 95.
4 'A Trety of þe Stodye of Wysdome Þat men clepen Beniamyn', in *The Cloud of Unknowyng and Related Treatises*, ed. P. Hodgson, Analecta Cartusiana 3 (Salzburg and Exeter, 1982), p. 134.
5 Richard of St. Victor, *Benjamin Minor*, cap. 74, *PL*, 196, col. 52. Translated as 'The Benjamin Minor or The Twelve Patriarchs', by G. Zinn in *Richard of St. Victor*, Classics of Spirituality (London, 1979), p. 131.

or, as the *Cloud* author puts in *A Tretyse of þe Stodye of Wysdome þat men clepen Beniamyn,*

> . . . Beniamyn is borne, and his moder Rachel diȝeþ. For whi in what tyme þat a soule is rauischid abouen hymself by habundaunce of desires & a greet multytude of loue, so þat it is enflawmyd wiþ þe liȝt of þe Godheed, sekirly þan dyȝeþ al mans reson.[6]

In their readings Richard of St Victor and the Middle English translator agree with Alan of Lille, who presents a similar line of progression in his *Anticlaudianus* where Phronesis is instructed to leave behind the chariot in which she has been travelling so far. This chariot has been drawn by the horses of the senses who were curbed by reason and her journey has been directed by the command of reason, yet she is allowed to ascend to the higher reaches of knowledge only if she leaves reason behind, going on accompanied by hearing and theology alone:

> Sed soli Fronesi ducatum spondet et ipsi
> Consulit instanter, precepti robur eidem
> Consilio miscens, ut currum deserat, ipsos
> In celo deponant equos comitemque relinquat
> Inferius, que sit stabilis custodia tanti
> Depositi, currum sistens, frenansque iugales,
> Ne si currus, equi, Racio, nitantur in altum
> Tendere, nec talem dignetur habere uiantem
> Semita celestis, alios experta meatus,
> Erret equs, nutet Racio, currusque uacillet.
> Explentur mandata dee uotisque fauetur;
> Stat Racio, sistuntur equi, quadriga quiescit.
> Omnibus exclusis, solum regina secundum
> Consorti concedit equm, qui parcius ipsum
> Admiretur iter nec multum deneget, ipsos
> Ascensus, fractus freni melioris habena.

> (But she [theology] pledges guidance to Phronesis alone and strongly advises her, adding the force of command to the same advice, that she leave the car behind, give the horses in charge to her companion in the heavens [Reason] and leave her below to be a reliable guardian of a charge so great, securing the chariot and curbing the horses, lest, if Reason with the chariot and horses should struggle upwards and the celestial path, acquainted with different wayfarers, should not deign to accept such a traveller, the steeds would miss the way, reason would falter and the chariot reel. The instructions of the goddess are fulfilled and her wishes find favour. Reason remains, the horses are secured, the chariot is stationary. Discarding all the others, the queen grants her companion the second horse alone [hearing], as

[6] 'Beniamyn', p. 144.

he, trained by a more effective rein and bit, would be less affrighted at that
road and would baulk but little at that upward journey.)[7]

Interestingly, Richard of St Victor also invokes the sense of hearing when he
explains the requirement for reason to remain behind in terms of the human
senses being overwhelmed by divine inspiration. If reason is not abandoned then the soul cannot respond fully to the 'thunder of the divine
voice':

> Ad tonitruum itaque divinæ vocis auditor cadit, quia ad id quod divinitus
> inspiratur, humani sensus capacitas succumbit, et nisi humanæ ratiocina-
> tionis angustias deserat, ad capiendum divinæ inspirationis arcanum in-
> telligentiæ sinum non dilatat. Ibi itaque auditor cadit, ubi humana ratio
> deficit.
>
> (And so the hearer falls down at the thunder of the divine voice because the
> capacity of human sense succumbs to that which is divinely inspired, and unless
> it abandons the limitations of human reasoning it does not expand the bosom of
> understanding in order to hold the secret of divine inspiration. And so there the
> hearer falls, where human reason fails.)[8]

Although it is a voice which is used to represent the divine inspiration, it is
significant that the metaphor of hearing is left behind, just as reason must
be, and an abstract figure of secret understanding is substituted. There is a
similarity here with the notion of *scientia*, which Balbus linked with what
one hears, and which is also valued, but must ultimately be superseded.

All the above accounts agree in presenting a form of progression in which
reason is crucial, and even attains a sort of appreciation, albeit not the
highest that can be achieved in this world. The powers of reason and reasoning can result in a type of knowledge which is valuable, both in itself
and in terms of preparation for the higher, more abstract form of understanding which comes with contemplation. In particular, reason forms the
core of self-knowledge, which is a crucial precursor to any attempt to approach an understanding of God, by whatever route. Richard of St Victor
makes clear the necessity of such self-knowledge when he expounds the
signification of Joseph:

> . . . et Dei cognitio, et sui ex ratione percipitur. Longe post Joseph
> Benjamin gignitur, quia animus qui in sui cognitione diu exercitatus,
> pleneque eruditus non est, ad Dei cognitionem non sustollitur? . . . Alio-
> quin si non potes cognoscere te, qua fronte præsumis apprehendere ea
> quæ sunt supra te?

---

7 Alan of Lille, *Anticlaudianus*, 5, 246–61, ed. R. Bossuat (Paris, 1955). Tr. J.J. Sheridan, *Alan
   of Lille, Anticlaudianus* (Toronto, 1973), p. 147.
8 *Benjamin Minor*, cap. 82, *PL*, 196, col. 58; Zinn, pp. 139–40.

(. . . knowledge of God and self are learned from reason. Benjamin is born long after Joseph because the soul that has not practised over a long time and been educated fully in knowledge of self is not raised up to knowledge of God. . . . If you are not able to know yourself, how do you have the boldness to grasp at those things which are above you?)[9]

The explanation is retained in the Middle English version where Joseph – discretion – learns not only to reject deceit in others but is also the means by which perfect self-knowledge may be attained. To this is then added a warning that without such self-recognition any such attempt to comprehend God is not only doomed to failure but is also highly presumptuous: there are some things it is not seemly for mortals to know about the divine:

> And also by þis ilke Joseph he is not only lernyd to eschewe þe deceyte of his enemyes, bot also of a man is led by hym to þe parfite knowyng of hymself.
> . . .
> For first I wolde a man lered hym to knowe þe vnseable þinges of his owne spirit, er he presume to knowe þe vnseable þinges of God. And he þat knoweþ not ȝit hymself, and weniþ þat he haue getyn somdele knowing of þe vnseable þinges of God, I doute it not þat he ne is disceyuid. And forþi I rede þat a man seke first besily for to knowe hymself, þe whiche is maad to þe ymage and þe licnes of God, as in soule.[10]

This is precisely the charge that Ymaginatif levels at Wil at the end of Passus XI.

Wil has enraged Reson at B.XI.373 by daring to ask why he does not direct mankind as he does the rest of the world. The response he gets is a rebuke for not suffering more and the recommendation that he should be more patient rather than butting in where he has little business and less understanding. It later transpires that, in this post-lapsarian world, no one can live without sin, and so it follows that it would be impossible for Reson to order all things so that mankind did no wrong. Were it possible to achieve such a state of affairs through the use of reason alone, it would have been achieved long ago. Alford agrees with Reson here, declaring that it 'is not for the will to question reason – taken either as transcendent order or as the faculty perceiving it'.[11] Yet, given that Reson can be regarded as flawed, it is not necessarily wrong for Wil to challenge him. The difficulty is that Wil has not yet achieved the requisite degree of self-knowledge and so falls into the category of the untutored presumptuous; a point Ymaginatif makes forcibly in his initial rebuke to Wil at B.XI as he drums home both Reson's

---

9 *Benjamin Minor*, cap. 71, *PL*, 196, col. 51; Zinn, p. 124.
10 'Beniamyn', pp. 142–43.
11 Alford, 'The Role of Reason . . .', p. 214.

lesson and Wil's own realisation that he has learnt the value of sufferance by showing a lack of it:

'Now I woot what Dowel is,' quod I, 'by deere God, as me thynketh!'
And as I caste up myne eighen, oon loked on me and asked
Of me, what thyng it were? 'Ywis, sire,' I seyde,
To se muche and suffre moore, certes,' quod I, 'is Dowel.'
'Haddestow suffred,' he seide,'slepynge tho thow were,
Thow sholdest have knowen that Clergie kan and conceyved
                                moore thorugh Reson –
For Reson wolde have reherced thee right as Clergie seide.
Ac for thyn entremetynge here artow forsake:
Philosophus esses, si tacuisses'. (B.XI.407–414a)

Wil has begun to recognise the point of what Reson has said on his own, but Ymaginatif reinforces the lesson by the use of the simile of the drunken man in the ditch (B.XI.425–432) and so ensures that Wil understands not only what Reson said but also why he, Wil, was affected by it. Ymaginatif makes Wil realise the impact of shame and, by extension, the power of an argument driven home by affective force.

By thus supporting Reson, Ymaginatif is acting true to the view of imagination as the helper of reason which is found most notably in the *Benjamin Minor*. As Richard of St Victor says, reason cannot function without imagination since without imagination reason knows nothing: *Nam sine imaginatatione, ratio nihil sciret*.[12] He later elaborates on this statement by declaring that reason is incapable of thinking about invisible or spiritual things unless imagination provides it with images of visible things from which it can work up to the consideration of invisible things:

ad invisibilium cognitionem numquam ratio assurgeret, nisi ei ancilla sua, imaginatio videlicet, rerum visibilium formam repraesentaret. Per rerum enim visibilium speciem surgit ad rerum invisibilium cognitionem.

(Reason could never rise to the consideration of invisible things unless her hand-maiden, namely imagination, presented images of visible things. For through the sight of visible things it rises to the consideration of invisible things.)

So it is in keeping with the role of imagination that Ymaginatif should both illustrate and reinforce what Reason's views.

Furthermore Ymaginatif declares that he has followed Wil all his life, in sickness and in health, and never been inactive. Indeed he has frequently tried to move Wil to consider his mortality and his standing in life, but so far to no avail (B.XII.1–19). Again all these traits tally with the presentation of imagination found in the *Benjamin Minor* where Rachel's handmaid, Bala,

---

12 *Benjamin Minor*, cap. 5, *PL*, 196, col. 4.

is taken to represent the imagination. Bala is constantly at work and cannot be silenced, a characteristic which leads to her being called a 'jangler' in the Middle English translation of the treatise.[13] Yet Imagination is far more than the essential but potentially distracting attribute it seems to be at first. It is also the faculty which is able to envisage the future, whether good or bad, as Richard of St Victor makes clear by his reading of the two sons of Bala, Dan and Naphtalim, as the Sight of Pains to come and the Sight of Joys to come respectively.[14] Langland's Ymaginatif displays both these sides as he urges Wil to reflect on his life so far and of the need to reform lest it be too late:

> And manye tymes have meved thee to mynne on thyn ende,
> And how fele fernyeres are faren, and so fewe to come;
> And of thi wilde wantownesse whan thow yong were,
> To amende it in thi myddel age, lest myght the faille
> In thyn olde elde, that yvele kan suffre
> Poverte or penaunce, or preyeres bidde.   (B.XII.4–9)

He then goes on to attack Wil for wasting his time meddling with verses when he could go and say his prayers, and neatly counters Wil's defence (that if he knew what Dowel, Dobet and Dobest were he would happily go and devote himself to a life of prayer and never work more) by presenting him with a list of those to whom the search and acquisition of knowledge brought nothing but shame, disappointment and downfall occasioned by pride. This ability to call up images of others as well as projecting probable consequences of Wil's own way of life demonstrates that Ymaginatif more than simply Wil's imaginative ability. He is, like Reson, a full allegory of his name. He therefore contains elements of both the mortal, or natural, aspects of imagination and the supernatural aspects which enable prophecy. E.N. Kaulbach points out that Ymaginatif actually 'blurs the distinctions between natural and supernatural knowledge', to which A.J. Minnis adds that he is the power which facilitates movement between these two forms – between *scientia* and *sapientia*.[15] When one then takes into consideration his role as part of the poetics of *Piers Plowman*, which A.V.C. Schmidt has expounded in *The Clerkly Maker*, one becomes aware of the variety and complexity of this figure. It is a richness that Langland exploits to the full.

An ability to call up images to illustrate an argument is a defining characteristic of any definition of the imagination and it is one of which

---

[13] 'Beniamyn', p. 129.

[14] See 'Beniamyn', p. 134.

[15] E.N. Kaulbach, 'The "Vis Imaginativa Secundum Avicennam" and the Naturally Prophetic Powers of Ymaginatif in the B-Text of *Piers Plowman*', *JEGP*, 86 (1987), pp. 496–514 (p. 496). See also A.J. Minnis, 'Affection and Imagination in *The Cloud of Unknowing* and Hilton's *Scale of Perfection*', *Traditio*, 39 (1983), 323–65.

Langland's Ymaginatif takes full advantage. He passes rapidly from point to point, illustrating each part of his speech with a reference to a tale or a simile, designed to make the whole argument more easily accessible and memorable. Within the space of ten lines we have been presented with such widely disparate images as Solomon and Sampson from the Bible, the respected classical author Virgil, Felice, from the romance *Guy of Warwick* and the historical figure of Rosamunde, Henry II's mistress who was thought to have been poisoned by Queen Eleanor. These contrasting characters are followed over the ensuing two hundred lines by illustrations and references from the Bible, similes of men going to war or swimmers and non-swimmers falling into rivers, discussions of the significance of peacocks and larks, and explanations of Trajan's redemption from hell. It is not that Ymaginatif deals with less high-powered aspects of theological theory than Reson or indeed Clergie, but rather he uses figures and images far more to bring his words to life.[16] As A.J. Minnis has pointed out, Ymaginatif teaches primarily through *exempla*, a form designed to work by stimulating the imaginative process, thus eliciting at least a felt response if not an intellectual one as well.[17] This argument has been taken further by Hugh White, who suggests that the felt response evoked and employed by Ymaginatif reveals how problematic the process of discovery is, but cannot offer any final conclusions.[18] Clearly, this tallies with the notion of Imagination as a handmaid who is necessary in order to achieve understanding, but cannot itself explain or understand. By showering Wil and us with examples of the various fates of others who have embarked on the quest for knowledge, Langland queries not only our understanding of knowledge, but also renders the intellectual pursuit of God itself problematic. For the questions that are constantly raised at this point in the poem are first: what is the role of faith in a religion which declares that all who believe and have been baptised will be saved, yet warns against ignorance as against the dangers of the blind leading the blind (B.XII.171–189) and secondly: where can men find reliable guidance or role-models for behaviour when an emperor can be saved through acting according to his pagan principles, despite not being baptised while those who are baptised can still be refused entry to the divine banquet (as Scripture's text of XI.112–14 showed)? Even the value of learning itself is undermined as a guide since it can be used to save felons from Tyburn, hardly a recommendation in moral terms, although very practical for the felon involved.

---

16 J.S. Wittig provides an extensive and thorough discussion of Ymaginatif's far-reaching influence in terms of both *intellectus* and *affectus* in his article '*Piers Plowman* B, Passus IX–XII; Elements in the Design of the Inward Journey', *Traditio*, 28 (1972), 211–280.
17 A.J. Minnis, 'Langland's Ymaginatif and Late-Medieval Theories of Imagination', *Comparative Criticism*, 3 (1981), 71–103.
18 H. White, 'Langland's Ymaginatif, Kynde and the *Benjamin Major*', *Medium Aevum*, 55 (1986), 241–48.

While admitting the existence of such questions and problems, Ymaginatif does not offer any kind of definitive answer. Indeed any of his opinions which we could be tempted to regard as conclusive dictates are undermined by examples or alternative views which Ymaginatif himself introduces. Even his apparently re-assuring declaration *'salvabitur vix iustus in die iudicii;/Ergo salvabitur!'* (XII.279–80), which seems to assert that if one is just one will be saved, regardless of how ignorant of Christianity one may be, is cast under a shadow of doubt when Ymaginatif selects Trajan as his proof. Since Trajan was regarded as the ultimate example of salvation through good works, regardless of learning, he ought to be the ideal case in point for Ymaginatif, yet this reference to Trajan must surely recall his previous presence in the poem where his case proved to be more complicated than it at first appeared. For Trajan gained salvation through the prayers of a pope, Pope Gregory, who surely had learning to his credit as well as faith. Furthermore, this reference also summons up echoes of the crises which occasioned that inner dream; the fear that as many are called and only few are chosen, there is no guarantee that one is a member of the chosen few rather than of the rejected many.

Instead of attempting to resolve such knotty problems through debate Ymaginatif tends to refer to other personifications as providers of solutions, in particular Clergie, while he himself stresses that humility and self-knowledge are required to be able to accept Clergie's teachings and so achieve any form of understanding. In fact, far from offering definite hope and consolation, Ymaginatif's main function seems to be to discomfort the dreamer and so force him to re-assess his intellectual standing and expectations.

This view of Ymaginatif's role is reinforced by the fact that his encounter with Wil ends with a dramatic affirmation of faith, not knowledge. There can be no certainty concerning who is saved or how one finally achieves salvation for, were it possible to achieve it by following a set of rules, the necessity of faith would be denied. Hence Ymaginatif's assertion 'Wheither it [the law] worth or not worth, the bileve is gret of truthe' (289). He is deliberately moving away from the approach to salvation through a knowledge based on judgement and learning towards one based on the operation of faith and ultimate hope and trust in God. His final texts are ones of declaration of faith:

> And wheither it worth or noght worth, the bileve is gret of truthe,
> And a hope hangynge therinne to have a mede for his truthe;
> For *Deus dicitur quasi dans vitam eternam suis, hoc est fidelibus.*
> *Et alibi, Si ambulavero in medio umbre mortis* &c. (B.XII.289–291a)

Yet there is a final paradox, for his parting words are not a re-affirmation of this belief, but an implied acknowledgement of the need for learning to match the text and its faith, for it is the *gloss* of the text which directs its reader to a sense of the value of truth and value to mankind. Hence even this apparent affirmation is subtly undermined and revealed as more complex than it at first appears.

If Ymaginatif's function is recognised as one of discomforting the dreamer in order to bring about an affective reaction which may prompt change or greater self-knowledge, it is a function he fulfils to the utmost. As Passus XIII opens the dreamer is not only thinking over all he has seen, as he has done previously after his dreams, but is actually wandering the country almost out of his senses. His discomfort and need to re-assess his intellectual standing has been so profound that he even removes himself from the accepted norms of society in order to try to come to some kind of greater understanding of all that his dream, inner-dream and subsequent encounter with his own imaginative faculty have signified.

We are given an indication that it is the action of the imagination and its effect that will be of interest, rather than the faculty itself, in the choice of the form 'ymaginatif' instead of 'imaginacioun'. This point has been made by J.S. Wittig:

> The poet's choice of the '-if' ending, when he could have just as easily written 'imaginacioun', suggests that, like Richard, Langland intended to stress the activity rather than the 'faculty'.... it is only now when the dreamer has been disposed by fear and shame that Imaginatif is able to help him.[19]

It is certainly true that Wil is deeply affected by his encounter with Ymaginatif, as his waking reaction shows, yet it must be remembered that Ymaginatif does not dispute the need for reason and learning; in fact he explicitly endorses both, not only in his first exchange with Wil in Passus XI.411–13 but also throughout Passus XII, where he declares

> ... yet is clergie to comende, and kynde wit bothe,
> And namely clergie for Cristes love, that of clergie is roote.
>
> (B.XII.70–71)

Indeed learning and reason are as essential as sight:

> And right as sight serveth a man to se the heighe strete,
> Right so lereth lettrure lewed men to reson.   (B.XII.103–104)

Conversely, Ymaginatif also provides examples of those who were saved despite being ignorant of Christian learning (among these are Trajan and the felon of Good Friday). So a paradox is set up in which learning is both to be desired and yet not to be sought unnecessarily, and reason is both necessary

---

[19] Wittig, 'Elements in the Design of the Inward Journey', pp. 270–71.

and yet fundamentally limited, just as Clergie and Kynde Wit are shown to be in lines 225–226. There are some questions which suggest themselves, but which cannot, nor ought not to be enquired into in depth:

> Ac why that oon theef on the cros creaunt hym yald
> Rather than that oother theef, though thow woldest appose,
> Alle the clerkes under Crist ne kouthe the skile assoille:
> *Quare placuit? Quia voluit.*
> And so I seye by thee, that sekest after the whyes,
> And aresonedest Reson, a rebukynge as it were . . . (B.XII.214–219)

The only answer possible to the question of why one thief rather than the other should be saved can only be 'because God willed it so' and this must serve. To enquire further is to be guilty of vain curiosity.[20]

Ymaginatif's attitude to reason, learning and faith can be seen to combine the acknowledgement of a use for questioning, with a recognition of the notion of vain curiosity, resulting in the idea of the necessity for an intellectual humility which seeks to know fully what it is right to know, but does not question beyond the bounds of what is suitable for a mortal, flawed, intellect. So Ymaginatif both endorses Reson and supports Clergie, but he also includes the need for a reaction to ideas and language which is affective, which can evoke the powerful reaction to which he and Wil referred at the very beginning of their encounter:

> 'Pryde now and presumpcion paraventure wol thee appele,
> That Clergie this compaignye ne kepeth noght to suwe.
> For shal nevere chalangynge ne chidynge chaste a man so soone
> As shal shame, and shended hym, and shape hym to amende.'
> . . .
> 'Ye siggen sooth, by my soule,' quod I, 'Ich have yseyen it ofte.
> Ther smyt no thyng so smerte, ne smelleth so foule
> As shame, there he sheweth hym – for ech man shonyeth his felaweshipe.
> Why ye wisse me thus,' quod I, 'was for I rebuked Reson.'
> (B.XI.421–24; 433–36)

The fact that Ymaginatif is about to leave Wil after this brief exchange indicates that he made his appearance in order to convince Wil of the efficacy and even necessity of moving the affective elements of the soul, not just the rational, and it is this point that is at the heart of his subsequent argument with Wil. It is the argumentative and inquisitive Wil who detains him and provides room for the ensuing conversation – an exchange which,

---

[20] For a review and discussion of the sin of curiosity since Augustine see Richard Newhauser's article, 'Augustinian *Vitium Curiositatis* and its Reception', in *Saint Augustine and His Influence in the Middle Ages*, ed. E.B. King and J.T. Schaefer (Sewanee, 1988), pp. 99–124.

as has been shown, results in an acknowledgment of the need for learning, but equally in an affirmation of the need for intellectual humility and a willingness to respond to affective elements of knowledge and faith.

This emphasis on the need for the learner to have the correct disposition in order to learn is also found in Richard Rolle's *De Emendacione Vitae*, translated into English by R. Misyn in 1434, roughly a century after it was written. Rolle's views on learning appears under the section dealing with meditation:

> Truly if þou despise techynge of doctours, & trow þi-selfe better may fynde, þen þa tech þe in þer writynge, know itt forsoith, cristis lufe þou sal not taste. ffond sayinge truly it is : god taght þame, qwhy þerfore sal he not tech me? I answere þe, for þou art not slike as þa were. þou art prowd & sturdy, & þa wer lawly meek, þu presumand of god askyd no-þing, bot þame-self vndyr all mekand toke conynge of sayntis. ¶ Þerfore he taght þame þat we in þer bokes suld be taght.[21]

Here we find many of the elements of Ymaginatif's speeches: the respect for learning and the authority of 'doctours', the rebuke of the pride which leads one to dispute the need of learning, or of teachers, and the stress on humility and a proper disposition if one is to learn.

Hence it is possible to regard Ymaginatif as supporting the orthodox view, rather than challenging it. In disconcerting the dreamer and perhaps the reader too, he is not undermining the whole fabric of learning and authority, nor indeed querying the fundamental tenets of society. In fact he is complying very much with the ideas of the role of the imagination both as the helper and supporter of reason and as the faciliator of movement between *scientia* and *sapientia*, between the discourses of *logos* and *verbum* and between natural and supernatural concepts. In addition it is Ymaginatif who voices and explains the purpose of affective language rather than just using it as Scripture and the friars of Passus VIII do. It is not out of character, then, for him to be at once very closely connected with the rational and intellectual processes (both their strengths and weaknesses) and also be the figure who leaves Wil 'witlees nerehand', having relied more upon evoking a response from Wil through reference to others than on using the methods of debate or definition. Langland does not side with one approach to understanding or use of language at the expense of the other. Elements of both the deductive and the affective approach are evident in *Piers Plowman* as he explores the extents and limitations of each, just as Ymaginatif both supports and modifies our attitude towards Reson.

---

21 Richard Rolle, *De Emendacione Vitae*, tr. R. Misyn in 1434 as *The Mending of Life, or the Rule of Living*, ch. 7. 'Of Meditacion', ed. R. Harvey, EETS o.s. 106 (London, 1896), p. 120.

Part Two

KNOWLEDGE THROUGH REASON

'Thirst for knowledge and greed for explanations never lead to a thinking inquiry. Curiosity is always the concealed arrogance of a self-consciousness that banks on a self-invented ratio and its rationality. The will to know does not will to abide in hope before what is worthy of thought.'[1]

1 Martin Heidegger, 'A Dialogue on Language', *On the Way to Language*, tr. P.D. Hertz (London, 1971), p. 13.

6

The Power of a Trained Mind

Wil's search for definitions of Dowel, Dobet and Dobest, which dominates Passus VIII–XIV, provides a framework for the more detailed exploration of authority and the use of language to be found in the Vita of *Piers Plowman*. Its similarity to the Dialogue form, as Wil passes from figure to figure, collecting definitions and directions as he goes, connects this section to the deductive approach to knowledge. This similarity evidently struck medieval readers also, as the explicit of the Oxford manuscript Bodleian MS Laud 581 reads: *Explicit hic dialogus petr[i] plowman*. The exception to this overall structure is the sojourn in the Lond of Longyng, contained in the inner-dream; yet even this episode is brought into the general domain of the rational by the intervention and interpretation of Ymaginatif. For the main part, then, the figures Wil encounters in the two linked dreams of B.VIII–XIV are predominantly concerned with acquiring knowledge by means of deduction and definition.[2] They are interested in knowledge as *scientia*, to be approached and debated in suitable terms.

Given the concern with right counsels and correct judgement that has dominated the Prologue and first seven passus of the text, and given the respect accorded Reson in those, it is not surprising to find ourselves involved in scholarly debate. After all, Wil has asked to be taught the truth and how to know the false; he did not ask how to know good or to gain

---

2 These passus seem to make a complete section, particularly in the B-Text where the end of Passus XIV coincides with the end of the Haukyn episode. In the C-Text the rubrics indicate that the scribes perceived a new section beginning with Passus XVIII and labelled it accordingly *Passus primus de Dobet*; but this division occurs within a dream and indeed in the middle of an exchange between Wil and Liberum Arbitriium. I have therefore regarded the first section as lasting until Wil's waking at C.XVIII.179, which clearly marks a dividing point, although, as Pearsall notes, its rather puzzling position suggests an incomplete revision at this point.

A.J. Minnis in 'Langland's Ymaginatif' treats Passus B.VIII–XII as a complete unit and defends his selection accordingly. However, as Clergie's banquet and the figure of the Doctor in particular are the culmination of the themes raised and developed in the previous vision, it seems sensible to treat the two dreams as a whole.

feelings or inclinations which could provide the 'goostly desires' mentioned in the Middle English *Beniamyn,* where a distinction is drawn between the two approaches and types of understanding:

> Þorow reson we knowe, and þorow affeccioun we fele or loue. Of reson springeþ riȝt counselles & goostly wittes, and of affeccioun springeþ goostly desires and ordeyned felynges.[3]

It is, therefore, entirely in keeping with the movement of the poem up to the beginning of Passus VIII that Wil should seek counsel and guidance from figures connected with intellectual excellence and theories of preaching, without first reflecting that this type of knowledge or 'truth' may not be the 'good' he seeks.

The unspoken assumption of all the personifications concerned with *scientia* is that theology itself is a science and therefore to be approached through the methods of reasoning and teaching appropriate to similar sciences, i.e. rational argument, deduction and the arts of rhetoric. Naturally it is a rather special science; the *Summa Theologica* attributed to Alexander of Hales explains:

> . . . sunt principia veritatis ut veritatis, et sunt principia veritatis ut boni- tatis. Dico ergo quod aliae scientiae procedunt ex principiis veritatis ut veritatis per se notis; haec autem scientia procedit ex principiis veritatis ut bonitatis et per se notis ut bonitatis, quamvis occultis ut veritatis. Unde haec scientia magis est virtutis quam artis, et sapientia magis quam scien- tia; magis enim consistit in virtute et efficacia quam in contemplatione et notitia.
>
> (. . . there are the principles of truth as truth, and there are the principles of truth as good. Therefore I say that other sciences proceed from the principles of truth as truth known as themselves; but this science proceeds from the principles of truth as good and known for themselves as good, although hidden in regards to truth. Whence this science is rather one of virtue than of art, and a wisdom rather than a science; for it consists more in virtue and the achieving of virtue than in study and intellectual knowledge.)[4]

The first type of principle – *veritas ut veritas* – can be proved to be true in its own terms, but the second type can only be demonstrated to be good, not true, as the actual rationale behind it remains ineffable. Hence, although one can deduce the existence of theological knowledge, the first-hand experience

---

[3] 'Beniamyn', p. 129. For a discussion of this difference of attitude see V. Gillespie's essay 'Mystic's Foot: Rolle and Affectivity', in *The Medieval Mystical Tradition,* ed. Marion Glasscoe (Exeter, 1982), pp. 199–207.

[4] Alexander of Hales, *Summa theologica,* Tractatus introductorius, q. 1 de doctrina theolo- giae, cap. iv, art. 2, resp. 2, p. 9b. The translation is mine, based on that given in Minnis-Scott, p. 216.

of it remains beyond the powers of the human mind. Thus theology is distinct from the other sciences because its most reliable knowledge comes from affective rather than deductive reasoning. The desire to retain the link with deductive methods of enquiry, and with it the kudos of the classification of science, is evident here, but at least Alexander of Hales allows that theology is perhaps so special a science that it is in fact a wisdom (*sapientia*). Giles of Rome (d.1316) could not countenance such slippage of terms, preferring to expand the definition of *scientia*, when he uses it in his Prologue to the *Song of Songs*, to include speculative and practical branches, rather than lose the term altogether:

> Bonitas vero spiritualis, quia non dependet ex operibus exterioribus, immo ex habitu caritatis, et ejus operibus; sacra pagina quae ad talem bonitatem ordinatur, practica dici non debet. Sicut ergo scientia quae ordinatur ad speculationem, non dicitur practica, licet speculari, sit quoddam opus; sed suscipit nomen ex speculatione, et dicitur speculativa: sic et theologica quae ordinatur ad affectionem sive dilectionem caritatis, quia hujusmodi opera non sunt exteriora, ab eis debet denominari specialiter theoligica, et debet dici affectiva vel dilectiva, et non practica.
>
> (. . . because spiritual goodness is not dependent upon exterior actions but rather upon the condition and works of charity, holy writ, which is directed towards this sort of goodness, should not be called practical. The science which is directed towards speculation is not called practical, even though to speculate is a kind of work, but instead derives its name from speculation and is called 'speculative'. Likewise theology, which is directed towards the affection of love or charity (because works of this sort are not exterior), must derive a special name from these qualities and must be described as affective and concerned with love, and not as practical.)[5]

Some blurring of the boundaries between deductive and affective discourses is apparent here, but these schoolmen wished to retain their foothold on the terra firma of rational argument and proof, however speculative their subject. This desire to analyse and understand concepts in purely deductive terms is analogous to Wil's reaction at the end of Passus VII, where he places his dream in the context of authorities, biblical dreams and the tenets of the Church. Finally he invests Dowel with the highest significance as the pleader for human souls:

> Forthi I counseille alle Cristene to crie God mercy,
> And Marie his moder be oure meene bitwene,
> That God gyve us grace here, er we go hennes,
> Swiche werkes to werche, while we ben here,
> That after oure deth day, Dowel reherce
> At the day of dome, we dide as he highte. (B.VII.196–201).

---

5 Giles of Rome, Prologue to *Commentary on Songs of Songs* printed in *S. Thomas Aquinas Opera Omnia* (Parma, 1852–72), Vol. XIV, p. 389. See Minnis-Scott, p. 247 and note.

The ambiguity of 'he' here allows for the conflation of Dowel with God, which perhaps creates a link between Wil's desire to understand Dowel and the scholars' exploration of theology. It is logical, then, for Wil to turn to figures drawn from the world of deductive theological debate for advice and interpretation of Dowel. One feels that it is a reasonable assumption that these figures, not only the friars but also the later personifications of intellectual capabilities such as Wit and Clergie, who are clearly learned in religious matters, should be the best guides in this area. In fact this assumption is gradually undermined.

Wil's meeting with the Franciscans at the beginning of Passus VIII signals the start of his dedication to the path of deductive enquiry. Wil himself enters most obviously into this realm with his cry of '*Contra*', with its echo of educated debate, which is endorsed by the rest of the line: 'quod I as a clerc, and comsed to disputen'. Wil realises that he not only sounds like an educated man, but also that his speech is like that of formal debate – a dispute.[6] He thus moves the poem into a more 'academic' register by using the Latin as a device to indicate the sort of exchange he has embarked upon. His reply to the friars' assertion that both Dowel and Do-evil are with them is more an excercise in intellectual point-scoring than an attack on the moral and affective justification of their claim. His case relies heavily on logical progression from premiss to conclusion and the binary opposition of the terms Dowel and Do-evil. Thus his argument runs that since the righteous (among whom it is presumed the friars would count themselves) sin seven times a day, which is Do-evil, and since Dowel and Do-evil cannot be in the same place at the same time, then, logically, Dowel cannot always be with the friars.

This is Wil's first attempt to engage in the type of dispute which tries to prove that an opponent's premiss is faulty and, from the point of view of the deductive approach to knowledge, his reason for attacking the friars' argument and his own rigorous logic are acceptable, if perhaps a bit glib. Unfortunately for him he has chosen to do battle with far more skilled disputants than himself and has even furnished them with the wherewith-all to defeat him. For, by introducing the text, '*sepcies in die cadit iustus*' he has given them the opportunity to embark on the parable of the man in a boat, which he appears neither to comprehend, nor be able to question. He retires confused, defeated by the friars' greater rhetorical skill:

> 'I have no kynde knowyng' quod I 'to conceyve alle thi wordes.
> (B.VIII.58)

---

[6] Full discussion of this and the dual development of sermon and theological argument are to be found in David D'Avray, 'The Transformation of the Medieval Sermon' (D.Phil. thesis, Oxford, 1976) and *The Preaching of the Friars: Sermons diffused from Paris before 1300* (Oxford, 1985).

For their part the friars acquit themselves perfectly, with an explanation which is completely orthodox and fails to convince only because their listener, by his own admission, is unable to understand it. At first it seems that Wil is the only one at fault, an impression which is re-enforced by the reader's automatic assent to his admission, but in fact the friars also fail in their task. They have rendered their teaching incomprehensible by not suiting their words to their audience's abilities. It is true that they do not deliver a *tour de force* of theological learning, but their explanation seems designed to triumph over Wil's attempt at argument rather than ensure he understands the doctrine they present. Their success in disputation is a failure in preaching.

From their introduction in the Prologue (B.58–67) to the final collapse of Unitee in the last passus friars are treated with mistrust. Such mistrust was by no means unique to Langland, or even the fourteenth century, as Wendy Scase and Penn R. Szittya have shown,[7] but the general anti-fraternal feelings had a revival in the late Middle Ages which was expressed in the literature. In Langland the suspicion of friars engendered in the reader is based on the picture of gluttonous, avaricious and power-greedy friars which appear throughout the text. However, although such personal corruption is clearly reprehensible, the most serious accusation is that they abused their education and ability with language to mislead others. In the Prologue the friars are introduced as those who 'glosed the gospel as hem good liked' (B.Prol.60), an ability which is also credited to friars by Chaucer in *The Summoner's Tale* where Friar John declares 'glosyng is a glorious thyng, certeyn'.[8] Yet in order to be this clever with words it is necessary to have a great deal of knowledge – an attribute rarely denied the friars by even their most bitter opponents. Corrupt they may be, ignorant they are not.

The importance vested in words and their use, especially when purporting to intrepret or give some indication of religious knowledge, meant that there was not only great suspicion of those who are too adept with words but also an appreciation of the power they could wield, which, blended with a natural dislike of those who were not obviously living up to what they preached, resulted in a growing mistrust of polished speakers and clever arguers. It is this suspicion that Chaucer used to comic effect in *The Pardoner's Tale* and *The Summoner's Tale*, both of which provide instances of clever speakers being caught out. Langland clearly found it an altogether more disturbing tendency.

The figures who represent the approach to knowledge through reason are

7 Wendy Scase, *'Piers Plowman' and the New Anti-Clericalism*, Cambridge Studies in Medieval Literature, 4 (Cambridge, 1989). Penn R. Szittya, *The Antifraternal Tradition in Medieval Literature* (New Jersey, 1986).
8 *The Summoner's Tale*, 1793, p. 130.

particularly open to question, since their approach relies on language as an accurate tool used by reliable authorities. If one is to learn from them it is crucial to make use of one's own discriminating abilities rather than simply accepting what these figures say on trust. When Wil next dreams, after leaving the friars, the figures which populate his visions are of a different order from those who have appeared so far.

It is Thoght who directs Wil down the road that the friars pointed out to him, and in doing so signals the shift in the poem towards reliance on inner guides and assurance from the internal faculties rather than the external forces of Church and State. However, since the combination of thought and will is essential for both approaches to knowledge there is no indication that Wil is about to embark on an exclusively deductive search for knowledge. Instead the text reveals how easily one can fall unawares into a definable way of thought and enquiry, as Wil and Thoght happen upon Wit, thence to Studie and Clergie, in an increasingly deductive progress which is a natural result of the sort of conversation they have been having for the last three days:

> Thoght and I thus thre daies we yeden
> Disputyng upon Dowel day after oother –
> And er we war were, with Wit gonne we mete.

(B.VIII.115–117)

Although Wil has not deliberately decided to follow the deductive route, the form of discussion he has been holding with Thoght has made it more probable that he will go down this path. They have been 'disputyng'– employing the form of enquiry which relies upon debate to explore the implications of terms, constantly re-defining them in an effort to understand more exactly.[9] Thus, consciously or otherwise, Wil has begun his move towards using the rational, deductive method of discovery. Yet the move is a subtle one as the terms used to speak of Dowel, Dobet and Dobest retain the register of language Wil has used so far as 'in londe' (B.VIII.126) recalls the enquires of 'Where Dowel dwelleth' of VII.13.

In the C-Text revision of Thoght's request to Wit Langland increases the association between Church and State, which has been evident throughout the previous passus, and emphasises the fact that their discourses overlap by stressing that the spiritual entities, Dowel, Dobet and Dobest, necessarily have social aspects and connotations too. The B-Text has:

---

[9] As A.J. Minnis points out, the vocabulary of this section is largely drawn from the terminology of a 'dispute'; see 'Langland's Ymaginatif . . .', p. 71.

> Wher Dowel and Dobet and Dobest ben in londe
> Here is Wil wolde wite if Wit koude teche;   (B.VIII.126–127)

– whereas the C-Text adds an acknowledgement that the law and society in which Dowel, Dobet and Dobest live, is also an important consideration:

> Whare Dowel and Dobet and Dobest ben in londe,
> Here is oen wolde ywyte, yf Wit couthe teche;
> And what lyues they lyue and what lawe þei vsen,
> And what þey drede and doute, dere sire, telleth.   (C.X.123–26)

The emphasis on the law and what Dowel, Dobet and Dobest fear continues Wil's previous insistence on knowing what Dowel, Dobet and Dobest are in this world – 'How Dowel, Dobet and Dobest doon among the peple.' (B.VII.112). The terms used reveal that Wil is asking how these personifications operate in human and experiential terms rather than as intellectual concepts. The C-Text stresses this element of Wil's enquiry with its shift from abstract noun to concrete verb – 'Dowel and Dobet and ho doth best of alle' (C.X.109). Throughout the passus which follow, the intellectual figures respond to this demand to know what Dowel is among the people in terms of government and social action. The replies Wil receives never satisfy him, and it becomes increasingly clear that these figures are unable to give him an answer to the question he is really asking – how individuals may come to know and understand Dowel in terms of their own lives, a far more personal knowledge. Nor are they able to tell him outright that he is not seeking his answer in the right way. These figures are capable of imparting a great deal of factual knowledge, which could be helpful, but they are not the appropriate sources for the type of knowledge Wil is seeking.

It is not only Thoght who tends towards the deductive route, Wit also shows signs of the move towards the intellectual and analytical method of discovery, while simultaneously retaining links with the more direct use of language of Prologue – Passus VII. Wit's choice of the metaphor of the Castle of Kynde at B.IX.1–24 with its familiarity and vividness, reminds us of the opening of the whole poem and so we feel included in the discourse of the text, not distanced or shut out by a final shift into difficulty. Furthermore, its fundamentally secular nature prevents a sudden jump from the things of everyday life into esoteric regions of theological concepts. However, the fact that the image is secular and even mundane is not to say that such a metaphor lies outside the sphere of scholastic, deductive discourse. As we have seen the use of metaphor was regarded as not only legitimate, but even desirable, in order to add persuasive force to an argument. Moreover, the choice of this particular image – a castle – recalls the link between Church and State that we saw operating in the Prologue. Although the far reaches of academic excercise were undoubtably elitist (requiring a sophisticated education not open to the poorer and less leisured classes), it was bound up with secular affairs through its roots in the forms of rhetoric and language practised in the Roman courts and Senate.[10] The fact that those most trained in the use of this language – clerics – were often those who held the administrative posts perpetuated the link between the language of theological debate and that of government and law. The result was to create a coterie of thinkers, administrators and clergy who shared common modes of discourse, and the attitudes and assumptions that went with them. This state of affairs has been recognised and summarised by Foucault in 'Text, Discourse, Ideology':

> ... any system of education is a political way of maintaining or modifying the appropriation of discourses, along with the power and knowledge they carry.[11]

It is also a way of perpetuating the belief that one particular approach to knowledge is preferable to any other as every system of education appropriates a discourse, sending its pupils down a predetermined track of enquiry.

Although Wit uses a secular image, he moves the debate on to a different plane by using his image allegorically, not just figuratively. He thus shifts the process of discussion and discovery into a more theoretical form, one step further towards the abstract reasoning of the deductive method of enquiry and away from Thoght's simpler definition. Dowel becomes 'Sire Dowel', and thus is given a definite social position and so is no longer just any man who fulfils his station in life consciensciously. As Wit's explanation proceeds we move further into the realms of theological argument as the original image becomes the starting point of an extended exegesis. Dowel as an injunction to be followed ('do well') is left behind and becomes a noun which cannot have the exhortative force of an imperative. Hence it is in the position of a concept which can be analysed and made the basis for *distinctio* and *disputatio*, in an attempt to understand it without making us feel that perhaps we ought to abandon all this intellectualising and actually go and do it. So Dowel is moved into the sphere of rational and deductive discourse and is left open to the analysis of the grammarians and scholastics, and Wil is committed to the search for *scientia*, at least for the time being.

These hints that Wil has finally entered the scholastic realm are confirmed by Studie's dismissal of Wit at the beginning of B.IX and C.XI where she invokes the familiar argument of not throwing learning in the way of those incapable of understanding and respecting it, and thereby places Wit and

[10] R. McKeon's article, 'Rhetoric in the Middle Ages', gives a brief survey of the adaptation of Roman rhetoric to theological and ecclesiastical uses.
[11] Michel Foucault, 'The Order of Discourse', *Untying the Text*, ed. R. Young (London, 1981), p. 64.

herself in the class of the learned, while simultaneously implying that Wil is not one of them:

> ... *Noli mittere*, man, margery perles
> Among hogges that han hawes at wille.
> Thei doon but dryvle theron – draf were hem levere
> Than al the precious perree that in paradis wexeth.
>
> (B.X.9–12; C.XI.7–10)

This passage contains not only the final assurance that we have entered the region of the deductive discourse. It also signals the start of the process of undermining both the approach to knowledge through reason and the personifications who represent it. As Wil ventures further into the intricacies of rational, deductive understanding, Langland renders the various figures ambiguous by revealing their limitations as well as their assets and so queries their authority. Studie's argument for elitism in education and the sharing of knowledge may have Biblical authority, but it was nonetheless problematic; if knowledge was not made available how were people to come by it? And this became an even more pressing problem as the channels originally set up for transmitting religious knowledge – the Church, preachers and theologians – were regarded increasingly as corrupt.

Langland reflects the dissatisfaction with the representatives of the Church and in particular those who had some control over learning, in the alterations made in Studie's speech in the C-Text, which indicate that her mind runs on earthly lines and restricts even her metaphors to the temporal and secular. The B-Text reading 'that in paradies wexeth' becomes 'þat eny prince weldeth' which, while it may make more sense on a purely surface level as it matches real pearls to real pigs, loses the metaphorical and religious dimension appropriate to a theologian's language. The meaning is the same, but our attitude to Dame Studie differs: in the B-Text she can be counted as one who regards theological knowledge as part of the riches of paradise, while the C-Text Studie merely compares temporal and secular hogwash with equally temporal and secular riches. Suspicion is cast even on Studie's appearance by the simple use in the C-Text of 'lokede' and 'semede' (C.XI.3) whose ironic force gradually makes itself apparent as our reactions towards this figure become increasingly ambivalent. In contrast the B-Text description of Wit as 'lene' and Studie as 'lene of lere and of liche both' is in their favour, as this thinness indicates a separation from worldly joys heightened by comparison with the fatness of the Doctor and the general connotations of gluttony, a topic which will be treated fully when the figure of the Doctor of Divinity is discussed.

The process of undermining is repeated as she reels off her list of achievements, which is impeccable; but having begun with writing Scripture's bible, directing her to Sapience and glossing the Psalms, it becomes increasingly temporal. Initially this acts as a reminder that even the humblest craft requires the help of knowledge, and that the means of mastering the simplest tasks are the same as those required for the most complex i.e. study. In this case her order is that of most prestigious application to least, however her confession 'I loke dymme' is a little disturbing, and her following assertion that

> Ac Theologie hath tened me ten score tymes:
> The moore I muse therinne the mystloker it semeth,
> And the depper I devyne, the derker me it thynketh.
> (B.X.182–84; C.XI.129–31)

– raises a query about her suitability as a guide to the Bible and glossed Psalter, which she has just declared herself to be, and yet which seem to surpass her understanding. At least this is the case until the following line is given full consideration: 'It is no science, forsothe, for to sotile inne' (B.X.185); or as the C-Text puts it even more explicitly: 'Hit is no science sothly bote a sothfaste bileue' (C.XI.132). If theology is not a science then perhaps there is another way of approaching theological matters and discussing them. Perhaps the need for intricate arguments is obviated and there is no reason to refuse knowledge to those people who, like Wil here, are deemed unfit or unable to learn. Perhaps even Studie is less vital than she seemed.

This statement casts doubt upon the validity of the type of enquiry to which Studie has just directed Wil for the knowledge he wishes to gain, and the results of which she spent her first speech castigating. The definition of theology as a science was a complex issue; to have such classification rejected by a figure which personifies one of the necessary steps towards achieving intellectual knowledge of any science – i.e. study – must call into question not only that particular definition and attitude to knowledge but also the figure itself. So Studie in effect undermines her own *raison d'être* in theological investigation. If theology is indeed a 'sothfaste bileue' and therefore 'no science . . . to sotile inne' then it is surely Studie's duty to turn Wil away from his vain, and possibly vainglorious, search and onto the correct path. If she encourages him to continue, or does not attempt to dissuade him, she is running the risk of inciting him to satisfy an empty, and so potentially sinful, curiosity.

One way out of the paradox (although not a complete resolution – Langland rarely resolves his carefully posed paradoxes) lies in recognising that, in this section above all others, the dreamer himself is acting as a personification. As will or desire he is crucial element in any choice (it is after all the faculty which urges one on to choose and subsequently follow any given path) and at this juncture that will is bent upon achieving *scientia* not *sapientia*, because at this point he has yet to comprehend the difference. Studie is fulfilling her role and helping Wil on the way he desires to go, just as Wit did and as Thoght has requested two passus before, where he had presented the dreamer to Wit as a fellow-personification:

> Here is Wil wolde wite if Wit koude teche. (B.VIII.125)

Without this will to learn the hearer is stony ground to the seeds of knowledge.[12] One must have the desire to learn before it is possible to do so, otherwise one will never put in the required effort. So much is common sense, but Augustine adds a further dimension in *De Magistro* where the amount of wisdom given to each soul is said to be in direct proportion to the quality and quantity of will present:

> Ille autem, qui consulitur, docet, qui in interiore homine habitare dictus est Christus, id est incommutabilis dei uirtus atque sempiterna sapientia, quam quidem omnis rationalis anima consulit, sed tantum cuique panditur, quantum capere propter propriam siue malam siue bonam uoluntatem potest.
>
> (Our real Teacher is he who is listened to, who is said to dwell in our inner man, namely Christ, that is, the unchangeable power and eternal wisdom of God. To this wisdom every rational soul gives heed, but to each is given only so much as he is able to receive, according to his own good or evil will.)[13]

In the light of this, Thoght's assurance that it is Wil who wants to learn takes on greater significance. It also helps to explain Studie's action, as ultimately it is the will which dictates what type of knowledge it will acquire.

However, Dame Studie must not be reduced simplistically to a kindly figure who is forced to follow the dictates of the will. The last words of her 'token' to Clergie and Scripture indicate that she takes a certain pride in being the founder of the science 'folk to deceyve' (B.X.215).[14] It is this side of her that Helen Barr pinpoints, seeing in her ease with Latin quotations and ability to supply *auctoritates* as required, a skill which has been shown to be all too open to abuse in the case of Lady Meed (B.III.331–53).[15] This is certainly the case later in the poem, where the figure of the Doctor is used to destroy finally the implicit trust in academic authority, but at this point the

---

12 This can be true of the B-Text only, as 'Wil' is replacd by 'oen' in the C-Text. This change has the effect of preventing Wil from being too closely indentified with the deductive route at this point. Langland uses a similar ploy at B.XII.215, C.XV.190 where he ensures that Wil is not associated exclusively with the affective path represented by Pacience.

13 Augustine, *De Magistro*, XI.38, CCSL, 29, p. 196. Tr. J.H.S. Burleigh, *Augustine's Earlier Writings*, Library of Christian Classics, VII (London, 1953), p. 95.

14 The omission of these lines in the C-Text, in which Studie's speech ends on an injunction to 'love lelly', simplifies the figure of Study by restricting her to religious knowledge.

15 Helen Barr, 'The Use of Latin Quotations in *Piers Plowman* with special reference to Passus XVIII of the B-Text', *Notes and Queries*, 33 (1986), 440.

use of quotations merely serves to link Dame Studie firmly to the intellectual line of enquiry that she herself queries. Given the strength of this link it comes as no surprise that Wil ignores, or forgets, Studie's limitations, despite the fact that she herself pointed them out (B.X.182–184) and goes 'wightly [his] wey' to reach the intellectual attributes of Clergie and Scripture, trusting that they will lead him to knowledge. He does not pause to consider that this intellectual route may not be the only one available as he travels 'withoute moore letyng', and indeed his assumption is not challenged until Scripture makes use of her affective ability to show him that his trust in deduction and the powers of reason have gone too far. Even this proves of no avail; it requires Ymaginatif and the sojourn in Middelerthe to jolt Wil out of the habit of seeking definitive answers that he develops in this section. It is only then that he recognises the truth of Studie's words: 'Ymaginatif herafterward shal answere to youre purpos' (B.X.117; omitted in C).

By telling Wil that Ymaginatif will provide the answers he seeks (or at least put him in the way of knowing what he wants to know) Studie is revealing that not only is she an essential element in the deductive path to knowledge but she is also aware of other approaches to understanding. For it is indeed Ymaginatif who makes Wil aware that he is looking in the wrong place for the answer to his question about Dowel and the way to salvation. It is only by being discomforted and reminded of the power of shame and affective, emotive response in driving home knowledge, that Wil is persuaded to move away from his dependence on intellectual authorities which he evinces in Passus VIII–XI. Given his preference for the deductive path at B.X.111, it is an ironic paradox that Wil follows the implications of Studie's skill with words and continues to pursue the deductive path to knowledge, but in doing so fails to question the meaning of her remark about the role of Ymaginatif. Had he paused to use the methods of the schoolmen on Studie's reference to Ymaginatif he might have chosen a different course of action; as it is Wil maintains his direction and so encounters the personification of learning – Clergie.

7

The Progression to Learning and the Role of Scripture

Having moved on from Studie, Wil has no difficulty in finding Clergie and Scripture. We may presume this is because he follows Studie's directions correctly and does not deviate from his chosen path in any way; indeed, he specifically mentions that he is unable to stop before he has met Clergie:

> And til I com to Clergie I koude nevere stynte.
> I grette the goode man as the goode wif me taughte,
> And afterwardes the wif, and worshiped hem bothe,
> And tolde hem the tokenes that me taught were. (B.X.220–23)

The fact that Wil both meets and greets Clergie first is important here, for it is an indication that he has finally arrived at a position of learning and, through that, come to a certain type of understanding of Scripture. In other words the appreciation of Scripture that Langland presents initially is one which is attained by the scholastic and deductive route to knowledge. Naturally, an understanding of Scripture is also the goal sought by the affective route to knowledge, but that aspect of Scripture herself is hidden at first. It is typical of the process of undermining that occurs throughout *Piers Plowman* that it is Scripture herself who, after demonstrating her connections with the deductive route reveals that the affective path is just as vital to full understanding. Wil's encounter with Clergie and Scripture is thus both an achievement of a goal and the beginning of the end of the deductive approach to knowledge.

Wil receives a warm welcome from Clergie and Scripture precisely because he was 'of Wittes hous and with his wif Dame Studie'; these are the necessary credentials which ensure that he has come through the required training and will give due respect to the form of knowledge in which they excel. The preoccupation with authorities becomes manifest as St Augustine, himself an *auctor*, is reinforced by reference to his 'auctores', the

Evangelists, and through them to Christ, the ultimate authority, the whole capped with a suitable scriptural quotation:

> Austyn the olde herof made bokes,
> And hymself ordeyned to sadde us in bileve.
> Who was his auctor? Alle the foure Evaungelistes;
> And Crist cleped hymself so, the same bereth witnesse:
> *Ego in patre et pater in me est; et qui videt me videt et patrem meum.*
>
> (B.X.241–244a)

It is even more explicit in the C-text, with its enthusiasm for books which becomes a celebration of the various types of authority, from the writings of such esteemed figures as the Church Fathers and prophets of the Bible to the testimonies of those close to Christ (the apostles) and to God (the angels) to the Divine itself, and so to the *logos*, the Divine Word which finds a pale reflection in Augustine's own prolific writing:

> Austyn þe olde herof made bokes:
> Ho was his auctor and hym of god tauhte?
> Patriarkes and prophetes, apostles and angelis –
> And þe trewe trinite to Austyn apperede
> And he vs saide as he sey, and so y bileue,
> That he seyh þe fader and þe sone and þe seynt spirit togederes,
> And alle thre bote o god, and herof he made bokes,
> 3e, busiliche bokes! ho beth his witnesses?
> *Ego in patre et pater in me est; et qui me videt, patrem*
> *meum videt qui in celis est.*   (C.XI.149–156a)

Both Clergie and Scripture fill their speeches with *auctores* and *auctoritates* and Wil proves himself able to match their disputes and enter the fray with his own contribution, which is equally well substantiated by Biblical quotations and references, even employing an example used also by John of Bromyard:[1]

> Ac I wene it worth of manye as was in Noes tyme
> Tho he shoop that ship of shides and of bordes:
> Was nevere wrighte saved that wroghte theron, ne oother
> werkman ellis,
> But briddes and beestes and the blissed Noe
> And his wif with hise sones and also hire wyves;
> Of wrightes that is wroghte was noon of hem ysaved.   (B.X.396–401)

---

[1] John Bromyard, *SP*, s.v. 'Verba Dei', f. 180r, see p. 111 below. For a detailed discussion of the use of this simile in *Piers Plowman* see G. Rudd, 'The State of the Ark: A Metaphor in Bromyard and *Piers Plowman* B.X.396–401', *Notes and Queries*, 37 (1990), 6–10.

He has become a learned man who produces a fully-fledged argument instead of a contracted and imperfect syllogism, as he did when challenging the friars. Yet the power of his ability is directed towards proving how inadequate Clergie and Scripture's teachings are by querying the very basis of their arguments – the sanctity of the *auctores*:

> Then Marie Maudeleyne who myghte do werse?
> Or who worse dide than David, that Uries deeth conspired?
> Or Poul the Apostle that no pite hadde
> Cristene kynde to kille to dethe?   (B.X.419–422)

Wil has become enough of an adept to be able to query Clergie and Scripture in their own terms.

Once again Langland has raised the question of how much the character of an *auctor* affects his authority. As Wil astutely points out, the very authorities one is taught to revere, Solomon and Aristotle, are actually declared by Holi Church to be in hell (B.X.375–86). Merely helping to build the Ark did not qualify the carpenters for a place on board. It is not enough to be part of the building process of the ark of the Church without knowing what it is for: as Wil says, if he actually followed the type of life led by Solomon or Aristotle he, too, would be damned – or drown, to continue the analogy. Not content with this, Wil also directly challenges the form of teaching, and this time without the apologetic admission of lack of knowledge with which he left the friars. Now that he has acquired the skills necessary to understand Clergie and Scripture from his time in Studie's school, he is not defeated by simple eloquence as he was by the Minorites, and so is able to declare the hollowness of their speeches; for all their fine words they have not actually taught him anything – and this time not because he is not able to understand:

> 'This is a long lesson' quod I 'and litel am I the wiser!
> Where Dowel is or Dobet derkliche ye shewen.'   (B.X.369–370)

This outburst applies to both Clergie and Scripture and is tantamount to an accusation that they are failing to teach properly. They are not matching their form to their listener and are in effect misusing, or even abusing, their ability to use words. Here, then, simple admiration for eloquence even when coupled with knowledge, is rejected and St Augustine's reservations in *De Dialectica* brought to bear:

> Quamvis enim nec disputationem deceat ineptum nec eloquentiam oporteat esse mendacem, tamen et in illa saepe, atque adeo paene semper, audiendi delicias discendi cupido contemnit et in hac imperitior multitudo quod ornate dicitur etiam vere dici arbitratur.
>
> (For although disputation should not be inept nor ought eloquence be deceptive yet in the former often, indeed nearly always, the desire for learning scorns the

pleasures of hearing and in the other the more ignorant mass judge that what is said ornately is said truly.)[2]

Clergie and Scripture have laced their speeches with learning and also made them highly eloquent; in so doing they have laid themselves open to the criticism of taking more delight in the form and rhetoric of their texts than whether or not they are making themselves understood. In Robert of Basevorn's eyes, this is introducing an illegitimate or 'secondary purpose': his opinion of someone who does this is damning: *adulter est verbi Dei, quod reputatur mortale* (he is an adulterer of the word of God, which is considered a mortal sin).[3] It may be to this aspect of Scripture's speech that Wil is objecting when he accuses her of obscurity, since such erudition is inappropriate in an explanation addressed to him. For, although Wil is no longer to be numbered among the 'more ignorant mass', he is still close enough to it and distant enough from the educated coterie to see that the instruction offered by Clergie and Scripture is useless to him.

It would be inaccurate to suggest that either Clergie or Scripture intend to confuse Wil, but they could be accused of misdirecting their skills. Clergie in particular reveals himself as having a narrow sphere of reference as he moves from definitions of Dowel, Dobet and Dobest in terms of increased education – Dowel is faith in what is taught (X.246); Dobet puts words into practice (X.249–255); Dobest corrects others (X.256–258) – into a description of the ideal of the religious life and how debased that ideal has become. Not surprisingly, for him heaven on earth is to be found in the cloister –

> For in cloistre cometh no man to chide ne to fighte,
> But al is buxomnesse there and bokes, to rede and to lerne
>
> (B.X.299–300)

– but this happy state of affairs is no longer to be found since religion is now 'a rydere, a romere by streets' (X.302). He seems to be offering Wil a way to discover Dowel which is in fact closed to him because the conditions in which it might be achieved no longer exist. When he goes on to envisage the time to come when these hypocrites will be overthrown, his use of metaphors of rulers and new government only confuse Wil further. In the end Wil does not engage with Clergie's views; they are neither confirmed nor refuted but left for the reader to make of what they can.

Clergie's position is left in this rather ambiguous state as he is pushed to one side and Scripture takes over the task of answering Wil's question:

> 'Thanne is Dowel and Dobet,' quod I, '*dominus* and knyghthode?'
>
> (B.X.328)

---

[2] Augustine, *De Dialectica*, Book VII; ed. and tr. B. Darell Jackson (Dordrecht, 1975), pp. 102 and 103.

[3] Robert of Basevorn, ch. V, p. 242; tr. p. 125.

Wil is still moving in the same linguistic sphere as he was in the Prologue-Passus VII where descriptions of right spiritual living were couched in terms of secular estates. The use of the connotations of knighthood is an image drawn from notions of government and so links with Clergie's use of the castle to which he has sent his sons to learn from the lord of life. In the same way it connects with the Castle of Kynde, Wit's image for the dwelling place of Dowel (B.IX.1–2). So Wil's terminology retains links with the language of *scientia*, but in being answered by Scripture he is drawn away from this imagery towards the realms of the more emotive, figurative language of the approach to knowledge as *sapientia*. Yet although she replies to this query about Clergie's speech (B.X.329–332) Scripture does not provide an adequate solution to his original question; indeed her speech is less obviously relevant than Clergie's, which at least contained definitions of Dowel, Dobet and Dobest (B.X.230–263). Despite this she avoids being dismissed as easily as Clergie by exercising another aspect of her nature and switching from the embodiment of scripture as source for theological quotations to the figure of affective Biblical writing.

This affective aspect of Scripture has hitherto been hidden, uncalled for because Wil approached her through study and learning – Studie and Clergie. In terms of intellectual enquiry her main function is as a treasury of *auctoritates* – a true thesaurus, an endless source of tags and topics for disputation. However the point of Scripture is that she is just as attainable by non-scholastics as scholatics, as the Bible is available to all, even if only through the readings and citations provided by a preacher. More importantly, one does not require advanced learning to understand at least some portions of the Bible, such as the actual events recorded in the Gospels, or the examples set by Christ and his followers. Such accessible elements provided the basis for the defence of using *exempla*, as Hugh of St Victor (c.1127) pointed out:

> If as they say, we ought to leap straight from the letter to its spiritual meaning, then the metaphors and similes, which educate us spiritually, would have been in vain. . . . Do not despise what is lowly in God's word, for by lowliness you will be enlightened to divinity.[4]

The accessibility provided by such lowly language is not an attribute of the more removed authorities of Greek philosophers and some of the Church Fathers, whose writings would be available to only the educated clergy or well-off layman, and would have demanded some degree of education to understand.

---

[4] Hugh of St. Victor, *De Scripturis*, V 13–15, quoted and discussed in relation to the practice of glossing in B. Smalley, *A Study of the Bible in the Middle Ages* (Oxford, 1952), p. 93.

Scripture, of course, contains not only parables but also more complex forms of affective writing, such as the Psalms and the Song of Songs. With such resources she cannot be rejected as irrelevant in the same way as Clergie can. This dual nature means that although her first speech contains elements of the same general style as Clergie's, such as the citation of Cato (B.X.335), she is also able to make reference to more figurative discourses, by including prophets and poets with the law-giving patriarchs (X.336). It is this speech, not Clergie's, that Wil endeavours to refute with a learned reply, rooted in the intellectual knowledge he has just been seen to acquire at Studie's school. In the end, however, this proves inadequate when dealing with a figure who has the resources of affective discourse at her disposal. Wil involves himself in a long disputation, backed-up by allusions and references and matching her style with his own. He strikes at the foundations of the structure of her speech – countering *auctoritates* with *exempla* – but is still defeated as Scripture imitates his tactics in a masterly stroke.

She refutes his criticism that she speaks obscurely by thrusting him into the inner dream, which reveals truth in the mirror of Middelerthe, and so proves to him by experience what showing darkly truly means, while simultaneously revealing how little he knows. It is a nice irony that she does this by means of a Latin *auctoritas* which describes Wil all too accurately: *multi multa sciunt et seipsos nesciunt* (B.XI.3). Wil breaks down in frustration; despite his carefully acquired mastery of the academic and rational style of understanding it seems that there is always more to learn before he finally discovers Dowel. More to the point he must learn in a different way: he is still lacking in the faith which, as St Bonaventure said, is essential if his academic knowledge is to be relevant to his spiritual quest:

> Fides enim elevat ad assentiendum; scientia et intellectus elevant ad ea quae credita sunt intelligendum.
>
> (For faith raises [the mind] to the point of assent, while knowledge and understanding raise it to the point where it can understand what it has believed.)[5]

Wil is so anxious to understand he has forgotton the importance of belief.

By shocking him into the inner dream, Scripture makes it possible for Wil to explore many of the objections he raised in his refutation of her speech. It also brings to the fore the full significance of Wil's accusation 'derkliche ye shewen' as the visions of Middelerthe are revealed through a mirror (B.XI.9). By recalling the familiar idea of seeing through a glass darkly (*in speculum aenigmate*, 1 Cor.13:11), Wil has unconsciously introduced the notion of the world and the scriptures as enigmatic showings of God's will

---

[5] Bonaventure, *Commentary on the 'Sentences'*, Proem, Q.2 conclusio, resp. 5, *Opera Omnia*, vol. 1, p. 11b; tr. Minnis-Scott, p. 226.

and His world which it is the aim of theology to unravel. However, according to Aquinas, although mankind is capable of recognising the existence of the universal good, which is God's good, and is also able to desire it, the human soul is not able to achieve it:

> mens humana universalis boni cognoscitiva est per intellectum, et desiderativa per voluntatem: bonum autem universale non invenitur nisi in Deo.
>
> (The human soul is able, through intelligence, to know goodness in its universality, and, through the will, to desire it. But the universal good is nowhere found except in God.)[6]

It is significant that Aquinas refers to the operation of intellect and will here, for he was a staunch defender of the approach to knowledge through reason and the intellectual faculties. As the above quotation reveals, he considers that if the human intellect cannot attain a thing, it is beyond mortal grasp.

This view, that the final goal of universal good is unattainable by the intellect and will is reflected in *Piers Plowman*. Clergie, as the personification of the educated cleric, has used words to explain and instruct, and failed, just as Studie failed and Wil himself fails. Scripture turns away from words to direct 'showings' in dream, which are also made highly emotive and experiential; Wil is 'ravysshed right there' (B.XI.7). In keeping with this sudden shift to affective teaching Scripture delivers what is for Wil the most moving address of the poem – but it is not a full-length sermon, despite the fact that we are told she 'preched'; all we are given is the theme and Wil's reaction:

> This was hir teme and hir text – I took ful good hede:
> '*Multi* to a mangerie and to the mete were sompned;
> And whan the peple was plener comen, the porter unpynned the yate
> And plukked in *Pauci* pryveliche and leet the remenaunt go rome.'
> Al for tene of hir text trembled myn herte.
>
> (B.XI.111–115; cf. C.XII.44–48)

The C-Text actually labels Scripture's speech a 'sarmon' and indeed we are given its 'teme' and 'text', but this loose use of the term by no means indicates a sermon based on the use of *auctoritates* and *distinctiones*. Again the C-Text is helpful here as it has 'tales' for 'text'. The tautological emphasis of the B-Text 'teme' and 'texte' is dropped in favour of drawing attention to the fact that this is an affective speech making use of *exempla* – 'tales', and as such is surely an emotive address not a theological discussion. In neither

---

6   Aquinas, *De Regimine Principum*, VIII, ed. S.P. D'Entrèves; tr. J.G.Dawson, *Aquinas Selected Political Writings* (Oxford, 1965), pp. 46 and 47.

version are we given the 'sermon' itself, the text alone being sufficient to move Wil, especially since it is expanded enough to recall its complete context in Matthew 22:14. Furthermore the text is taken from a parable, the form of Biblical teaching which leant authority to the use of affective language – 'tales'. However, even here the advantage of having some degree of learning is mentioned. The uneducated are in danger of being cast into despair by a mis-application of the meaning of the theme that only few are chosen; if they assume that they are one of the many rather than the few this theme could make them desert the faith altogether:

> Ac the matere that she meved, if lewed men it knewe,
> The lasse, as I leve, lovyen thei wolde
> The bileve of Oure Lord that lettred men techeth.   (B.XI.108–110)

Alternatively, these lines could be implying that if the 'lewed' knew the scriptures directly, with the type of 'knowyng' sought by Wil, they would be less impressed by the interpretations of the 'lettred'. Such a reading could fit the context of the inner dream, which presents the alternatives to the intellectualism of the outer dream.

These alternatives are shown to strike home in Wil's reaction to Scripture's address: the scholastic arguments have baffled and enraged him, but his heart never 'trembled' at them. So, when the authority of books is next invoked it is swept away vigorously, even though it was Scripture who introduced the iconoclast by a literary reference:

> 'Ye, baw for bokes! . . .
> Lawe withouten love,' quod Troianus, 'ley ther a bene –
> Or any science under sonne, the sevene arts and alle!'
>
> (B.XI.140, 170–71)

Trajan is advocating authority based on experience: he is standing up and presenting himself as a case in point, offering a totally different basis for knowledge in which authorities are used to back experience, not studied for their own sake and used to interpret experience.[7] Yet he himself owes his power as an *exemplum* to the fact that his name and character have been preserved (and greatly enhanced) by books – and in particular by the account of St Gregory in the *Golden Legend*, which he himself cites (B.XI.160). The intricacies of this character will be fully explored later when Trajan is examined as an instance of authority based on experience; here his relevance

---

7 In the C-Text as punctuated by Pearsall, much of Trajan's speech and in particular his attack on learning is given to Rechlesenesse. This renders the reliability of this attack more problematic as it is presented by a clearly unreliable character, but does not actually affect the present argument, for which the important fact is that Wil is being shown that there are alternatives to any purely rational approach.

rests on his claim to cast aside all trust in books while simultaneously basing his right to make such statements on the deference due to one who figures honourably in the *Legenda Sanctorum*.

Although such empirical knowledge is clearly a sharp contrast to the logical and deductive discourse of intellectual enquiry, its introduction by no means necessitates or even implies anti-scholasticism. A writer was not forced to abandon the use of learning in order to write affectively or figuratively, but nor did the use of learning necessarily assume the endorsement of the academic canon's views. A case in point is Christine de Pizan, who is careful to portray herself as an educated woman in the prologue to her *Book of the City of Ladies* and then goes on to challenge the notion that every opinion of the canon's respected philosophers and authorities must be accepted as true without question. The three ladies who come to enlighten her and tell her how to build her city declare that, despite her learning, she is in fact blind and so shuns what she knows to be true from her own experience, preferring to believe the 'many strange opinions' of her authorities instead. Christine then goes on to illustrate that the lives and characters of various famous, or infamous, women could bear different interpretations from those usually provided by the established authors, by re-telling several familiar tales in very unfamiliar ways. Medea is praised for beauty, being noble 'with an upright heart', and for her skill with herbs and command of the elements rather than being presented as a witch and murderess. Similarly Ariadne earns her place in this compendia of famous women because she is credited with inventing dyes and being especially skilled in treating wools and threads. Her competition with Pallas is relegated to an aside and Boccaccio's claim that people were better off before woollen clothing is sharply refuted.[8] Christine's writing thus requires some degree of learning in order to understand how she changes and challenges the premisses she attacks, but she is not esoterically academic, providing in *The Book of the City of Ladies* and *The Treasury of the City of Ladies* compendia of tales which could be regarded as *exempla*, and blending the emotive and deductive discourses in her own language.

In *Piers Plowman* this recommendation of a combination of the two discourses, introduced in the figure of Scripture and supported by Trajan's words, is strengthened by Ymaginatif, who takes up the case introduced so forcefully by Trajan. In Passus XII Ymaginatif reminds Wil of the value of learning, but warns him against losing sight of its limitations:

> Clergie and kynde wit cometh of sighte and techyng,
> As the Book bereth witnesse to burnes that kan rede:
> *Quod scimus loquimur, quod vidimus testamur,*

8 Christine de Pizan, *The Book of the City of Ladies*, tr. E.J. Richards (London, 1983), pp. 4–6, 69, 81–82.

> Of *quod scimus* cometh clergie, a konnynge of hevene,
> And of *quod vidimus* cometh kynde wit, of sighte of diverse peple.
> Ac grace is a gifte of God, and of greet love spryngeth;
> Knew nevere clerk how it cometh forth, ne kynde wit the weyes:
> *Nescit aliquis unde venit aut quo vadis &c*
> Ac yet is clergie to comende, and kynde wit bothe,
> And namely clergie for Cristes love, that of clergie is roote.
>
> (B.XII.64–71)

This defence of Clergie is expanded in the C-Text which presents Ymaginatif's appreciation of Clergie as complementary to and working from the basis provided by Kynde Wit. This leaves the question of Clergie's limitations to be exposed fully later in the passus, but allows for a clearer statement of the necessity for learning and the learned:

> So grace is a gifte of god and kynde wit a chaunce
> And clergie a connynge of kynde wittes techyng.
> And ȝut is clergie to comende for Cristes loue more
> Then eny connyng of kynde wit but clergie hit reule.
> For Moyses witnesseth þat god wroet and Crist with his fynger;
> Lawe of loue oure lord wroet long ar Crist were,
> And Crist cam and confermede and holy kyrke made
> And in soend a sign wroet and saide to þe Iewes:
> "That seth hymsulue synneless, sese nat, y hote,
> To strike with stoen or with staf this strompet to dethe."
>
> *Quis vestrum sine peccato est*
> Forthy y conseile vch a clergie to honoure.   (C.XIV.33–43)

The use of language in these two passages is revealing. The B-Text version is an illustration of the value of learning as Ymaginatif first quotes a Latin text and then expands upon it to show how clergie and kynde wit have different sources but equal merit. The speech itself is a demonstration of the use of clergie since his proof would not be possible, or comprehensible, without a basic understanding of Latin and knowledge that the text *Nescit aliquis unde venit aut quo vadis* is an allusion to description of the movement of the Holy Spirit in John 3:8. It is after this that the B-Text goes on to the story of the condemned woman as a further illustration of the theme that Christ mitigated the Old Law, which demanded her death by stoning, without undermining it. Ymaginatif is drawing here from both the deductive and affective traditions and interweaving them in a way that is itself indicative of his argument for the use of learning and the exemplary proof of the tales. The C-Text, however, omits the use of integrated Latin and English and relies much more heavily on the power of the story to drive home the point. The Latin that is used is not essential to the speech, although it provides the appropriate references to the Bible. This is, of course, a use of the Latin as *auctoritas* and as such could be regarded as coming from the more academic

94

tradition. However, this is really a case of citing a text in order to 'place' it, and then continuing by using the story from which it is taken as the basis of argument rather than analysing the words of the text themselves. Despite these differences the effect of both Trajan's interruption and Ymaginatif's defence of learning in each text is to qualify the unadulterated use of Clergie while also preventing his utter dismissal.

For the exploration of the uses of various discourses in *Piers Plowman* the interpretation of Ymaginatif as a personification of the imagination and helper of reason is less important than the effect he, and the inner dream which precedes him, have upon the dreamer. It is vital to bear in mind the context of these episodes because, following the experience of the inner dream and encounter with Ymaginatif, Wil returns to the academic sphere and finds himself confronting the epitome of the corrupt scholar in the shape of the 'maistre of divinitee'. This time Wil is conducted by Conscience and Scripture, the latter being present only as a silent server at the banquet and, in the C-Text, under the supervision of Reson. Most importantly Pacience makes his appearance; more *exemplum* than authority, he is reminiscent of Piers in his confidence in his own rectitude and concomitant humility. In the C-Text this likeness is made explicit as he asks for food:

> Ilyk Peres the ploghman, as he a palmere were.   (C.XV.34)

The entry of Pacience and the evocation of a less complex approach to knowledge indicated by his humility and his similarity to Piers as both honest workman and devout pilgrim, indicates that the banquet scene is to contain a further comparison of the emotive and deductive approaches to knowledge.

8

The Doctor – The Last Word in Scholasticism

The Doctor is the culmination of the exploration of the academic quest; clearly he epitomises all the faults of that mode of thought and discourse, the result of over-interest in intellectual knowledge and delight in scholastic ability for its own sake. Here a major role of the previous personifications becomes evident as the various aspects they embody are brought together and travestied in the figure of the doctor. Despite Spearing's view that 'they appear most often simply as preachers' and so 'do not have to be interpreted allegorically in themselves, but are more likely to use the medieval preacher's technique of allegorical exegesis on Scriptural texts',[1] it is in fact vital to interpret these characters by means of their names. By calling the figures Wil meets in this section 'Wit', Studie', 'Clergie' and 'Scripture' Langland is indicating that they are symbols of different ways of using intellectual knowledge, abilities and resources, and must be read as such. To this extent they are personifications which demand individual assessment, i.e. precisely 'to be interpreted allegorically in themselves', and their differing use of exegesis and other explanatory and linguistic techniques are a part of their signification as allegories. They are graded figures on the intellectual or academic scale, who offer for examination various aspects of intellectual ability which, if put together in unfortunate or wrong combinations, can result in the Doctor. If these figures are regarded 'simply as preachers' the significance of their names, roles and positions in the poem is totally ignored.

After such a long sojourn in the realm of personifications, relieved only by the short section of waking following Ymaginatif and the almost surreal inner dream, it is refreshing to be presented with a figure who, while clearly a caricature in a dream, is nevertheless a recognisable type, part of the waking world. He is introduced into the poem as a man of learning; his title 'maister' indicates his position as an educated man and therefore one who may be presumed to have advanced theological knowledge. However he is

---

1 A.C. Spearing, 'The Art of Preaching', pp. 68–90.

also a friar. It seems that Langland wished to emphasize this fact, for in the C-Text the initial description of the Doctor explicitly states that he is 'a mayster, a man lyk a frere' (C.XV.30). The B-Text version initially describes Wil's ignorance about this important friend of Clergie – 'What man he was I nyste' (B.XIII.25). However, after some forty-four lines we infer that this Doctor of Divinity is a friar, as Wil protests against him, citing 2 Corinthians 11:26, *'Periculum est in falsis fratribus'* (B.XIII.66a). This impression is later confirmed by Pacience's words:

> And thanne shal he testifie of a trinite, and take his felawe to
> witnesse
> What he fond in a forel after a freres lyvyng. (B.XIII.93–94)

As a friar the Doctor is linked with the two Franciscans who started Wil down this particular path of enquiry, which culminates in the encounter of Wil and the Doctor. Langland is surely creating a resonance here, through which our reservations about the first two friars are echoed in our reactions to this one.

In addition to these pre-existing doubts about the character of friars the combination of 'frere' and 'maister' immediately introduces a tension, for, although many friars earned the right to be called 'maistre' by gaining a degree, it implies a social position which the friars were not supposed to seek. The fact that, despite their vow of humility, friars frequently did expect such position is humorously exploited by Chaucer in his exchange between frere John and the lord in *The Summoner's Tale*:

> 'Now, maister,' quod this lord, 'I yow biseke –'
> 'No maister, sire' quod he 'but servitour,
> Thogh I have had in scole that honour.
> God liketh nat that "Raby" men us calle,
> Neither in market ne in youre large halle.' (2184–88)

The point was that the friars' humility and recognition of Christ as their Master ought to preclude the possibility of any friar allowing himself to be called 'maister'. The scriptural basis for this position is the command in Matthew 23:7 and 9:

> ... be not ye called Rabbi: for one is your Master, even Christ; and all ye are brethren. . . . Neither be ye called Masters; for one is your Master, even Christ.

The Biblical context is an injunction not to become like the scribes and pharisees who 'love the uppermost rooms at feasts and the chief seats in the synagogues'. In the light of this it is disturbing that this man, so respected for his intellect by Conscience, should be accorded the most prestigious seat at Conscience's table.

Yet to regard Conscience as blind or unreliable because of his respect for the Doctor would be to over-simplify matters. Theologians were often respected figures, not automatically objects of satire, even in vernacular literature, as is shown by the fact that the Spicers Play, *The Annunciation and Visitation* (number XII in the York Mystery cycle), is introduced by a doctor of theology who makes use of Latin quotations – all of which are translated – and provides brief exegeses for the Biblical images he employs.[2] It is a nice touch that this play, which is so concerned with words (annunciation) is introduced by a man whose profession means he is involved with words, their power and implications, and above all with the explanation and transmission of the message of the incarnate Word, the *logos*. Furthermore, since Conscience regards the Doctor as a theologian, rather than a friar, his use of the title 'maister' does not necessarily present the Doctor as an object of suspicion. However, the emphasis upon this title, which earns him the position 'mooste worthi' in Conscience's estimation and at his table, brings to a head all the tensions centred on the issue of office. As a friar he is a preacher as well as a speculative theologian, and as such

> injungit se in officium cujus finis per se est facere alios bonos.
>
> (enjoins upon himself a duty whose end in itself is to make others good.)[3]

As we have already seen, this duty involves being a good example in life as well as being a purveyor of good words. Instead this doctor acts like the stereotypical gluttonous and rich abbot attacked in the *Apocalypsis Goliae*[4] whose total debauchery earns him a place under the seventh seal of the poem, indicative of the highest point of corruption. This gluttony is an outward manifestation of his actual ignorance in spiritual matters, which becomes increasingly obvious throughout this episode.

---

2 *The Annunciation and Visitiation*, play no. XII in *York Plays*, ed. R. Beadle, York Medieval Texts 2nd series (London, 1982), p. 110.

3 Robert of Basevorn, ch. IV, p. 241; tr. p. 123.

4 Previously attributed to Walter Map, this poem is printed in *Latin Poems Commonly Attributed to Walter Mapes*, ed. T. Wright, Camden Society Old Series XVI (London, 1841), where it appears under the full title *Apocalypsis Goliae Episcopi*. Wright also provides two English translations, one Tudor/Stuart, the other of 1625, testifying to the continuing popularity of the theme. The poem is mentioned briefly in Jill Mann's *Chaucer and Medieval Estates Satire*, p. 18, and also in the Schmidt and Pearsall editions of *Piers Plowman*. While the poem may serve as an analogue to *Piers* in that its general anti-clerical attitude is similar, it is significantly different in being not only a travesty of religious lives and abuses painted with a broad brush, but also in allocating each type of divine their own exclusive vice: the friars are indeed greedy, but their greed mainly takes the form of avarice to which gluttony is only incidental. It is the abbot who is the arch glutton, and the monks who are totally debauched.

The connection between food, words and knowledge is of long standing.[5] In Christian terms it has its roots in the tree whose fruit bestowed knowledge of good and evil, this symbolism being given an extra layer of signification in the Last Supper, where Christ, the Incarnate Word, offers the bread and wine, transforming bodily food into spiritual sustenance. The same metaphorical meaning of the notion of feeding as a spiritual as well as physical act forms the basis of the command 'Feed my sheep', given by Christ to Peter, founder of the Church and precursor of all the priests to follow, in John 21:15–17. The idea that the ministers of the Church are responsible for nourishing the souls of their flock is re-enacted in every Eucharist. St Augustine also recognised the notional link between food and knowledge, giving it a wider range of reference, though still within a Christian context, as he underlines the need for knowledge to be presented in a way suited to its receivers:

> Sed quoniam inter se habent nonnullam similitudinem vescentes atque discentes; propter fastidia plurimorum etiam ipsa, sine quibus vivi non potest, alimenta condienda sunt.
>
> (But since there is some comparison between eating and learning, it may be noted that on account of the fastidiousness of many even that food without which life is impossible must be seasoned.)[6]

So, both food and knowledge are essentials of life, but both must be presented in a way that will make them digestible.

In his portrayal of the Doctor, Langland combines this metaphor of words as food with the traditional satire of the religious as gluttonous to arrive at the image of a man who is incapable of eating the plain food of penitence presented to Wil and Pacience, but instead dines on richer, more costly dishes:

> . . . thei eten mete of moore cost – mortrews and potages:
> . . .
> He eet manye sondry metes, mortrews and puddynges,
> Wombe cloutes and wilde brawen and eggs yfryed with grece.
> (B.XIII.41, 61–62)

It becomes increasingly obvious that the Doctor is as unable to understand the simple faith which Pacience represents as he is to swallow the food he eats. The C-Text makes this point explicitly:

> Ac of this mete þat mayster myhte nat wel chewe. (C.XV.46)

---

5 E.R. Curtius cites many of the instances and references of the use of the metaphor of knowledge as food in *European Literature in the Latin Middle Ages*, 2nd edn, pp. 134–37.
6 Augustine, *De Doctrina Christiana*, IV.2.28, CCSL, 32, p. 135; tr. p. 136.

The image of the glutton shovelling in more food than he needs from dishes specially prepared for him, designed to entice the appetite and shared only with his associates, merges with that of the theologian who delights more in the presentation and phrasing of an argument than in discovering the truth of the point under discussion. There is added criticism in the word 'chewe', which implies that the purer doctrines of Pacience yield no quibbling little details or niceties for such theologians to chew over.

This greedy acquisition of every type and aspect of knowledge is directly opposed to the meditative or contemplative approach to God which, though equally demanding, attempted to pass beyond the bounds of language and the limitations of reason. Some followers of this approach, such as the *Cloud* author, advocated the concentration on one mono-syllabic word in order to concentrate the mind, rather than employing the highly verbal methods of analysis which developed within scholasticism. Even Hilton, whose language and approach to understanding are more accessible than the *Cloud* author's, stated that those who adopted a contemplative form of life ought to avoid discussion and argument, even to the extent of refraining from drawing a fellow-sinner's attention to a fault in charity. To do so could be too combative and out of place in a life devoted to discovery through introspection:

> to þe or to oni oþer wilk haþ stat and þe purpos of lif contemplatif, hit falliþ nouȝt for to leeue þe kepyng of ȝoure self and biholden and vndir-nemen oþer men of heere defautes, but if hit were ful gret neede, so þat a man scholde perissche but ȝe vndirnemid him.[7]

Interestingly, Hilton adopts a similar attitude when dealing with the issue of food. He devotes some space to advising moderation in eating, but warns against the lure of starvation; since food is a bodily need it is as much a sin to ignore it as to over-indulge it.[8] The crucial factor in each case is need. It is this which determines how much food one should take and also how much knowledge. One should not strive to know more than is necessary, more than one ought to know – which is exactly what Ymaginatif tells Wil:

> Adam, whiles he spak noght, hadde paradis at wille;
> Ac whan he mamelede aboute mete and entremeted to knowe
> The wisedom and the wit of God, he was put fram blisse.
> And right so ferde Reson bi thee – thow with thi rude speche
> Lakkedest and losedest thyng that longed noght to doone.
> Tho hadde he no likyng for to lere thee moore. (B.XI.415–420)

---

[7] Hilton, *Scale*, Book 1, ch. 17:1, ed. B.E. Wykes (1957: rpt. Michigan, 1989), p. 112.

[8] Hilton, *Scale*, Book 1, ch. 72, p. 219. Hilton does not make an explicit connection between food and knowledge, but his use of the phrase 'savourless knowledge', in *Scale*, 1, ch. 4 indicates that he thought in terms of the common metaphor of knowledge as food.

Underlying this speech is the link between Original Sin and greed, the desire for the fruit of the Tree of Knowledge. Although this link might lead us to expect that gluttony is always regarded as a reprehensible sin, as indeed has been the case in Langland's treatment of the Doctor of Divinity, Hilton treats it peculiarly lightly. His tolerant criticism of it is as follows:

> ffor a man sinneþ nouȝt comunli dedli in glotonye, bute if he be encombred wiþ oþer dedly synnes biforn don.[9]

It transpires that this leniency springs from the recognition that gluttony is based on the bodily need for food, which, being a requirement of nature is not of itself sinful, as Hilton immediately goes on to state:

> And, þerfore, þou schalt nouȝt arisen agein þe ground of þis synne, as þou schalt agains alle oþer synnes. ffor þe ground of þis synne is onli nede, wilk may nouȝt ben eschaped.

Clearly the fact that one must eat means that gluttony cannot be overcome by denying oneself any opportunity which might lead to this sin, even if only in thought, since such action runs the risk of cutting out food altogether and leading to wilful starvation.

The doctrine of seeking to know only what one ought to know had to be treated with similar caution by the thinkers of the time as the laudable desire for knowledge could easily turn into a greed for learning which overstepped the bounds of permitted knowledge, leading to intellectual pride. The eating of the apple of the Tree of Knowledge and the subsequent expulsion from the Garden of Eden illustrated how sinful such action could be. So a difficult path had to be trodden between the two in an effort to extend learning without falling into error. Bonaventure solves this difficulty by differentiating between knowledge sought for specific theological ends and knowledge sought to satisfy curiosity:

> dicendum, quod omnes illae auctoritates intelliguntur de perscrutatione curiosa, non de perscrutatione studiosa.
>
> (it must be said that all these authorities are understood as referring to enquiry pursued to satisfy curiosity, not to studious enquiry.)[10]

By making the distinction between curiosity, which is potentially sinful, and studious enquiry, which is not, Bonaventure makes it possible to give credit to writers' ideas and the knowledge they present without necessarily having to agree with their theology. Their information could be right, but

9 Hilton, *Scale*, Book 1, ch. 72, p. 220.
10 Bonaventure, *Commentary on the Sentences*, Proem, Q.2, conclusio, Resp. 1, 2, 3, *Bonaventura*, vol. 1, p. 11a; tr. Minnis-Scott, p. 226.

irrelevant to Christian doctrine, so the need to decide whether or not a pagan author was sinful does not arise. However, rather than making it possible to justify any enquiry, Bonaventure's division actually begs the question of when studious enquiry becomes curiosity and *vice-versa*, and also how one can justify curiosity.

This seems a far cry from Langland's attack on gluttony, both in the person of the Doctor and in the wonderfully vivid Gloton of the deadly sins (B.V.297–385), but in fact both the attacks on greed and on excess learning concentrate on precisely the area where need cannot be a mitigating factor. Gloton does not seek food and drink because otherwise he will die, nor does the Doctor of Divinity seek learning because he is in danger of falling into deadly sin or misunderstanding if he does not achieve it. Moreover, not only does Gloton consume more food than he needs and the Doctor more knowledge, but also their greed is a waste and abuse of resources which are badly needed by others. The description of society in the half-acre of Passus VI has shown how the wasters' over-indulgences, coupled with their refusal to work, creates a general famine as Hunger affects all the people in Piers' community, not just the wasters and false beggars. Equally, in the banquet scene Wil actually seeks to benefit from the learning which the Doctor possesses, but the Doctor uses, or displays, this learning only for his own satisfaction; he does not translate his words into actions, nor does he really attempt to make Wil understand the answer to his question by defending it against Pacience's view. Instead he attempts to preserve his standing as a learned man by ridiculing Pacience's words as a mere tale. Both the Doctor and Gloton are eager to acquire what they desire for themselves, but not so ready to share it with others. So it is that when criticising both bodily and mental gluttony Langland strikes at an area where resources are being abused, whether those resources be food or knowledge, and so there is a fundamental and culpable lack of accord between teaching and practice. Wil stresses the connection between abuse of resources and abuse of office in his criticism of the Doctor which centres on his hypocrisy:

> 'Ac this Goddes gloton' quod I 'with hise grete chekes,
> Hath no pite on us povere; he parfourneth yvele.
> That he precheth, he preveth nought . . .' (B.XIII.77–79)

The accusation is clear: here is a man whose theoretical knowledge of Dowel does not guide the way he conducts his life.

Not only is Wil's criticism justified on its own account, but it also indicates a development in his attitude and understanding. The above words, addressed to Pacience, reveal Wil's greater awareness of the responsibilites held by a preacher as he points out how the Doctor's behaviour detracts from his position because he does not follow his own teachings. Yet the fact that Wil speaks to Pacience only here, rather than shouting out in abrupt interruption, and, at Pacience's bidding, refrains from open accusation until the Doctor has condemned himself out of his own mouth, show that he has also learnt patience itself, and even a touch of humility. The lesson delivered by Reson and endorsed by Ymaginatif has found its mark. When he does speak he reveals that he is now able to find fault with a scholar and defeat him on his own terms, just as the friars were able to do to him at the beginning of Passus VII. They conquered Wil by means of greater argumentative skills, without needing to strike at the premiss of his case; now Wil attacks the Doctor by pointing out that if his definition of Dowel is correct he is not fulfilling its requirements. Either the doctrine or the proclaimer is at fault:

> 'By this day, sire doctour' quod I 'thanne in Dowel be ye noght!
> For ye han harmed us two in that ye eten the puddyng,
> Mortrews and oother mete – and we no morsel hadde.
> And if ye fare so in youre fermerye, ferly me thynketh
> But cheeste be ther charite sholde be, and yonge children dorste
> pleyne!' (B.XIII.105–108)

Gluttony is not simply indulgence; it is also an abuse of available resources. Just as the refusal by some to share out food will lead to the actual starvation of others, so the refusal to share out knowledge will lead to the starvation of some people of the Word. As a theologian and preacher it is the Doctor's duty to proclaim the Word of God, the Bread of Life, the food of the soul. As John Bromyard stated, *Verba dei debent habere pronunciatores et auditores* (The Word of God must have proclaimers and listeners).[11] Bromyard's brief statement declares the need for hearers as well as proclaimers, an equal balance which recalls the view that the listener is a responsible part of the process of disseminating the Word.

This topic of mutual responsibility has already been explored by Langland in the half-acre scene (B.VI). Piers has promised to provide for all those on the half-acre, but is divided about how to act towards the wasters who will only work when starvation makes them. He acknowledges that Hunger's remedies will work, but is not sure that he has the right to put them into practice. He recognises that even these wastrels are 'My blody bretheren, for God boughte us alle' (B.VI.207), and that he has a duty to love and help them all as they have need (208–9). The same point is made in Passus VII where Langland refers to both Gregory and Jerome who advocated giving to all who asked, for it is impossible for man to know who is truly deserving and who is not:

> For wite ye nevere who is worthi – as God woot who hath nede.
> In hym that taketh is the trecherie, if any treson walke –

---

11 John Bromyard, *SP*, f. 180r.

For he that yeveth, yeldeth, and yarketh hym to reste,
And he that biddeth, borweth, and bryngeth hymself in dette.
(B.VII.76–79)

This quandary about how to divide resources deals with the same principles as the banquet scene. Wil's situation at the banquet is similar to Piers',
but he is on the opposite side of the equation, being the receiver rather than
giver. He is attempting to gain knowledge and has equipped himself as well
as he could to receive it, but is thwarted because the Doctor of Divinity is
either unwilling or incapable of giving any such knowledge to him. In each
case both Wil and Piers have fulfilled their side of the bargain, but are
defeated because others will not fulfil theirs. To return to Bromyard's statement, the obligation is upon both *pronunciatores* and *auctores*.

The two related areas of social and educational obligation, which have
been the central concerns of the poem, are finally conflated as it becomes
increasingly obvious that this banquet of Passus XII is like those Dame
Studie attacks for lavishness and elitism combined with a disregard for the
spirit of the letter discussed, which results in the needy being chased away
while the diners delight in rich food and refined arguments about the
Trinity. Such characters have lost any understanding of what proper enjoy-
ment is as they take their pleasure in debauchery and excess:

Ac murthe and mynstralcie amonges men is nouthe
Lecherie, losengerye and losels tales –
Glotonye and grete othes, this game they lovyeth.
Ac if thei carpen of Crist, thise clerkes and thise lewed,
At mete in hir murthe whan mynstrals beth stille,
Thanne telleth thei of the Trinite how two slowe the thridde,
And bryngen forth a balled reson, and taken Bernard to witnesse,
And puten forth a presumpcion to preve the sothe.
Thus thei dryvele at hir deys the deitee to knowe,
And gnawen God with the gorge whanne hir guttes fullen.
Ac the carefulle may crie and carpen at the yate,
Bothe afyngred and afurst, and for chele quake;
Is non to nyme hym neer his noy to amende,
But hunsen hym as an hound and hoten hym go thennes.
Litel loveth he that Lord that lent hym al that blisse,
That thus parteth with the povere a parcell whan hym nedeth!
(B.X.48–63)

Over-indulgence in food is clearly linked with abuse of knowledge as these
diners fill in the lulls between minstrels with irrelevant and irreverent quips
and displays of clever argument. They have the right information but they
put it to the wrong use, just as they have enough food to feed themselves
and the poor outside, but choose to gorge themselves and hound the de-
prived. The knowledge they have does them no good, in fact it does them

actual harm, as their amusements lead them into blasphemy and away from the practice of the doctrine they bandy about. The scene Scripture describes is one which bears out Jill Mann's claim that 'a perversion in eating and drinking leads to a perversion in words and vice versa.'[12] Given this connection it is clear that such theologians as the Doctor are as much wasters as the false beggars and minstrels who are vilified in the Prologue (33–45).[13] The link is strengthened when both minstrels and friars are seen to be abusers of words, who delight in their ability to play with language, rather than in the message it bears. Furthermore, their dubious relation with language is surely the reason why Lyere, who embodies the abuse of the power of words, finds a haven with both groups following the debacle of Mede's wedding in Passus II:

> Lightliche Lyere leep awey thennes,
> Lurkynge thorugh lanes, tolugged of manye.
> . . .
> Ac mynstrales and messagers mette with hym ones,
> And withhelden hym an half yeer and ellevene dayes.
> Freres with fair speche fetten hym thennes,
> And for knowynge of comeres coped hym as a frere;
> Ac he hath leve to lepen out as ofte as hym liketh,
> And is welcome whan he wile, and woneth with hem ofte.
> (B.II.216–17, 228–33)

It is no wonder that learned men of the type described by Studie and represented by the Doctor take pleasure in secular minstrels rather than in 'he that hath Holy Writ ay in his mouthe / And kan telle of Tobye and of the twelve Apostles' (B.X.32–33). For the lewed minstrels and the lax theologians are of the same order of men.

---

[12] Jill Mann, 'Eating and Drinking in *Piers Plowman*', *Essays and Studies* n.s. 32 (1979), 34.

[13] The connection between friars and minstrels is discussed in detail by Penn R. Szittya, who makes it the basis for his chapter on *Piers* in *The Anti-Fraternal Tradition in Medieval Literature*, see esp. pp. 248–265. Szytta's query about why 'hunger should be an appropriate problem at the end of the poem' is surely answered by the fact that the link between food and knowledge has become so strong that any reference to eating contains within it a reference to hunger for knowledge as well.

9

Speech as God-Given Resource

A s Wit states, to waste words is as bad as wasting any other resource. He begins by giving as a definition of Dowel the example of one who refrains from wasting either words or time and, by avoiding sin in these areas, avoids becoming entangled in other forms of sin too. However, he does not leave the matter there, but expands it to include all levels of living, not just the high ideal offered by Dowel. It becomes clear that an irresponsible attitude towards speech and, indeed, how one spends one's time, is something to be avoided by all:

> He dooth best that withdraweth hym by daye and by nyghte
> To spille any speche or any space of tyme:
> *Qui offendit in uno, in omnibus est reus.*
> Tynynge of tyme, Truthe woot the sothe,
> Is moost yhated upon erthe of hem that ben in hevene;
> And siththe to spille speche, that spire is of grace,
> And Goddes gleman and a game of hevene.
> Wolde nevere the feithful fader his fithele were untempred,
> Ne his gleman a gedelyng, a goere to tavernes.   (B.IX.97–104)

Underlying this speech is an attitude akin to that of Scripture who denounces the debauchery of the banquets where true minstrels who sing of the glory of God are ignored in favour of those who provide less enlightening entertainment (B.X.48–63). Yet, despite first appearances, Wit is not being a kill-joy who disapproves of any form of entertainment at all; instead he is advocating a delight in the correct use of language, which recognises it as an offshoot of grace. The words 'gleman' and 'game' and the image of the fiddle tuned to be played properly, all reveal that speech used properly can be as much fun (if not more as it is also without sin) as the more usual illicit uses associated with tavern life. Nevertheless, speech is a 'spire of grace', an approach to the Divine Word, the creating power; as such the ability to speak and to use words properly brings with it a responsibility to use that gift to good end. To 'spille speche' implies that words are poured out to no purpose, the potential they bear for communicating knowledge left

106

unexploited. This tallies with Henry of Ghent's assertion that the method of passing on knowledge must suit the way it is learned so that the knowledge in question is made accessible to those wishing to acquire it:

> necessarium est quod modus tradendi huius scientiae sicut et cuiuslibet alterius sit conformis modo sciendi, vt tali modo tractetur quo competentius ab homine sciri possit.
>
> (It is, therefore, essential that the mode of handing down this knowledge [theology], as with any other subject, matches the method of learning it, so that men may be able to acquire knowledge of it more readily.)[1]

For Henry it is an essential qualification for a teacher that he has enough authority for the listener to believe his words and carry out his teaching. As he puts it, what is required is:

> . . . docentis auctoritas, ut auditores sibi credendo obediant.
>
> (. . . authority in the teacher, so that the listeners by believing [what he says] may obey him.)[2]

The aim of the teacher of theology is that his listeners should obey his words. This will happen only if he has enough credibility for his audience to believe that his words are worth listening to and for this to be the case he must have integrity as a teacher, which will then dispose his audience to believe his lessons, and so be more likely to carry them out. In a rather paradoxical way the audience has the power to endow a teacher with authority: if they believe him they trust him, and so give him the reputation he needs to be a respected and authoritative speaker. This is the case even for priests, whose authority comes from the Church; for, as we have seen, if their conduct alienates their congregation they run the risk of undermining their teaching, despite the fact that the message may be sound even when the teacher is not.

The implications of Henry's words are that, although the teacher must have authority as a communicator, that authority actually comes from the attitude of his audience, rather than from a higher power. The power of the audience and its views of those who address it is dealt with more explicity in his *quaestio* on women's ability to preach. Each of the objections to women preachers that he puts forward rests upon the way women are perceived, even where other causes are the apparent reasons for disqualifying them. It is worth remembering that all his objections rest upon how he himself perceived women and so, in this aspect at least, Henry stands as a representative of a potential audience.

Henry regards women as incapable of fulfilling the requirements for a

1 Henry of Ghent, *SQ*, XIV, q. i, resp. f. 100rD.
2 Henry of Ghent, *SQ*, XI, q. ii, resolutio, f. 77vP.

preacher because they are easily seduced from truth, they are physically too weak to speak in public, they are the inferior sex, and their words (and very presence before a crowd of men) would divert men into sinful thoughts. Each one of these objections rests on the audience's attitude towards the speaker. This becomes obvious when one takes into account the fact that Henry admits that if a woman has knowledge there is no reason why she cannot address other women on theological matters. She is not considered too easily seduced from the truth for a female audience, nor too weak to speak to one and, naturally, objections based on sexual inferiority or erotic effect on the audience would not have to be taken into account when the listeners are all women. In effect it is men's refusal to admit authority in a woman which denies it to her; and hence prevents her from being an effective preacher. As Henry admits the matter is not one of ability or deed but of authority or power: '... non de facto, sed de iuris permissione.'[3]

From the teacher's point of view it is thus essential to win the approval of the potential audience and hence convince his auditors of his authority. When dealing with an uneducated audience this could be effected by fine words, references to *auctores*, use of suitable *exempla* or, if the preacher were unscrupulous, by such trickery as false relics and bulls – depending on the level at which he preached and the level of his corruption (the archetype is provided by Chaucer's Pardoner). On the other hand, from the standpoint of the listener who is concerned to know what he should believe, it is essential to be able to assess what he hears. Ideally he needs enough knowledge to be able to say whether or not a particular interpretation is correct, an argument sound, an authority cited properly. If he has not got this knowledge, he must be willing to challenge and question the speaker in order to ascertain whether the figure in front of him is qualified to teach him, or whether, in fact, he is a charlatan. In other words he needs to make himself proof against trickery and not allow himself to be impressed by outward appearances of authority. The moment the audience ceases to believe in the teacher's authority and his right to teach his ability to teach them has gone. Seen in this light the power of the listener becomes apparent.

The proviso is that the listener must be willing to learn and want to understand fully what is said, otherwise he will simply accept the words of his teacher and his authority without question and so be in no position to carry out his principles in an intelligent manner. At worst such a listener may totally misunderstand what he is told and so fall into error (Haukyn (B.XIII–IV) is a case in point). Wil, however, clearly does want to learn;

---

3 Henry of Ghent, *SQ*, XI, q. ii, resolutio, f. 77vO.

witness his repeated questions and, more importantly, his attempts to argue
and discuss the dogma presented to him by the various figures on their own
terms. This reveals his desire to understand properly what he is told and
also to understand how he ought to act. In effect this section presents Wil as
student gradually fulfilling his obligation to become a fitting auditor of
God's Word. As Clergie says: 'In scole there is scorn but if a clerk wol lern.'
(B.X.301).

As Wil acquires greater understanding and so proves himself a willing
pupil, he becomes increasingly well-qualified to judge the authority of the
figures he meets in this section. His dismissal of Clergie and Scripture as
misguiding because they do not tell him what he wants to know, and his
utter disgust at the Doctor, are all indications of his greater, but by no means
infallible, awareness that not all who preach are reliable guides. The Doctor
himself is a different case: he will not even consider that Pacience – that
lowly figure at his side-table – could have spoken truthfully, nor merit any
authority whatsoever. He cannot or will not recognise the validity of an
alternative discourse and attempts to undermine Pacience's words by redefining them as romantic notions – 'a dido . . . a disours tale' (B.XIII.172) – for
entertainment only. He ostentatiously refuses to lend credence to Pacience's
speech in an attempt to persuade others to do likewise and thus destroy
Pacience's authority; instead he destroys only his own.

The Doctor's actions reveal him to be severely flawed: he is too caught up
in the material world to be able to practise what he preaches, or even to
admit the truth of one better qualified to teach, i.e. Pacience. However,
despite being associated with wasters and idlers, he is not totally rejected. It
is only his behaviour which is at fault; what he says is sound doctrine,
which is not disputed by any of the guests at the banquet. Pacience himself
prevents Wil from lambasting him out of hand (advising him to wait until
the Doctor's own words betray his moral corruption) and when Wil does
contest his words it is on the grounds of misuse of learning rather than the
irrelevance of this kind of knowledge. This is not a case of misguided
curiosity, but an instance of a man having the right knowledge, but not
acting upon it. Similarly it is Clergie, the personification of learning, who
undermines all that the Doctor represents by his refusal to match the Doctor's definition with one of his own because he recognises that his expertise
in deduction and learned enquiry is insufficient for a proper definition of
Dowel:

'I have sevene sones,' he seide, 'serven in a castel
Ther the lord of lif wonyeth, to leren hem what is Dowel.
Til I se tho sevene and myself acorde
I am unhardy,' quod he 'to any wight to preven it.
For oon Piers the Plowman hath impugned us alle,
And set alle sciences at a sop save love one;

And no text ne taketh to mayntene his cause
But *Dilige Deum* and *Domine quis habitabit.* (B.XIII.119–126)

To have such a speech given to Clergie is possibly surprising since it appears to present learning as useless. However, Clergie's words demonstrate that he knows that his learning has limitations, which must be recognised if learning itself is to be useful in the search for understanding. In this he is similar to Studie and Pacience, who, as James Simpson has pointed out, 'underline the inadequacy of grammatical knowledge'.[4]

Despite such limitations, learning, in the B-Text, is not utterly deserted as an ultimately futile pursuit. Instead Conscience departs admitting he may well need Clergie in the future. Even his dramatic rejection of learning is couched ironically in an idiom which would give him the best of both worlds as he declares he would prefer to have perfect patience and yet reject only half of Clergie's books:

> Me were levere, by Oure Lord, and I lyve sholde,
> Have pacience parfitliche than half thi pak of bokes!
>
> (B.XIII.200–201)

Conscience is not just accepting that learning has its place; he is also advocating a combination of learning and faith which will result in a thorough understanding. This is reflected in his parting shot that Pacience must be 'oure partyng felawe and pryve with us bothe'. With such a combination and balance 'ther nys no wo in this world that we ne sholde amende' (B.XIII.206–7).

The C-Text is far more extreme: here (in Passus XV) Peres suddenly bursts onto the stage to speak for himself, pushing Clergie and the Doctor into the background. His abrupt and unheralded entrance in line 138 follows Clergie's speech which invokes the example of Peres as the reason why he, unlike the Doctor, will not offer a definition of Dowel:

> 'Now þou, Clergie,' quod Conscience, 'carpe what is Dowel.'
> 'Haue me excused,' quod Clergie, 'be Crist, but in scole,
> Shal no such motyef be meued for me, bote þere,
> For Peres loue þe palmare зent, þat inpugnede ones
> Alle kyne connynges and alle kyne craftes,
> Saue loue and leute and lowenesse of herte. (C.XV.128–33)

By appearing at the end of Clergie's speech and immediately giving his own opinion, Peres seems to brush aside the need for learning, even when it acts as a spokesman and supports his position. The compromise latent in the B-Text is abandoned in the C version as Reson leaps after Peres as soon

---

[4] J. Simpson, 'The Role of *Scientia* in *Piers Plowman*', p. 63.

as he vanishes and when Conscience leaves Clergie his parting words do not offer the combination of learning and patience present in the B-Text, but are an unequivocal affirmation of the power of Pacience alone:

> Lettrure and longe studie letteth fol monye,
> That they knoweth nat,' quod Concience, 'what is kynde Pacience.
> Forthy,' quod Concience, 'Crist y the byteche,
> With Pacience wol y passe, parfitnesse to fynde.'   (C.XV.181–84)

It is a more final ending to a dramatic scene than the B-Text admission that Clergie may yet have a place in the action of the poem.

Yet even in the C-Text the fact that Clergie is left standing and Reson has leapt out of the text, never to reappear, does not mean that there is no place at all for learning. The caution is that they must eventually be abandoned in order to reach a different type of understanding, which does not become merely theoretical as it has in the case of the Doctor of Divinity, but actually affects one's conduct. The personifications of the intellectual faculties have played a part in helping Wil reach the point where he can begin to understand what Dowel is and how to achieve it. Even the Doctor has been useful in acting as a catalyst. His presence and the obvious discrepancy between his words and deeds have brought about the climax which results in the break between Conscience and Clergie as Pacience becomes the next guiding figure in the poem.

So, despite the drama of the end of the banquet it is clear that Ymaginatif has been proved right, and learning cannot be dismissed; even a sinning preacher has his uses, since he can still say the right things. John of Bromyard holds the same view:

> Tales enim sunt sicut fabricatores arce Noe: per quam alii servabantur et salvabantur et ipsi in diluvio perierunt.
>
> (For such people are like the builders of Noah's ark, through which others were helped and saved but they themselves perished in the flood.)[5]

Or, as Henry of Ghent puts it rather less vividly:

> Se habet enim hoc modo doctor ad instruendum alium secundum habitum huius scientiae: sicut artifex quidam ad operandum artificium secundum habitum artis. De artifice autem dicit Philosophus in fine primi politicae: quod non oportet eum habere vitutem ad hoc enim quod sit bonus faber potens facere bonos cultellos nulla virtus moralis in eo requitur sed solum perfectio artis fabrilis.
>
> (For this is the situation of a teacher in instructing someone else according to the mode of this science: he is like a craftsman in creating a work of art according to

---

5 John Bromyard, *SP*, s.v. Verba Dei, f. 180r.

the rules of his art. Moreover, about art the Philosopher says at the end of his first book of politics: it is not necessary that it should have virtue; for in as much as a man is a good craftsman able to make good little knives no moral virtue is required in him, but only the perfection of the art of metalwork.)[6]

For both John and Henry the important thing is that the teacher should transmit his message properly, thereby enabling others to learn what ought to be done and act accordingly. Learning has a place, therefore, since without it neither the teacher nor the pupil could learn how to act and where to find guidance. Yet, as Henry shows, it is essential that both teacher and learner should be aware of the limitations of their roles: it is not necessary for a knife-maker to live virtuously to be a master craftsman and pass on his skill, since his pupil has come to learn from him, not to imitate his way of life. So, in John's instance, those who had the skills necessary to build the ark did not understand how the result of their expertise – the ark itself – could benefit them, but those who knew its purpose did not have the practical knowledge to construct the ark and so could only build it by using others' skills. It appears, then, that any knowledge can be useful but is likely to be limited in itself; its full potential can only be realised by those who unite knowledge and understanding. Thus, even those writers who did not embrace the approach through reason still accorded learning a place in the process of understanding. Hilton is one such writer, as is apparent in his outline of the three steps of contemplation. Here reason and learning take their place in the first stage:

> Þe first lith in cnowynge of God and of gostly þinges, geten bi reson, bi teching of man, and bi studie in Holy Writ, withouten gostly affeccioun and inly sauour feled bi þe special ȝieft of þe Holy Ghost. Þis partie han specially some lettred men, and grete clerkes whilk bi long studie and trauail in Holy Writ comyn to þis cnowyng, more ore lasse, after þe suteltee of kyendly wit and continuance of studie vpe þe general ȝifthe þat God ȝyues ylke man þat haþ vs of reson. Þis cnowyng is good, and hit mai be callid a partie of contemplacion in also mikil as hit is a siht of Sothfastnesse and a cnowynge of gostly þings. Neuerþeles, hit is bute a figure and a schadue of verreie contemplacion.[7]

Knowing is good, and is a starting place for proper understanding, but it is not an end in itself.

The result of the banquet episode is not to declare all learning useless but rather to question whether one can expect scholarly knowledge to yield final answers to what is, above all, a spiritual quest. Thus Wit and Clergie

---

6 Henry of Ghent, *SQ*, XI, q.v, resp. 1, f. 80rK.
7 Hilton, *Scale*, Book 1, ch. 4, p. 89. This acceptance of learning (albeit as the lowest rung on the ladder) and the relationship between learning and greed, helps to make sense of his leniency towards the glutton later in *Scale* 1.

are valued for the knowledge they have, whereas Studie and the Doctor both show the results of over-emphasis and misapplication of the learning the other two supply. Scripture is left as an ambiguous figure, fundamental to both the deductive and affective approaches to knowledge and so both necessary and susceptible to abuse. Hence she is given a place as the server of Pacience and Conscience and, in the C-Text in an image reminiscent of the government of Passus III–IV, is under the guidance of Reson, who is thus placed in the position of watchdog. Although Reson does not speak he is given a clear place in the hierarchy as the channel through which Clergie's directions pass:

> Thenne was Resoun radde, anoon riht aftur,
> That Conscience comaunde sholde to do come Scripture
> And bring breed for Pacience ... (C.XV.52–54)

Such great respect for reason as a judge of what should and should not be believed is evident in Henry of Ghent, among others:

> quod solis testimoniis credere, vel homini, vel scripturae, sine reddita ratione fatuum esset.
>
> (To believe something on testimony alone, either human or scriptural, without the reason being declared, would be fatuous.)[8]

For Robert of Basevorn and St Augustine (whom Robert paraphrases) reason is necessary for evaluating and validating an authority which is questioned by an equally authoritative source:

> Unde dicit quod ubi deficit auctoritas, rationi insistendum est, sine qua nec auctoritas est auctoritas.
>
> (This is why he says that where authority is lacking, we must rest on reason, without which even authority is not authority.)[9]

It is an area also tackled by Peter Abelard in the Prologue to his *Sic et Non* where he points out that the Gospels often differ on details and yet it must be assumed that the Gospel writers wrote the truth, so it is reasonable to attribute such discrepancies to scribal error. He also points out that the most authoritative combination of attributes is justice and wisdom, or in different terminology, learning and reason. He goes on to quote the second book of Cicero's *De Officiis*:

> Iustitia cum sine prudentia satis habeat auctoritatis, prudentia sine iustitia nihil valet ad faciendam fidem. Quo enim quisque versutior et callidior,

---

8 Henry of Ghent, *SQ*, IX, q. iii, arg. 1, resp. f. 72rP.
9 Robert of Basevorn, ch. X, p. 246; tr. p. 130.

hoc invidiosior et suspectior detracta opinione probitatis. Quamobrem intellegentiae iustitia coniuncta quantum volet habebit ad faciendam fidem virium. Iustitia sine prudentia multum poterit; sine iustitia nil valebit prudentia.

(Whereas justice without wisdom [reason without learning] has a certain amount of authority, wisdom without justice has not the strength to command belief, for the more shrewd and cunning a man is, so is he all the more hated and suspect once he has lost his reputations for probity. So justice coupled with wisdom will have as much power as it wishes to command belief. Justice without wisdom will have much power, but wisdom without justice none at all.)[10]

We have been given an example of this in the way Wil rejects the guidance of the Doctor of Divinity because he is a clever but apparently immoral man.

Reason is here being used to its best advantage as an arbitrator, much as recommended by the translators of the Wycliffite Bible, yet it is reason working within a precise domain, as described by St Bonaventure:

Et quod obiicitur, quod credibile est supra rationem; verum est, supra rationem quantam ad scientiam acquisitam, sed non supra rationem elevatam per fidem et per donum scientiae et intellectus.

(As for the objection that what relates to belief is above reason, it is true that it is above reason as far as acquired knowledge is concerned. But it is not above reason that has been elevated by faith and by the gift of knowledge and understanding.)[11]

Bonaventure thus comes to a concept of a perfect dialogue between reason and faith in which each illuminates the other.

This notion that knowledge and learning form a useful basis for the later stages of understanding is reflected in *Piers Plowman* as Langland presents his readers with various types and shades of learning in the intellectual figures from the Friars and Wil to the Doctor of Divinity and Clergie. As he introduces these various characters he also presents possible reactions to learning and its uses. The result is that Wil is no longer overawed by educated people like the friars but yet he is aware that the knowledge they have may be worthwhile. When he accuses the Doctor of not living up to the text he preaches, he does not assume that the text and teaching must also be unsound (B.XII.64 following; C.XV.70 following). This more moderate reaction is tantamount to an admission that, as a learner, he too has a responsibility to try to understand the knowledge he seeks.

---

[10] Abelard, *'Sic et Non': A Critical Edition*, eds. Blanche B. Boyer and Richard McKeon (Chicago and London, 1976), p. 95. Translation from Minnis-Scott, p. 131.

[11] Bonaventure, *Commentary*, Proem, q. 2, concl. resp. 5, p. 11b; tr. p. 226.

In this highly complex section Langland presents what could be termed a Scale of Scholastic Perfection which reveals that intellectual knowledge cannot lead infallibly to the wisdom Wil requires. In doing so this section shows that there is a difference between *scientia* and *sapientia* and that it is vital to understand what one is looking for and thus be able to choose the best means of attaining that end rather than be misled by impressive-sounding ways and so run the risk of following the wrong course, blind to its limitations and corruptions. It takes the profoundly disconcerting encounter with Ymaginatif, following hard on the heels of the Land of Longing and visions of Middelerthe, to shake the dreamer out of his blinkered acceptance of the authority of knowledge as *scientia*. Yet he has also attained a respect for learning in its right place, and is now better equipped to understand and assess what follows; the cry 'I have no kynde knowyng!' is not heard again.[12]

---

[12] The meaning of this phrase 'kynde knowing' has been examined closely by Sister Mary Clemente Davlin in 'Kynde Knowynge as a Middle English Equivalent for Wisdom in *Piers Plowman*', *Medium Aevum* 50 (1981), 5–17. Her view is endorsed by James Simpson in his essay 'The Role of *Scientia* in *Piers Plowman*', pp. 49–55. Simpson concentrates on the figure of Dame Studie and shows that there was a strong tradition of ironic use of scholastic terminology to undercut academic discourse. His general appraisal of this figure is more favourable than that I have offered here, as he gives her more credit for knowing her own limitations. While this is a valid point, I feel that the alterations made for the C-Text indicate that in the B-Text she is to be regarded warily.

Part Three

KNOWLEDGE BEYOND REASON

The abuse of rational argument leads to a distrust of reason; the worried turn to revelation as an alternative.[1]

1 Beryl Smalley, 'The Bible and Eternity: John Wyclif's Dilemma', *Studies in Medieval Thought and Learning* (London, 1981), p. 399.

10

Knowledge Beyond Reason

For the majority of Passus VIII to XIV the tendency is towards the deductive discourse and form, descended through the university dispute from rhetoric and dialectic. This tendency has led to this section of *Piers Plowman* being termed the 'scholastic' section, since the influence of medieval scholastic theological interests and attitudes towards language are apparent within it. The characters display their ability to furnish apt quotations (Scripture), apply and expand topics (Studie) and embark on academic enquiry (Clergie and the Doctor). Definitions, *distinctiones* and fine arguments abound, hence the number of definitions of Dowel, but there is little evidence of its practice: the teaching offered is that of words rather than example. The alternative form is not forgotten by Langland, but is refused voice at this stage: it is present in the figures of Pacience and Piers, both instances of the *exempla* which are essential for illustrative discourse, but easily ignored by the university dispute. Their presence is a reminder that there is an alternative, but their lowly position at Conscience's banquet reveals that this mode of speech is greatly marginalised by the narrow intellectualism given prominence at this point in the poem.

Pacience is mentioned as coming after Scripture with Clergie and Conscience, which seems to imply equality, but in fact he and Wil are physically set aside at the banquet:

> And thanne Clergie and Conscience and Pacience cam after.
> Pacience and I were put to be mettes,
> And seten bi oureselve at a side borde. (B.XIII.33–36)

They are not ignored, just as the deductive discourse does not necessarily deny the fact that there could be an alternative, but they clearly have no part in that discourse. Their presence is thus acknowledged, but they are not a part of the general table. In a similar way the marginalisation of Piers, the most constant *exemplum* in the poem, is not a permanent setting aside of him as no longer relevant and so finally discarded. Instead it is a deferral, which admits that there may come a time when the discourse, for which

119

Piers is a symbol, may come into its own. In these terms the treatment of Piers is even more striking than the treatment of Pacience. In the B-Text Piers is not even granted an appearance, but is present only in the indirect form of Clergie's reference and Conscience's subsequent remarks:

> 'I am unhardy,' quod he, 'to any wight to preven it [Dowel].
> For oon Piers the Plowman hath impugned us alle,
> And set alle sciences at a sop save love one;
> And no text ne taketh to mayntene his cause
> But *Dilige Deum* and *Domine quis habitabit*;
> And seith that Dowel and Dobest arn two infinites,
> Whiche infinites with a feith fynden out Dobest,
> Which shal save mannes soule – thus seith Piers the Plowman.'
> (B.XIII.122–129)

Here, in a speech which is reminiscent of Holi Chirche's words on love and its power in Passus I (B.I.140–207), Clergie admits that his form of discourse is incapable of understanding and defining Dowel because the true definitions, those given by Piers, lie outside the realms of his language. By declaring love to be the only worthwhile science Piers not only dismisses all other sciences, all other ways of knowing, but also destroys the very idea of a science and redefines it, for love is not a science in the usual sense of the word. It cannot be arrived at through derivation or definition, but like theology, for which in part it stands here, it must be regarded as a special case. Furthermore his mode of expression is markedly different; Piers uses no texts – no *auctoritates* – except one exhortation to love God and one reference to the Psalms, one of the most figurative books of the Bible. It is no wonder, then, that Clergie finds himself unable to give Conscience the definition he seeks; his language has been taken away from him.

Even Conscience is at a loss because he cannot 'kanne' Clergie's words, cannot understand them intellectually, and is instead thrown back on the simple assertion 'ac I knowe wel Piers./ He wol noght ayein Holy Writ speken, I dar wel undertake.' (B.XIII.130–31). With these words Conscience treats Piers as a figure whose opinion is to be deferred to without question, and by so doing makes him into an authority. It is the first time since the end of Passus VII that Piers has been deferred to in quite this manner; Clergie has respected him enough to enquire further into the claims he makes, but has done so by sending his sons to a higher authority, the lord of life, not by referring to Piers himself. Yet, despite this remarkable change of status, Piers is immediately set to one side and excluded from the discourse as Conscience moves on from Piers to Pacience:

> Thanne passe we over til Piers come and preve this in dede.
> Pacience hath be in many place, and paraunter knoweth
> That no clerk ne kan, as Crist bereth witnesse.
> *Pacientes vincunt* &c. (B.XIII.132–34a)

Conscience's words form a reference which simultaneously brings Piers into the discourse by allusion, and debars him from it by declaring that further discussion in this vein must wait until Piers himself makes an appearance. By turning to Pacience immediately afterwards Conscience opens the poem to the language of affective discourse, thus beginning the disruption of the domination of *scientia*'s approach and language.

In contrast the C-Text version actually includes Piers, but his presence is profoundly disconcerting as he suddenly bursts in and just as suddenly disappears, 'wiste no man aftur/ Where Peres the plogman bycam, so priueyliche he wente' (C.XV.149–150). The intrusion of the central *exemplum*-figure of the poem into this most academic scene in a way reminiscent of Christ's appearances and subsequent mysterious disappearances after the Resurrection, undermines its security and breaks the circle of discourse which it has created. For it is an intrusion of an actual figure who can be seen, felt and acknowledged into a theoretical and abstract debate. There is no need of discussion if the object or end being debated and described can be shown and immediately comprehended.

These instances show the power of affective language and also portray it as incompatible with the discourse of the rational approach to *scientia*. Yet, while it is true that highly deductive reasoning had little use for figurative language as a mode of expression, this is not to say that any form of rational discourse precluded the use of illustrative speech. As the example of Clergie shows, there is a certain overlap: he speaks of his seven sons doing service for the lord of life in his castle (B.XIII.119–20), which in itself is a figure of speech. However Clergie himself must wait until these seven sons, the seven arts, return, having themselves learnt from the lord of life; then, and only then, will he be able to understand and speak the language of Piers.

The encounter with the Doctor of Divinity and the responses Wil receives to his questions demonstrate the distrust of reason which arises in the reader as well as in Wil as a consequence of the abuse of rational argument. Wil's reaction seems to be to turn to the alternative form of understanding which is the aim of the path to knowledge as wisdom, or *sapientia*. This is demonstrated in his choice to leave Clergie's banquet in order to follow Pacience. For it is Pacience, with his highly figurative and affective use of language, and not Ymaginatif, who represents the real alternative to Reson.[2]

Pacience was first mentioned in the poem at B.V.622, where she (the quality being gendered as female at this point) is one of the seven sisters who act as porters to the gates of Truth. This first, brief, reference to Pacience is clearly to patience as the virtue which counterbalances the deadly sin of wrath. Later when the personification of patience becomes an

2 For further elaboration of this claim see A.V.C. Schmidt, *The Clerkly Maker*, pp. 82–83.

121

actual participant in the text, in Passus XIII, the character has expanded to contain extra aspects which are connected with the ideal of active patience (and also becomes male). There are echoes of the trusting faith of the ideal pilgrim as Pacience stands 'in pilgrymes clothes' (B.XIII.29) and his humility is made apparent as he asks for food for charity's sake and describes himself as a poor hermit (30). In fact humility is the outstanding characteristic of this figure of Pacience; he sits quietly at a side table (36), accepts with gratitude all that is given to him, calling it 'propre service' (51) and delights in his treatment while Wil sulks (61). However, it is an informed humility. Pacience accepts the position he is given and restrains Wil from indignant outburst, but he does not refuse to speak when called upon to give his definition of Dowel, Dobet and Dobest, and furthermore, Conscience's words of B.XII.133–134a indicate that Pacience is well qualified to discuss the meaning of Dowel; for *Pacientes vincunt*. Thus Pacience is presented as a figure who possesses a kind of knowledge which the educated 'clerkes' may know exists (hence his inclusion at the banquet at all) but choose not to use.

As the action of the poem progresses it becomes clear that Pacience is also a figure of patient poverty, for he has no belongings but goes forth like a pilgrim, carrying all he needs in his bag (B.XIII.216; XIV.37–38). The food he offers Haukyn as a cure-all is 'a pece of the Paternoster – *Fiat voluntas tua*' (B.XIV.49). It is this affirmation of the code of acceptance – 'thy will be done' – which epitomizes Pacience's stand-point. He advocates the primacy of faith over learning as a path to salvation, a view supported by the repeated use of the tag '*Pacientes vincunt*'.

Through the use of '*Pacientes vincunt*', and by showing Pacience to be knowledgable and abstemious, and through the very action of Conscience's banquet, which ends with Conscience leaving the Doctor of Divinity and Clergie in order to follow Pacience, Pacience is presented in opposition to the Doctor. He commands respect for his behaviour and his concern for his fellow citizens, which is revealed in his encounter with Haukyn, whom he attempts to look after and feed – a sharp contrast to the Doctor's relish for rich food obtained at others' expense (B.XII.40–45a). As well as being a contrast in demeanour, his language and the type of knowledge he offers are an alternative to those advocated by Clergie and the Doctor. His definition of Dowel, Dobet and Dobest is highly figurative as he presents a simple interpretation illustrated by recounting the exchange with love. He does not offer an explanation which pins down precisely what is meant by *Disce, doce, dilige inimicos* (B.XII.136), nor does he indicate a precise path to follow; instead his words, both to Conscience's guests and to Haukyn, are designed to evoke a more emotional response which will move the hearers to reform their lives, as indeed Haukyn does. Pacience's way of life and use of language consolidate the hints of the emotive discourse which have appeared occasionally so far (the inner-dream being the most vivid instance) and moves the text closer to the attitudes associated with the approach to knowledge as *sapientia*.

Within the range of affective discourses there were two main strands – the *via negativa* and *via positiva*. The *via positiva* used images in a creative and comparative way, building up from the familiar to the divine. Take the brightest thing known to man, the sun; consider how far its brightness excels that of all other things; so much and more does the goodness of God excel that of the most virtuous human. The *via negativa*, on the other hand, sought to free the mind from the need for images of any kind. Where they are used they are made deliberately surprising, shocking and literally almost inconceivable since they are used in a reverse, negative fashion, as Eckhart does when he states that calling God good is like calling the sun black:

> Got enist guot noch bizzer noch allerbeste. Wer dâ spraeche, daz got guot waere, des tacte im als unrechte, als ob es die sunne swarz hieße
>
> (God is neither good nor better, nor best of all. Anyone who says that God is good, is as wrong as if he were to call the sun black.)[3]

This seemingly perverse use of imagery is deliberately disconcerting in order to force the listener/reader to work out how it can be true. In the case of Eckhart's comparison it is because God is as far removed from our idea of 'good' as the sun is from the idea of black; the comparison is so inadequate it becomes useless. Yet positing such non-comparisons enables the thinkers to free themselves from even involuntary use of images and concepts which are by their very nature limiting. A variant is the use of the cloud images in *The Cloud of Unknowyng*. Here the cloud of unknowing and the cloud of forgetting block out the familiar world and prevent any other image entering either the reader's mind or the text. The clouds defy conceptualization, which is the point, while also eliciting feelings of dis-orientation and separation from both the real world and the world of images.

This divide in language reflected a similar choice concerning the type of life one led; as well as the active life, with its involvement in the world, or the contemplative's withdrawal, there was a rarer, third option of 'mixed life' which was active in that it advocated involvement in the world and the fulfilment of responsibilites to dependants, but it also made room for periods of contemplation in order to allow for spiritual growth, which would then enrich the active periods. The various 'lives' were regarded as distinct but adherence to one did not preclude eventually moving to another: one could progress through the Active to the Contemplative or

---

3 Meister Eckhart, Predigt 9, in *Meister Eckhart Predigten*, ed. E. Band, Deutsche Werke, I (Stuttgart and Berlin, 1936–58), 148. Tr. *Meister Eckhart: Teacher and Preacher*, Classics of Western Spirituality, ed. B. McGinn (New York, 1986), p. 257.

Mixed. It is possible to see an analogy with the use of languages in the deductive and affective discourses, or indeed within the two forms of language within the affective discourse, although the language associated with each *via* tended to remain more separate. Clearly it would be confusing to use images both positively and negatively in the same piece. When the mixed life is discussed, as it is by Hilton in both parts of his *Scale of Perfection* and also in Ruysbroek's *Seven Steps to the Ladder of Spiritual Love*, the type of language used is constantly affirmative.

It may perhaps be obvious that the negative way should be equated with the fully contemplative life. Just as the negative use of language sought to free its followers from the need for conceivable images and comparisons in order to express the experience of God, so the contemplative life aimed at removing its followers from involvement with the created world and the society around (whether or not that implied physical enclosure) in order to achieve a direct understanding of and communion with God – insofar as is possible in this world. Since Langland is not writing an advice-treatise to prospective contemplatives, as the *Cloud* author and Hilton are, he has little space for negative vocabulary. He is writing a poem of the type that demands images and which is fiercely concerned with society and the difficulties faced by the majority of his contemporaries. Strict adherence to esoteric doctrines cannot be relevant and would drive him into silence. This gradual progression towards silence is recognised by the *Cloud* author in his version of Pseudo-Dionysius, *Deonise Hid Divinite*:

> . . . whan we entren into þe derknes þat is abouen mynde, we schul not onliche fynde þe schortyng of wordes, bot as it were a madnes & a parfite vnresonabiltee of alle þat we seyn.[4]

The achievement of this darkness which is beyond conception is the aim of the negative way.

The level of contemplation which allows one to enter this transcendent state 'abouen mynde' is also the ideal for the positive way, but it is an ideal regarded as unattainable in this world. This is because it is a state which can be perceived more easily than achieved, since it involves coming to a point where words lose their meaning. As the positive way uses language in an affirmative manner to help understanding and expression, the state in which one surpasses the need for words must remain outside its sphere. Rather than seeking to achieve the disorientating effect of the *Cloud*'s

---

4 'Deonise Hid Diuinity', in *The Cloud of Unknowing and Related Treatises*, ed. P. Hodgson, Analecta Cartusiana 3 (Salzburg and Exeter, 1982), p. 126. See also the discussion of this passage in R.A. Lees, *The Negative Language of the Dionysian School of Mystical Theology: an approach to 'The Cloud of Unknowing'*, Analecta Cartusiana 107 (Salzburg, 1983), p. 241.

terminology, the *via positiva* deliberately uses highly emotive language in order to create a deeply emotional effect, which is intended to communicate depth of feeling and inculcate a desire to experience such emotions oneself. However, although the language and images, and the effects they produce, are often very powerful, they are cleansed of the taint of worldly associations by being applied to spiritual matters. An example of this process is the word 'ravysshed'. In secular language, 'ravysshed' implies swift seizure, legal or otherwise, and often the context indicates emotional if not actual sexual undertones. This is clearly the case when Chaucer uses it in his *Romaunt of the Rose* as Reson describes the kind of love which renders people irrational:

> ... that which makith thee woo,
> And bringith thee in many a fit,
> And ravysshith fro thee al thi wit. (*Romaunt* 5196–98)[5]

The emotional power of the word is retained when Hilton uses it to communicate the strength of feeling occasioned by his fervent belief in God. He declares that as one moves towards contemplation one is 'y-rauisched out of þe bodili wittes' and 'bi rauichinge of lufe, þe soule is oned for þe time and conformed to þe ymage of þe Trinite'.[6] The sexual overtones have been superseded, but the emotional power and the notion of being carried beyond the bounds of rationality remain. It is this power which Langland's uses when Wil declares himself 'ravyshed right there' (B.XI.7)

This deliberate use and yet transformation of the emotive power of words is typical of the affective discourse of the *via positiva*, but it is markedly different from the use of images and affective language within the deductive discourse, where the aim is to engage the audience's attention in order to move them on from the initial emotional position to the safer paths of rational analysis and deduction. It is also distinct from the attitude towards the use of emotional effect in the *via negativa*, for all such associations, even when they are used to indicate a totally different kind of experience, retain links with the tangible world, and the aim of the negative way is to break all such links. Far from seeking to capitalize on the possible power and accessibility of words and images, the negative way seeks to disentangle itself entirely.

It is not surprising, then, that Langland opts for the expression of the *via positiva*. Wil's words of Passus VIII illustrate both Langland's social concern and his linguistic preference:

---

5 Chaucer, *Romaunt*, p. 741.
6 Hilton, *Scale*, Book 1, ch. 8, p. 95.

Knowledge Beyond Reason:

For more kynde knowyng I coveite to lerne –
How Dowel, Dobet and Dobest doon among the peple.

(B.VIII.111–12)

The demand to know how these three qualities operate 'among the peple' precludes withdrawal from society, and the choice of the term 'Dowel', which first makes an appearance at the end of the Visio, requires the comparative terms of 'better' and 'best'. As the *Cloud* author points out,

> Where-so-euer þe best is set or nemyd, it askeþ before it two þinges a good & a beter; so þat it be þe best, & þe þryd in noumbre.[7]

One is therefore committed to not only a language of comparison, but more particularly of positive comparison. For to seek to discover how something may be done well and from that to see how it may be done better and then best, is to ascend a scale of comparison and illustration which works from what is most familiar to what is least familiar with the assumption that one is progressing towards a more accurate (though perhaps never complete) idea of what it is that consititutes the ultimate aim.

Despite the use of comparison and the judgment that it implies, even the positive form of expression seeks to go beyond the bounds of the deductive discourse of the rational approach to knowledge. For the point of comparison is its accessibility and its ability to strike the audience with an immediacy which is not possible if there is a long process of deduction to explain first. Once this has been achieved it is possible to lead the followers on to ever increasing heights of affective understanding, which may result in a direct apprehension of God.

This is not to say that the method of using images found in the deductive discourse is rejected altogether. Allegories could be explained and elaborated to prove various points of theology or ethics, as well as used for immediate, emotive effect. These two possible uses of images were recognised by Thomas Gallus, who considered both the intellectual and loving powers of the soul to be aspects of cognition which could act simultaneously. For him the intellectual power is like sight and hearing, which apprehend an object directly but are not affected by it, whereas the loving power is like taste, touch and smell, which involve a direct contact between perceiver and perceived and so is profoundly experiential:

> . . . duos esse sensus in intellectu – visum et auditum: tres autem in affectu, scilicet, gustum, tactum et odoratum . . .

---

7 *Cloud*, ch. 21, p. 29.

(. . . there are two senses in the intellect – sight and hearing; three in the affection, namely, taste, touch and smell . . .)[8]

Yet, although the two powers can act together, this is only possible in the initial stages of contemplation; as one ascends the levels of contemplation the deductive and rational powers are first refined and then left behind, allowing the soul to reach a state as near as possible to the ideal final point of communion with God. It follows from this that if the affective side of the soul can be touched, the effect is not only more immediate, but also potentially longer lasting.

The use of images for affective ends had an additional advantage: it required no previous training on the part of the audience to understand them. This point is made by Hugh of Balma (1289–1304) when he differentiates between knowledge of God and the other sciences:

Haec enim sapientia in hoc differt ab omnibus aliis scientiis, quia in hac primo oportet vsum habere seipso, quam verba intelligere, & practica hic praecedit theoricam. In alijs scientijs necesse est, primo verba intelligere, quam quae addiscitur, scientia habeatur.

(For this wisdom differs in this from all other sciences, because in this it is necessary to have some knowledge of the thing itself in order to understand the words and here practice precedes theory. In other sciences it is necessary first to understand the words so that, when they have been learnt in addition, one may obtain the knowledge.)[9]

It would appear from this that the desire for *sapientia* (which involves no academic training) would be more automatic than that for *scientia*, which clearly does. However, it seems that this is not the case, as the *Cloud* author recognised in *þe Book of Priuy Counseling*:

Late hem faste awhile, I preie þee, from here kyndely delite in here kunnyng; for, as it is wel seide, a man kyndely desireþ for to kunne; bot certes he may not taast of goostly felyng in God bot only by grace, haue he neuer so moche kunnyng of clergie ne of kynde. & þerfore, I preie þee, seche more after felyng þen after kunning; for kunnyng ofttymes disceyuiþ wiþ pride, bot meek louely felyng may not begile. Sciencia inflat, karitas edificat. In knowyng is trauaile, in feling is rest.[10]

The desire for 'kunnyng of clergie' may be a natural desire, but it is not to be trusted. People are inclined to place too much emphasis on learning and the

---

8 Thomas Gallus, *Commentary on the Canticles*, quoted and discussed in Lees, *Negative Language*, p. 279.
9 Hugh of Balma, *Viae Syon Lugent*, published in *S. Bonaventura Opera Omnia* (Cologne, 1609), vol. VII, col. 658–59; see Lees, *Negative Language*, p. 299.
10 *The Book of Priuy Counselling*, in *The Cloud of Unknowing and Related Treatises*, ed. P. Hodgson, Analecta Cartusiana 3, p. 98.

operation of the intellect and reason, they must turn away from these if they wish to attain a feeling of the divine. A similar point is made in *The Cloud of Unknowyng* itself and in such a way as to query the use of *auctoritates* so favoured by the deductive route. The author has just referred his readership to 'Denise bookes' for corroboration of what he has said, but hesitates to do more than give a general direction:

> On none oþerwise þen þus list me not alegge him, ne none oþer doctour for me at þis tyme. For somtyme men þou3t it meeknes to sey nou3t of þeire owne hedes, bot 3if þei afermid it by Scripture & doctoures wordes; & now it is turnid into courioustee & schewyng of kunnyng. To þee it nediþ not, & þerfore I do it nou3t. For whoso haþ eren, lat hem here, & whoso is sterid for to trowe, lat hem trowe; for elles scholen þei not.[11]

While the practice of citing others as authority for one's own views is a sign of meekness, all is well, but once it becomes an opportunity for a display of learning it is no longer praiseworthy and indeed must be avoided. For it is the meekness which is an absolutely necessary component of true wisdom as *sapientia*, whereas, although some level of learning is often present and can be useful, it is not essential. Significantly, this passage ends with a reference to Christ's own words as given in Matthew 13:9 just after the parable of the sower and the grain: 'He who has ears let him hear'. The parable itself is not explained to the assembled crowd, but only to the disciples. If one is in a position to understand the parables they will not need to be explained; if one is not one would not be able to understand them properly anyway. It is this view that Hugh of Balma echoes in his affirmation that in theological matters it is necessary to have some knowledge of theology in order to understand what is being said: the practice must precede the knowledge.

Yet, despite the initial accessibility of the emotive discourse, the rejection of reasoning and intellect it advocated could lead to a point as inaccessible and esoteric as that reached by a rigorous application of the deductive approach, since its final result was the total lack of images and reason, attainable by a few only. This stage is described by Ruysbroek in his *Seven Steps to the Ladder of Spiritual Love* as 'an intelligence in repose and empty of images, a clear contemplation of the divine light, and a pure spirit uplifted to the face of God'.[12] This is perfect contemplation, the 'perfect unreasonableness' of the *Denise Hid Divinite*. However, Ruysbroek is adamant that one ought not to remain in this state, precisely because of its esoteric and ultimately individual nature:

---

[11] *Cloud*, ch. 70, p. 70.
[12] Jan van Ruysbroek, *The Seven Steps of the Ladder of Spiritual Love*, ch. VI, tr. F. Sherwood Taylor (London, 1943), p. 56.

So we are to go out into the activity of the life of the sense, then again go in by love and cleave to God, and remain ever motionless in community with him. . . . Yet we must always be ascending and descending the steps of our heavenly ladder, in interior virtues, outward good works, the commandments of God and the precepts of Holy Church, just as has been said above.[13]

So Ruysbroek's preference is for a constant movement between the active and contemplative lives which would allow for the insight of the fully contemplative and the accessibility and social responsibility of the active. Hilton, too, advocates this way of life, which he initially moots in Book 1 of his *Scale of Perfection* and later develops in *Mixed Life*. It is a preference which is also found in *Piers Plowman* both in the type of language and in the type of life Langland presents as the optimum.

The most explicit statement of this preference within *Piers Plowman* is in B.XV where Anima is explaining the right use of knowledge to Wil. He cautions against intellectual pride and curiosity and goes on to cite St Bernard:

> *"Beatus est,"* seith Seint Bernard, *"qui scripturas legit*
> *Et verba vertit in opera* fulliche to his power." (B.XV.60–61)

Reading the Scriptures is not enough; one must also strive to put them into practice. In the same way achieving contemplation is good, but to realise the full potential of those moments of perfect communion one must return to the world and work in it. From this viewpoint the best life is one which draws from both the active and contemplative worlds and, by extension, the most effective form of language would be one which acknowledged both the deductive and the emotive discourses and so was accessible to both. Langland's solution is to intertwine elements of the two approaches in *Piers Plowman* in such a way that there are several passages that may be read in different ways, depending upon which particular approach is given precedence. As an illustration of this, and in an attempt to avoid the misleading impression given by disentangling the various threads of the poem, this chapter on the approach to knowledge beyond reason will open with a re-reading of the encounter with the friars at the beginning of the Vita.

Wil, awake and freshly embarked upon his quest for Dowel, asks the two friars if they know where he might find him (B.VIII.10–13). He asks *'pur charite'*, which invokes the fundamental principle of poverty and *caritas* and with it the idea of teaching the lewed in a way appropriate to them. The bulk of their reply is a *'forbisne'* – a parable which, with its evocative image,

---

[13] Ruysbroek, *Seven Steps*, ch. VII, pp. 60–61.

is in tune with the ideal of teaching the unlearned in ways they will be able to understand, here by force of example rather than argument. It is to be remembered that Wil cannot be regarded as one of the *docti* at this point. As we have seen, this method of teaching through example had the weight of Biblical precedent behind it in Christ's use of parables, and was often recommended in guides to composing sermons, especially *sermones ad populum*. In keeping with this attitude the friars do not offer a definition of Dowel – and in fairness Wil has not asked for one – instead they offer a picture of a man whose life is saved by Dowel 'charite the champion, chief help ayein synne'. Here Dowel is charity and, it transpires, the life of Dowel is the life that all men lead unless they wilfully choose to follow the flesh and the Devil and commit deadly sin:

> Ay is thi soule saaf but thow thiselve wole
> Folwe thi flessh and the fend after –
> Do a deedly synne and drenche so thiselve. (B.VIII.49–51)

The picture they present concurs with Hilton's statement that any men or women who have grace and charity will be saved because they will also have a natural inclination to God which will prevent them from falling into deadly sin:

> Bute an oþer man or a woman wilk is in grace and in charite haþ alwei a good general wil to God in his sowle, weþer he slepe or wake, ete or drinke, or wat dede þat he doþ; so þat hit be nouȝt iuel in þe selfe, bi þe wilk wil he chesiþ and disiriþ God a bouen alle þing and hadde lefere forberen al þe likyng of þis world þan his God, for luf of Hym. Þis wil, þouȝ hit be bute general, is of so gret vertue bi þe grace of oure Lord Ihesu þat þouȝ he falle bi frelte in luste and likynge of mete and drink, oþer swilk oþer sekenesse . . . it sauiþ and kepiþ hym from dedli synne.[14]

The grace of which Hilton and the friars of Passus VIII speak is available to all and operates as long as one does not voluntarily commit a deed which is obviously evil. For the intention is that people should be saved, not damned, but if they choose otherwise that is a different matter.

The type of life described here is that which requires the least effort on the part of its followers, for if they avoid conscious sin the natural will to do good, the action of synderesis, will direct them towards a life worthy of salvation. Of course, to say it requires least effort is not the same as saying it involves no effort at all; a definite attempt to avoid sin and do good must be made. This concurs with the definition of active life given in *The Cloud of Unknowyng*:

[14] Hilton, *Scale*, Book 1, ch. 72, p. 220.

Þe lower party of actiue liif stondeþ in good and honeste bodily werkes of mercy & of charite.[15]

So it would appear that the Dowel the friars are offering Wil corresponds to the active life – a life of good works, honesty and charity. There is no suggestion of withdrawing from the world, nor of the need for special training or education. This is a form of life open to all and sundry. If one can avoid entering wilfully into sin and also embarks actively on the 'good and honeste bodily werkes' of which the *Cloud* author speaks, one is as assured of salvation as one can be. Yet this is not to say that such a life is free from all sin, for, as Wyclif states, the nature of man is such that it is impossible for a man to follow the active life without some venial sin:

impossible est hominem vitam activam ducere nisi peccet venialiter.[16]

This view is acknowledged in *Piers Plowman* in B.XI where Reson ends his rebuke of the over-inquisitive Wil with the quotation from Cato *'nemo sine crimine vivit!'* (B.XI.402). Reson's use of this phrase from Cato's *Distichs* (I,5)[17] serves the double purpose of asserting that it is beyond the bounds of common sense to expect reason to be able to order any being to live contrary to its nature, which is in fact what Wil is demanding when he asks why Reson cannot make mankind live without sin, and also shames Wil by pointing out that he is just as sinful as the rest. Indeed Wil is in the act of falling prey to the sin of vain curiosity by wanting to know more than it falls to mankind to know. It is clear, then, that the best that can be hoped for is that by embarking on the active life one may avoid wilful, deadly sin, for one is always prey to the sinful results of one's own nature. Nonetheless, if followed fully, this way of life must merit salvation, as Wil himself acknowledges in his assessment of his second vision, where he weighs up the relative merits of the power of prayer and works (Dowel):

[I] demed that Dowel indulgences passed,
Biennals and triennals and bisshopes lettres,
And how Dowel at the Day of Dome is digneliche underfongen,
And passeth al the pardon of Seint Petres cherche.
. . .
And so I leve leelly (Lord fobede ellis!)
That pardon and penaunce and preieres doon save

---

[15] *Cloud*, ch. 8, p. 17.
[16] John Wyclif, 'Super Evangelia de Sanctis XX', *Johannis Wyclif Sermones*, ed. Johann Loserth (London, 1887–90), 2, 147. F.J. Steele includes a discussion of this particular text in his D.Phil. thesis, 'Definition and Depictions of the Active Life in Middle English Religious Literature of the 13th, 14th and 15th Centuries, including special reference to *Piers Plowman*' (Oxford, 1979), p. 76.
[17] The *Distichs* (a book of maxims ascribed to Cato) was often used in medieval schools as a basic Latin book. See Pearsall, *Piers Plowman C-Text*, p. 88, n. 17.

Soules that have synned seven sithes dedly.
Ac to trust on thise triennals – trewely, me thynketh,
It is noght so siker for the soule, certes, as is Dowel.

(B.VII.170–74; 177–81)

The Pardon and penance as well as prayers offered for the dead and advocated by the Church must have their place, but in Wil's eyes at least, Dowel appears to be the surer way to salvation, for the power of prayer cannot redeem those who have not at least tried to live a good life, insofar as they understand it. This is an issue which Langland introduced in Passus VII where he endorsed the importance of works by including even the merchants in Truth's pardon, provided they put their profits to good use. He explores it at greater length in Passus XI when he introduces the figure of Trajan, a man who was saved at the request of Gregory's prayers, but who merited consideration because of his honourable life.

The active life, then, is admirable when it is properly fulfilled, but it is the absolute minimum for a life which will lead to salvation; it is the place to start, but not necessarily to stay. If a soul remains at this level it will achieve a place in heaven, but it will be the lowest, as Ymaginatif declares is the case with Trajan and also the thief on the cross: 'For he is in the loweste of hevene, if oure bileve be trewe' (B.XII.212). Greater rewards are possible only with greater perfection.

It is clear by now that this way of approaching the question 'How may a soul be saved?' by working through imagined scenarios rather than defining the terms of the question is closer to the more figurative method of the emotive approach and contemplatives, than to the analytical rationality of the deductive way. Yet, although the medium is different, being that of parable rather than debate, the message is much the same; both ways of reading the encounter with the friars acknowledge the importance of Wil's recognition that he needs some kind of inner conviction if he is to understand the friars' words. This 'kynde knowynge' (B.VIII.60) involves an element of self-knowledge which is as necessary for the approach to knowledge which is based on the belief that true understanding comes from introspection as for that which relies on deduction. Hilton's statement is relevant here, as it was in the exploration of the deductive approach:

It nediþ a soule þat wolde haue knowynge of gostly þinges, for to haue first knowynge of itself. For it may not haue knowynge of a kynde aboue itself bot if it haf knowynge of itself; & þat is when þe soule is so gedred into itself, & departid from beholdynge of alle erþly þinges & from þe vse of bodily wittes, þat is feliþ itself as it is in þe owne kynde withouten a body.[18]

---

[18] Hilton, *Scale*, Book 1, ch. 30, pp. 122–23.

It is vital to note that for Hilton self-knowledge is a knowledge of one's own nature, one's 'kynde', which will lead on to an apprehension of the higher nature of God. This is a contrast to the attitude evident in the deductive approach where self-knowledge was a practice ground for reason. Hilton's words work from the assumption that human nature is related to the nature of God, but, obviously, is a pale reflection. Hence, he writes of the 'higher nature' of God which it is the aim of the emotive approach to apprehend in some small manner.

Such apprehension relies less on learning and rational knowledge than on understanding based on self-knowledge. When this is taken into account Wil's response to the friars –

> I have no kynde knowyng . . . to conceyve alle thi wordes,
> Ac if I may lyve and loke, I shal go lerne bettre.   (B.VIII.59–60)

– may be seen to refer to the emotive path to *sapientia* as much as the deductive route to *scientia*. Thus, depending on which attitude the reader favours when reading this passage, the emphasis given to the words is different, although the components remain the same. For the deductive approach the stress would fall on the recognition of the necessity for 'knowynge' and the need to 'lerne'; the alternative, affective, reading of the passage emphasises the desire for 'kynde' knowledge as a form of innate understanding based on inner conviction which is not gained by intellectual enquiry. Furthermore, Wil declares he will also 'loke' in order to learn – a reference to the use of imagery and apprehension of the immanent God reflected in the whole of creation (a view later illustrated in Kynde's revelation of Middelerthe) rather than sought in the analysis of texts demonstrated by the friars and Doctor of Divinity. It also echoes the emphasis on visual language preferred by the *Cloud* author and the concomitant preference for the use of evocative images rather than the forms of language which demand analysis and rational interpretation.

The type of knowledge with which these affective or mystic writers are concerned does not come solely from books and arguments but also, and more importantly, from experience and perception. Yet although this alternative to deductive learning is tacitly offered at this early stage in Wil's quest for Dowel, its possibilities are not taken up immediately; instead they lie dormant as Wil becomes involved with the scholastic method of discovery and learning. As J.S. Wittig[19] has pointed out, Wil is unwilling to make the effort a change of direction demands, preferring to exhaust first the possibilities of the deductive route, which has the appeal of being a seemingly more secure option as it provides precepts to follow and

---

[19] J.S. Wittig, '*Piers Plowman* B Passus IX–XII: Elements in the Design of the Inward Journey', *Traditio*, 28 (1972), 229.

authority figures to instruct and direct its pupils. In contrast the emotive path guides its adherents by advice and exhortation, encouraging its followers to experience the states of understanding it describes rather than defining them and offering a sure route to attaining them. The acolytes of this way are thus made to rely more upon their own perceptions, as such experiences as entering the cloud of unknowing cannot be taught in the way deductive and analytical skills can, since they necessarily demand active and emotional involvement from the practitioners. The aim of this approach is to guide the acolyte to a position of empirical knowledge similar to that of the guide but yet deeply personal. Unlike the teacher of the deductive path, this guide is thus the agent of authority rather than its manifestation. The emphasis shifts from what one knows to how one knows it.

11

Dowel, Dobet, Dobest and the Three Lives

Before embarking on an exploration of the parallels between Langland's Dowel, Dobet and Dobest and these lives it is as well to heed Hussey's warning.

> The error, I think, lies in the type of criticism that, having perceived some correspondences between Dowel, Dobet, and Dobest, and the active, contemplative and mixed lives, proceeds to equate the two triads, thereby limiting the interpretation of the former.[1]

The implication of these words is that, where such correspondences can be found, the mixed life is always to be regarded as the highest and so equated with Dobest. However, the attraction of such straightforward equations must be avoided since Langland drew on elements of the affective tradition and put them to his own use, without slavishly following any one set of definitions or hierarchy. Furthermore, although he uses the term 'active life' and indeed includes a personification of it *Piers Plowman* in the shape of Haukyn (*Activa vita* in the C-Text) he never refers to the mixed life as such, and his references to the contemplative are fleeting. Such allusions as are present are used as points of comparison with the form of life with which he was principally concerned, that is the life of the majority who have neither means nor opportunity to embrace the contemplative life. This means that the most exclusive way of life has little relevance in the poem and consequently the term 'Dobest' is the least thoroughly explored of the three. It seems that Dobest is a concept which must exist in order to give the others meaning, but which, of itself, has little relevance to the poem. Nevertheless, as Hussey implies, there are some correspondences between Dowel, Dobet and Dobest which are of interest.

---

[1] S.S. Hussey, 'Langland, Hilton and the Three Lives', *Review of English Studies*, 7 (1956), 132–50 (p. 133).

Dowel is the life lived according to the best codes of conduct available at the time in this far from ideal world. These codes need not be Christian, as the same basic defintion of Dowel applies to all, whether Christian or pagan. The point is to have lived as well as possible given one's individual circumstances. This understanding of doing well is clearly much the same as the description of active life given by Hilton in Book 1 of his *Scale of Perfection,* where he says that the active life consists of love and charity as manifested in good works.[2] In a Christian context such a life will obviously include the basic tenets of Christianity, but in fact the same code of conduct could be attained by non-Christians through the application of Natural Law alone. For Natural Law, as Sir Frederick Pollock pointed out, is based fundamentally on a notion of reason and the fitness of things:

> . . . an ultimate principle of fitness with regard to the nature of man as a rational and social being, which is, or ought to be, the justification of every form of positive law.[3]

As such, Natural Law will be in accord with Divine Law, but it is discoverable through the action of reason alone, and so could be applied by heathen and Christian alike:

> For the Law of Nature, by its very definition, was a rule of life and society discoverable by human reason apart from any special revelation or the decision of any particular authority. When discovered, again, it was admitted to be absolutely binding. Natural Law could not be in conflict with divine law, for it was a part of the divine law.[4]

Thus, Christian tenets are not strictly necessary in order to comply with Thoght's notion of Dowel; those of Natural Law will suffice. Any who follow this lowest stage of active life will indeed merit salvation, even a non-Christian. For it would be a breach of justice to deny salvation to someone who had lived a worthy life but had been ignorant of Christianity and so clearly could not be expected to live according to Christian religious beliefs. The element of ignorance is crucial here: if one had the opportunity to be baptized into the Christian faith but chose not to take it salvation would be denied, regardless of how well one lived. It is this possibility of meriting salvation through virtuous conduct alone which allowed the notion of the salvation of the righteous heathen to arise.

It is not surprising, then, that although Dowel made its first appearance in the obviously Christian context of the Athanasian Creed in Truth's

---

2 Hilton, *Scale,* Book 1, ch. 2, p. 87.
3 Sir F. Pollock, 'The History of the Law of Nature', *The Journal of the Society of Comparative Legislature,* 2 (1900), p. 418.
4 Pollock, p. 424.

Pardon to Piers, its later definition in Passus VIII has no such explicit and elitist Christian requirement:

> Whoso is trewe of his tunge and of his two handes,
> And thorugh his labour or thorugh his land his liflode wynneth,
> And is trusty of his tailende, taketh but his owene,
> And is noght dronkelewe ne dedeynous – Dowel hym folweth.
>
> (B.VIII.81–84).

According to this definition, all that is required is to live as honourably as one can and to earn a living honestly without taking more than one's due. In other words, to live according to the basic principles of a responsible person in society. Ruysbroeck provides a similar definition of 'the first part and the lowest way of the life of works' in his *Seven Steps of the Ladder of Spiritual Love*. The precepts of the Church must be followed 'in all good will', but the customs of society have a claim also:

> You must in all good will obey God and your superiors, complying with the usage and good practice of Holy Church, according to your powers and right discretion in accordance with the ordinary ways and conduct of good men and the custom of the land in which you dwell.[5]

Ruysbroek thus explicitly links his injunction with the precepts of the Church, but he states that one must follow this 'good practice' in a way that is dictated by one's society and circumstances. This gives the 'customs of the land' a high priority, almost equal to the practices of Holy Church, although as the first injunction is to obey God, this clearly take precedence.

So, we have a definition of Dowel which accords with the active life and consists of fulfilling one's station in life to the best of one's ability. Such a life is open to all, rich, poor and even heathen, since this form of life could be achieved by following the precepts of Natural Law and society alone. However, if one moves on to a better way of life, or ascends the ladder, other factors come into operation.

Thoght's definition of Dobet is clearly a progression from his conception of Dowel, but it does not exclude or supersede it. Thoght specifically says that Dobet does exactly what Dowel does ('right thus') and then adds to it ('dooth muche moore') he does not ignore it. This fact alone indicates that Dobet, as defined by Thoght, cannot be equated with the contemplative life, since such a life excludes active life entirely. In fact his Dobet is actively engaged in works of charity as he helps each according to their need:

> He is as lowe as a lomb and lovelich of speche,
> And helpeth alle men after that hem nedeth.

---

5 Ruysbroeck, *Seven Steps*, ch. V, p. 42.

The bagges and the bigirdles, he hath tobroke hem alle
That the Erl Avarous heeld, and hise heires;
And with Mammonaes moneie he hath maad hym frendes,
And is ronne into Religion, and hath rendred the Bible,
And precheth to the peple Seint Poules wordes –
Libenter suffertis insipientes cum sitis ipsi sapientes:
[Ye wise], suffreth the unwise with yow to libbe,
And with glad wille dooth hem good, for so God yow hoteth.
(B.VIII.86–95)

We have passed the point where Natural law alone suffices, and entered a life lived according to more exacting tenets but still involved with the world. This move is signalled by the introduction of the qualities of humility, illustrated by the simile of the lamb, and charity, demonstrated by the distribution of money to the poor. By this stage explicitly Christian terms have become part of the definition, as shown by the use of the figure of the lamb (with its association with the lamb of God) and the mention of the Bible. The reference to Dobet running into Religion seems to indicate that there is an element of contemplation or at least seclusion from the everyday world in this form of life. This neatly corresponds to a passage in *Cloud* where the author defines the higher stage of active life as one which to some extent overlaps the lower stage of contemplative life, but is distinct from the contemplative life proper:

> Þe lower party of actiue liif stondeþ in good & honeste bodily werkes of mercy & of charity. Þe hier party of actiue liif & þe lower party of contemplatiue liif liþ in godly goostly meditacions, & besy beholding. . . . Bot þe hiзer partye of contemplacion (as it may be had here) hongeþ al holy in þis derknes & in þis cloude of vnknowyng . . .[6]

So, despite the implication of Hussey's words that, insofar as comparison ought to be made, Dobet is to be seen as the contemplative life, Thoght's definition can be seen to describe the mixed life. Even though it may be tempting to assume that the casting aside of worldly goods and the seeking out of religion is a description of entering an enclosed life of contemplation, such a reading ignores the precise nature of the actions taken by Dobet.

Dobet has 'tobroke' all his 'bagges' and 'bigirdles' – the signs of stored treasure – and distributed his wealth. This is active charity which necessarily partakes of the world; equally his subsequent actions involve him with other people as he runs into religion in order to translate the Bible and then teach it: 'And precheth to the peple seint Poules wordes'.

This is a description of an apostolic life, one which combines study of the Scriptures with teaching it to others and also providing practical help. Note

---

[6] *Cloud*, ch. 8, p. 17.

that in keeping with this attitude Thoght's quotation from Paul, which advocates respect for the unlearned – *Libenter suffertis insipientes cum sitis ipsi sapientes* (2 Cor.11:19) – is translated. This avoids any elitism of language by making it accessible to everyone, not only those who have the right training and understand Latin. This in itself is a demonstration of Dobet's role, as the use of translation and explanation aptly illustrates within the tissue of the poem the definition contained in the text. Far from shutting out society and devoting himself to the enclosed life, Dobet is greatly involved in sharing the fruits of his labours, both manual and intellectual, with his fellow-men. This could be regarded as a type of life which constitutes an intermediate stage between the active and the contemplative, combining elements of both. The *Cloud* author describes this intermediate stage as the higher part of the active life and the lower of the contemplative. He also declares that neither form of life may be achieved without an element of the other:

> So þat a man may not be fully actiue, bot ȝif he be in party contemplatiue; ne ȝit fully contemplatiue (as it may be here), bot ȝif he be in partie actyue.[7]

This form of life is not, in the author's view, the highest attainable in this world (it must be remembered that this is a treatise on the contemplative life), but it is a stage through which one progresses before achieving the full contemplative life. This mixed life is meritorious in itself and, as its correlation with Dobet implies, is seen as a higher achievement than the active life of Dowel, and is often regarded as the highest form of life available to the majority, who are bound to the world by their responsibilities to those dependent upon them and so prevented from attaining the higher reaches of the contemplative life.

Another conception of mixed life regards it as possible only after some ability in contemplation has been achieved; it is possibly from this that the notion of mixed life as higher than contemplative, implicit in Hussey's article, has sprung. However, wherever this type of mixed life is referred to, it is clear that it involves a constant movement between the higher moments of contemplation and the lower, but socially more valuable, moments of active life. This is the case at the end of Ruysbroeck's *Seven Steps* and also in *The Book of Privy Counselling*. Ruysbroeck ends with the assertion that after attaining the peak of rapt communion with God, which is true contemplation,

> ... we are to go out into the activity of the life of sense, then again go in by love and cleave to God, and remain ever motionless in community with Him ... Yet we must always be ascending and descending the steps of our

7. *Cloud*, ch. 8, p. 17.

heavenly ladder, in interior virtues, outward good works, the command-ments of God and the precepts of Holy Church, just as has been said above.[8]

This tallies with Langland's image of Dobet running into religion where both the times of contemplation and the times of action are valid, but the times of action are based upon the results of the times of contemplation. It is also worth noting that Ruysbroeck specifically mentions all aspects of life as taking part in this Life; there is no strict segregation of internal, 'contempla-tive' virtues and external, 'active' work. Clearly this form of mixed life must allow for dialogue between internal and external, contemplative and active, God as perceived within each individual and God as codified in the pre-cepts of His Church.

Whether this mixed form of life is regarded as superior to the pure contemplative life or not, the element of dual involvement with the external world and the internal, spiritual world is constant. Full contemplatives are totally divorced from the external world, even to the extent of not taking thought for their livelihood. Similarly these are the only people who are not obliged to provide for themselves and contribute to the general welfare in tangible ways. The assumption is that the lives lived by such people benefit all, and so are counted as work, with contemplation being a most taxing form of spiritual labour. Thus the contemplative life qualifies as 'travail-lynge in preieres' and as such is included by Hunger in his definition of work:

> Kynde Wit wolde that ech a wight wroghte,
> Or in techynge or in tellynge or travaillynge in preieres –
> Contemplatif lif or Actif lif, Crist wolde men wroghte.
> The Sauter seith in the psalme of *Beati omnes*,
> The freke that fedeth hymself with his feithful labour,
> He is blessed by the book in body and in soule:
> *Labores manuum tuarum &c'*. (B.VI.247–252a)

Yet, although the contemplative is given a place in Hunger's relation of Kynde Wit's scheme, the emphasis is firmly on the active component as the citation of Psalm 127:1 concentrating on the bodily work of 'feithful labour' shows.

Following this scheme of parallels one would expect Thoght's Dobest to be equivalent to the full contemplative life. It is possible to find such corre-lations, but they tend to be vague and rely on the fact that there is no direct assertion that Dobest works in the world at all. He may judge and protect those who do, but such authority comes from lack of direct involvement, it is the authority of distance rather than of experience. His bishop's crosier is

---

[8] Ruysbroek, *Seven Steps*, ch. VII, p. 61.

not only a sign of temporal authority in the Church but also an outward sign of his inward merit; theoretically at least a bishop should have achieved a greater level of spiritual perfection than his flock. He is therefore regarded as removed from the generality of mankind and so superior and worthy of respect. Nevertheless he is, or ought to be, involved with the world – the crosier is a reminder of his role as shepherd with responsibilities for his flock; responsibilities which demand participation in society. His superiority to Dobet lies in his greater duties, not least in ensuring that those who preach in his bishopric are qualified to do so. Langland has already expressed his opinion of bishops who renege on this duty:

> Were the bishop yblessed and worth bothe his eris,
> His seel sholde noght be sent to deceyve the peple.   (B.Prol.78–79)

It appears, then, that Dobest is a more socially prestigious form of Dobet – both being levels of mixed life; the contemplative is acknowledged, but set aside as if belonging to another sphere of reference. This reluctance to engage with the notion of a fully contemplative life is also evident in Wit's definition of Dobest, which uses terms applicable to a withdrawn, contemplative life:

> That dredeth God, he doothe wel; that dredeth hym for love
> And noght for drede of vengeaunce, dooth therfore the bettre.
> He dooth best that withdraweth hym by daye and by nyghte
> To spille any speche or any space of tyme:
> *Qui offendit in uno, in omnibus est reus.* (B.IX.95–99a)

At this point in the B-Text, then, the contemplative life is clearly included and correlated with Dobest, but it is not elaborated. This lack of further description of Dobest is in keeping with the tenor of the poem, since there is no room in *Piers Plowman* for the fully contemplative life, except as an unattainable ideal. Indeed, it appears that Langland was not entirely happy with including even this brief a reference to the contemplative option at this point in the poem for, upon turning to the C-Text, we find that not only is this definition never developed, but it is omitted altogether. In its place there is an increased emphasis on the obligation to help and love our neighbours and enemies:

> Inwit and alle wittes closed been þerynne;
> By loue and by leute, þerby lyueth *Anima*,
> And lyf lyueth by inwit and leryng of Kynde;
> Inwit is in the heued and *Anima* in herte.
> And moche wo worth hym þat inwit myspeneth,
> For þat is goddes oune goed, his grace and his tresour,
> . . .

Euery man þat hath inwit and his hele bothe
Hath tresor ynow of Treuthe to fynden hymsulue.
 Ac fauntokynes and foles þe which þat fauten inwit,
Frendes shal fynde hem and fram folye kepe
And holy churche helpe to, so sholde no man begge
Ne spille speche ne tyme, ne myspende noyther
Meble ne vnmeble, mete noþer drynke.
 And thenne dede we alle wel, and wel bet ȝut to louye
Oure enemyes enterely and helpe hem at here nede.
And ȝut were best to ben aboute and brynge hit to hepe
That alle landes loueden and in on lawe bileuede.   (C.X.170–190)

Inwit is presented as the spark of God in everyone which must not be abused. As such it is common to all – except those unfortunates who are lacking in wits and who are therefore special cases – but with it comes certain obligations, as implied by the word 'leute' which has connotations of loyalty and dues. The main obligation seems to be to find Truth's treasure for oneself, with the implication that it will be found within oneself. This accords with the stress on the importance of self-knowledge and knowledge reached through and based on the certainty of one's own experience found in the affective approach to knowledge as *sapientia*. However, Langland avoids the notion that in order to know oneself one must withdraw from society. Instead he asserts that although such knowledge is internal it is manifested in helping those who cannot help themselves. Doing well is to be a friend to the 'fauntokynes and foles þe which þat fauten inwit'; doing better is to love our enemies and help them also; doing best is to engage in conversion in the attempt to bring all lands under the same rule of love as he recommends for the individual. Clearly such activities are not compatible with an enclosed life. Here, then, we have a very different attitude to the prerequisites of self-knowledge from those put forward by Hilton in Book 2 of his *Scale*.

Langland thus diverts our attention away from the individual towards the social. He re-defines Dowel and Dobet as doing good deeds to those obviously deserving, and then even to those who may seem to have forfeited their right to such help. From this he arrives at a Dobest which is far from the reclusive, uninvolved Dobest of full contemplation. Equally the B-Text references to active and contemplative lives are totally removed in the C-Text and replaced by an extended treatment of marriage (C.X.202–300), rounded off by a brief set of definitions of Dowel, Dobet and Dobest which again apply only to the life lived in the world:

And thus is Dowel, my frende, to do as lawe techeth,
To louye and to loue the and no lyf to greue.
Ac to louye and to lene, leef me, þat is Dobet.
Ac to ȝeue and to ȝeme bothe ȝonge and olde,

Helen and helpen, is Dobest of alle.
For þe more a man may do, by so þat a do hit,
The more he is worthy and worth, of wyse and of goed ypresed.

(C.X.301–307)

Notably, the definitions of Dowel and Dobet are the least changed; Dowel is
to live according to the tenets of Christianity and Dobet is to do this and
add the deeper understanding of faith to it. Dobest, however, is recast in
order to create a Dobest which is thoroughly active – the more a man does
the more worthy he is.

In neither version of the poem are Wit's definitions of Dowel, Dobet and
Dobest allowed to stand unassailed, as Dame Studie attacks his speech for
being inappropriate and so possibly misleading. However, she objects to his
words on the grounds that such interpretations will not suffice given the
state of the world, rather than because the definitions themselves are at
fault. This is the point of her graphic diatribe at B.X.17–70 (C.XI.14–129),
where her argument is that those who wish to know too much will blind
themselves to what Dowel, Dobet and Dobest are, and so never find them:

And tho that useth thise havylons to ablende mennes wittes
What is Dowel fro Dobet, now deef mote he worthe,
Siththe he wilneth to wite whiche thei ben alle.
But if he lyve in the lif that longeth to Dowel.
I dar ben his bolde borgh that Dobet wole he nevere,
Theigh Dobest drawe on hym day after oother.   (B.X.131–136)

The main tenor of Studie's speech, reiterated in her 'sign' for Clergie and
Scripture (B.X.170–217), is that knowledge is to be regarded warily; not all
knowledge is good, and a desire for learning for the sake of learning alone
can lead to mistaken notions, and so away from the path to truth. It is
because of this danger that Wil's search for a definition of Dowel, Dobet and
Dobest is so fiercely attacked. The tendency is that the more one indulges in
defining and examining these concepts the less likely it is that one will
actually follow them.

Studie is in many ways a true defender of mystic ideas. It is no accident
that in the instance she gives of the conceited lords at table using an *auctor*
to substantiate their specious arguments, the *auctor* chosen is St Bernard
(B.X.54). In view of the fact that he was one of the philosopher-mystics who
warned against relying on written authorities and was wary of the pursuit
of intellectual knowledge, it is a satirical comment on these prandial theologians. If they actually implemented St Bernard's teaching rather than
using him as authority in their debates they would be leading very different
lives. Given these reservations about learning, it is thoroughly in keeping

with her character that Studie should be the one who attempts to move Wil away from depending on the deductive, rational approach to knowledge as *scientia* and tries to steer him on the road to *sapientia* instead.[9]

However, the possibility of an alternative, latent in Studie's words, is not followed at this point; instead, Langland shifts ground slightly by going on to Clergie's definitions. As would be expected from a personification of clerical learning, Clergie's emphasis is on words. Hence Dowel is to believe the articles of faith, the written expression of the necessities of Christianity (or, in the C-Text XI.142–159, the Ten Commandments which are even more obviously the written expression of faith) and, in making the point, Clergie refers to Augustine for authority and beyond him to his authorities:

> 'It is a commune lyf,' quod Clergie, 'on Holy Chirche to bileve,
> With alle the articles of the feith that falleth to be knowe:
> . . .
>   'Austyn the olde herof made bokes,
> And hymself ordeyned to sadde us in bileve.
> Who was his auctour? Alle the foure Evaungelistes;
> And Crist cleped hymself so, the same bereth witnesse
> *Ego in patre et pater in me est: et qui videt me videt et patrem meum*
>   'Alle the clerkes under Crist ne koude this assoille,
> But thus it bilongeth to bileve to lewed that willen dowel.
> For hadde nevere freke fyn wit the feith to dispute,
> Ne man hadde no merite, myghte it ben ypreved:
> *Fides non habet meritum ubi humana racio prebet experimentum.*
> (B.X.230–248a)

The emphasis is on one's external conduct being a true manifestation of one's internal life, and more particularly on being what one seems to be, specifically being what one's words suggest one is. This emphasis is continued in the definition of Dobet that follows:

> Siththen is Dobet to suffre for thi soules helthe
> Al that the Book bit bi Holi Cherches techyng –
> And that is, man, bi thy myght, for mercies sake,
> Loke thow werche it in werk that thi word sheweth;
> Swich as thow semest in sighte be in assay yfounde:
> *Appare quod es vel esto quod appares.* (B.X.249–253a)

The appeal here is directly to 'the Book', albeit the Book as interpreted by the Church. Dobet has greater learning and understanding and so approaches Holy Writ more directly. Yet, even so, this is not an approach

---

[9] I agree with Carruthers here, who makes this point admirably in *Search*, p. 89.

which denies the need for a canon of interpretation. This Dobet follows the Bible, but it is a carefully annotated Bible.

The extended treatment of Dobet and Dobest is left out of the C-Text, as Langland simplifies the issue by using a different triad:

> Thus bileue and leute and loue is the thridde
> That maketh men to Dowel and Dobet and Dobest. (C.XI.161–162)

This re-wording has two effects on the reader of the poem. By being briefer it has the immediate and obvious result of tightening up the whole episode. Rather than mulling over yet another definition of Dobet and Dobest, and probably getting more confused, one is left with the impression of the importance of Dowel and then moved on to the inner dream. The second effect is that by making use of the alliterative form of the line Langland has emphasized the inter-dependence of the three components and also that one progresses from each stage to the next. This is a simple trick of para-rhyme, but because it works through sound and the use of instinctive connections (i.e. the teaming together of like sounds) it comes as a contrast to the intellectual effort required for the various interpretations of Dobet and Dobest which precede this brief statement.

In the B-Text, however, we are left with Clergie's version of Dobest to study. This lays a much greater emphasis on the judgemental aspect mentioned in Wit's definition:

> Thanne is Dobest to be boold to blame the gilty,
> Sythenes thow seest thiself as in soule clene. (B.X.256–57)

This is an assertion which is given greater force by being the opening of the definition than it would have had if it had occurred in the middle of a considered argument. As a result the difference between this ideal of Dobest and the ideal of the contemplative life are borne in upon us. The suggestion that Dobest has a right to judge others is directly counter to the emphasis on humility concomitant with perfect contemplation. Hilton expresses this point very clearly:

> . . . to þe or to oni oþer wilk haþ stat and þe purpos of lif contemplatif, hit falliþ nouȝt for to leeue þe kepyng of ȝoure self and biholden and vndir-nimen oþer men of heere defautes, but if hit were ful gret neede, so þat a man scholde perissche but if ȝe vndirnemid him.[10]

Yet if we bear in mind Langland's preoccupation with the individual in society it becomes clear that this Dobest acknowledges responsibility

---

[10] Hilton, *Scale*, Book 1, ch. 17, p. 112.

towards his fellows, and part of this responsibility is to use his greater insight to direct those around him.

This interpretation is substantiated by what follows, for Clergie himself seems to be aware of the dangers of his first reply, as his next words warn against the hypocrisy Hilton mentions. This is a theme he dwells on, elaborating the consequences not only for the potential hypocrites, but also for those who may be looking to them for guidance:

> Ac blame thow nevere body and thow be blameworthy:
> *Si culpare velis culpabilis esse cavebis;*
> *Dogma tuum sordet cum te tua culpa remordet.*
> God in the Gospel grymly repreveth
> Alle that lakketh any lif and lakkes han hemselve:
> *Quid consideras festucam in oculo fratris tui, trabem in oculo tuo, &c.*
> Why mevestow thi mood for a mote in thi brotheres eighe,
> Sithen a beem in thyn owene ablyndeth thiselve?
> *Eice primo trabem de oculo tuo, &c.*
> Which letteth thee to loke, lasse outher moore?
>   'I rede ech a blynd bosard do boote to hymselve –
> As persons and parissh preestes, that preche sholde and teche
> Alle maner men to amenden, bi hire myghte.
> This text was told yow to ben war, er ye taughte,
> That ye were swiche as ye seyde to salve with othere.
> For Goddes word wolde noght be lost – for that wercheth evere;
> If it availled noght the commune, it myghte availle yowselve.
>
> (B.X.258–270)

Not surprisingly, Clergie addresses most of his words to those whose positions involve teaching and the use of language. It is the teachers and preachers who are picked out for particular attention; it is to these that he directs his interpretations of his words. He makes the point all the more striking by changing suddenly to direct address: 'This text was told yow'. Those who deal in words have a responsibility to deal honestly – to make sure of their own conduct before criticising that of others. Even if their attempts do no more than keep themselves up to the mark, that in itself is still an achievement, and, in Clergie's terminology, it is an achievement of the word of God: 'For Goddes word wolde noght be lost – for that wercheth evere'. Here Langland is using Clergie to present a view of the obligations of the *logos* which is akin to Bromyard's assertion that the words of God must have proclaimers and hearers: *Verba Dei debent pronunciatores et auditores.*[11] The words of God must not be lost; those who have the ability to read them for themselves have a responsibility to pass them on to those who do not. The fact that this duty is one that Thoght has ascribed to Dobet

---

[11] Bromyard, *SP*, s.v. 'Verba Dei', f. 380r.

(B.VIII.91–94) is an indication of how unwise it is to seek for steadfast equivalents between Dowel, Dobet and Dobest and the three lives.

Clergie stresses the positive aspect – by ensuring the integrity of the preacher/teacher he ensures the integrity of the message. The Doctor of Divinity uses the same line of reasoning, but in reverse, hoping to assert his own integrity by asserting that of his message. Thus the interpretations he offers echo Clergie's, but his use of the quotation from Matthew 5:19 to support his claim implies that he is just as concerned to present himself in a favourable light as to provide a reliable reply to Wil's question:

> And Dobet is he that techeth and travailleth to teche othere;
> And Dobest doth hymself so as he seith and precheth:
> *Qui facit et docuerit magnus vocabitur in regno celorum.* (B.XIII.116–17a)

Again Dobet explicitly involves dealing with other people, whereas Dobest stresses introspection and concomitant removal from the daily life of the surrounding world, as increasing self-awareness is necessary to avoid being hypocritical. In the mouth of the Doctor such opinions have a degree of hypocrisy, or at least of lack of self-knowledge; yet when spoken by Pacience there can be no such reservation. As so often in *Piers Plowman* and particularly in the case of the Doctor, the doctrine is sound but the speaker is revealed to be suspect.

It is with Pacience's words that the final correlation of *disce, doce* and *dilige* with Dowel, Dobet and Dobest, which has been an underlying theme in many of the previous definitions, is made. Dowel has already been seen to be *disce* in the exhortations to obey and so learn the tenets of Natural Law or the Commandments; this is active life. Teaching requires both a knowledge of the principles taught and an engagement with others in order to teach them: it is a mixture of internal and external work. To place love above both these is typical of the affective approach to *sapientia*, which, as Hilton describes in Book 1 of the *Scale*, preferred to follow the example of John, the loving and loved disciple, rather than that of Peter, who was involved with leading and guiding later followers and was appointed to lead the Church on earth. Hilton uses the example of these two disciples and the difference between them as an illustration of the difference between the way of life befitting the contemplative and that suited to the active. The Last Supper provides a setting for his presentation of the idea of progression through an active life to contemplative:

> Þat þis is soþ, hit semiþ bi seint Iohn, whilk hadde þe stat of contemplatif lif, and Seint Petir, whilk hadde þe stat of actif lif. Whanne Oure Lord in His laste soper wiþ His disciplis atte priue stering of Petir to Seint Iohn, tolde Seint Iohn how Iudas schulde bitraie Hym, Seint Ion tolde hit nouȝt to Seint Petir as he askede; bute he tornid hym and leyde his heued vpon Cristes breste and was rauisched bi loue in to contemplacion of Godes

priuites, and so medfulli to hym þat he forȝat boþ Iudas and Seint Petir; in tokninge and techynge to oþer men whilk wulde be contemplatif, þat þei schulden disposin hem for to do þe same.[12]

John, the contemplative, has been prompted into action by Peter, the active life. The implication is that there must be an incentive for contemplatives to use their capacity for knowledge through contemplation. Hilton also indicates that the type of knowledge the contemplatives aim to achieve is not attainable by, or even communicable to, the active, for John does not attempt to impart his information about Judas to Peter. Instead the love which comes with such knowledge transports the contemplative beyond the realms of the active life into the realms of pure communion with God.

This total disinterest in things of the world is reflected in Pacience's speech which moves from the recommendation to learn, teach and love (*disce, doce, dilige*) to allusions to the Passion, the ultimate example of self-sacrificing love. Yet although the effect on the individual is to make the concerns of the world irrelevant, Pacience also points out that people who manifestly follow these precepts will be invested with authority and respect by those surrounding them:

> Kynde love coveiteth noght no catel but speche.
> . . .
> For, by hym that me made, myghte nevere poverte,
> Misese ne mischief ne man with his tonge,
> Coold, ne care, ne compaignye of theves,
> Ne neither hete, ne hayle ne noon helle pouke,
> Ne neither fuyr, ne flood, ne feere of thyn enemy,
> Tene thee any tyme, and thow take it with the:
> *Caritas nichil timet.*
>   And ek, have God my soule! and thow wilt it crave,
> Ther nys neither emperour ne emperesse, erl ne baroun,
> Pope ne patriark, that pure reson ne shal make thee
> Maister of alle tho men thorugh myght of this redels –
> Nought thorugh wicchecraft but thorough wit; and thow
>   wilt thiselve
> Do kyng and quene and alle the comune after
> Yyve thee al that thei may yyve, as thee for best yemere,
> And as thow demest wil thei do alle hir dayes after:
> *Pacientes vincunt.* (B.XIII.150; 158–171a)

Here, then, we have a direct expression of authority springing from the spiritual characteristics of people rather than their intellectual or political capabilities, or the social position they hold.

---

[12] Hilton, *Scale*, Book 1, ch. 17, p. 113.

Conscience's later application of Dowel, Dobet and Dobest to Christ's life can only enhance the credentials of the affective interpretations of these concepts. For Conscience uses far more figurative language than even Pacience does as he draws on scenes from Christ's life to illustrate and support his interpretations of Dowel, Dobet, Dobest. It is also significant that all the examples he cites are instances of Christ's active involvement with the world and concern for the people around him. Langland thus tacitly reinforces his constant theme of the importance of active and virtuous participation in society in order to 'do wel' in the world. Once again Dowel is concerned with knowing and obeying the laws, figured in Conscience's speech by the wine at the Canan marriage feast:

> In his juventee this Jesus at Jewene feeste
> Water into wyn turnede, as Holy Writ telleth,
> And there bigan God of his grace to do wel.
> For wyn is likned to lawe and lifholynesse;
> And lawe lakkede tho, for men lovede noght hir enemys;
> And Crist counseileth thus – and comaundeth bothe –
> Bothe to lered and to lewede, to lovyen oure enemys.
> So at that feeste first, as I bifore tolde,
> Bigan God of his grace and goodnesse to dowel;
> . . .
> He wroghte that by no wit but thorugh word one,
> After the kynde that he cam of; there comsede he Dowel.
>
> (B.XIX.108–116; 122–23)

The wine is interpreted as the law, but this is the law of the New Covenant 'to loveyn oure enemys'. This commandment is one of those given by Christ to supplement the Commandments of the Old Testament, which becomes the paramount commandment for the disciples and by which they are told they will be identified as followers of Christ:

> A new commandment I give to you, that you love one another; even as I have loved you, that you also love one another. By this all men will know that you are my disciples, if you have love for one another.
>
> (John 13:34–35)

It is worth remembering that the wine that Christ produces for the feast is generally acclaimed as being superior to that which was served initially (John 2:11).

After Dowel we naturally progress to Dobet, which Conscience represents by Christ's miracles. Miracles must be the ultimate combination of faith and works, since they necessarily involve the performers with the world, by acting directly upon those they heal and feed:

> And whan he was woxen moore, in his moder absence,
> He made lame to lepe and yaf light to blynde,

149

And fedde with two fisshes and with fyve loves
Sore afyngred folk, mo than fyve thousand.
Thus he confortede carefulle and caughte a gretter name,
The which was Dobet, where that he wente.   (B.XIX.124–29)

Thus Dobet is part of the world, yet is also marked out as different from it: it is therefore telling that Langland notes that this stage occurs only when Christ is no longer accompanied by his mother, his mortal half. Involvement with the world is a part of Dowel, but it is a philanthropic involvement, not an emotional one.

As before, Dobest receives the least attention. Rather than being explicitly defined it is placed in a context in which the implication is that Dobest involves total detachment and utter faith. Upon seeing and touching Christ, Thomas has been moved to a declaration of complete belief (B.XIX.172–76). The reply he gets is both a blessing and an assertion that future generations who attain utter faith will be redeemed by that belief:

"Thomas, for thow trowest this and treweliche bilevest it,
Blessed mote thow be, and be shalt for evere.
And blessed mote thei be, in body and in soule,
That nevere shul se me in sighte as thow seest nowthe,
And lelliche bileve al this – I love hem and blesse hem:
Beati qui non viderunt et crediderunt."

It is after this that the concept of Dobest is introduced:

And whan this dede was doon, Dobest he thoughte,
And yaf Piers power, and pardon he grauntede:
To alle maner men, mercy and foryifnesse;
To hym, myghte men to assoille of alle manere synnes,
In covenaunt that thei come and kneweliche to paye
To Piers pardon the Plowman – *Redde quod debes.*   (B.XIX.178–88)

From this we gather that Dobest is connected with the power to create faith, as Christ has just evoked it in Thomas. Dobest thus acts as a catalyst; its aim is to bring others to an experience of faith as complete as that of Thomas, but the believer must be predisposed to belief already. Here then Langland presents a Dobest whose role is like that of the affective writers, that is to bring believers to a state of recognition and understanding rather than to teach them rules to follow. As Langland presents Christ as turning from convincing Thomas to establishing the Church with his words to Peter, the implication is surely that the Church must aim to fulfil this role of inspiring faith in the world.

In the Biblical sequence of events the creation of the Church precedes the Assumption, the final move from the temporal sphere into the spiritual –

the ultimate detachment. In the sequence of events presented by Conscience this handing over follows from – and is perhaps prompted by – an affirmation of the blessedness of pure, strong faith which requires no empirical proof. In terms of *Piers Plowman*, however, the use of 'Piers' rather than 'Peter' signals a return to previous aspects of the poem and the Dreamer's quest, rather than new definitions of Dowel, Dobet and Dobest. We have come to a point where precise definitions of the Lives or of Dowel, Dobet and Dobest are no longer a paramount concern. They have served their purpose by increasing our understanding of how to live and also increasing our awareness of language in displaying the power and ambiguity of definition and the creative power of the word. The time has come for a final move away from any trace of a deductive, defining approach to knowledge and towards a more consistently affective discourse. Conscience has already signalled this move by using more metaphorical language than the preceding personifications and the process is continued as Wil abandons the realm of deductive discourse represented by Clergie's banquet and follows Pacience and Conscience into the world. Here the first person he encounters is representative of all ordinary people who try to follow the active life in order to 'do well' in the world. That person is Haukyn, the 'Actif man'.

12

Haukyn and the Paradox of the Active Life

The departure of Pacience and Conscience may signal a final commitment to the importance of belief, but the emphasis is on belief as illuminating knowledge rather than simple ignorant faith. Haukyn the Actif Man is an object case of how belief without understanding can lead to a travesty of the original faith; as such he is the diametric opposite of the Doctor. As such he is a rounder, more human figure than the Doctor, who, although a character from the waking world as opposed to a personified characteristic, is nevertheless a stereotype and so must fulfil the conventions of the greedy, corrupt, but learned friar. Haukyn is a representative of the ordinary man trying to do the best he can in the world as he finds it. He is typical, not stereotypical. Pacience's gentle explanation to Haukyn of true belief, and his answers to Conscience's questions, reveal just how far away from the ideal of Active Life (which he is trying to follow) Haukyn has strayed while yet following, in a fumbling way, what he is told to believe. Here the theme of the saved pagan is finally concluded, as it is approached from the other angle: instead of Trajan representing the Saved Heathen who was redeemed despite not holding the faith, by doing what he believed to be good, Haukyn represents the Christian whose hope of salvation rests solely on mercy rather than rewards because, despite following the commands and examples, even of Piers himself, he does not truly comprehend them, follows blindly, and so errs. He thus embodies Wil's fear that however hard one may endeavour to do what is right and so merit salvation by being numbered among the few who are chosen, one may still sin unwittingly and so be counted as one of the many.

Haukyn himself exists in the B-Text only; in the C-Text he becomes merely Activa Vita, a much simpler figure who personifies the Active Life and is a clear statement of the opposite of Pacience. Haukyn, however, brings together many of the themes of the poem: he is minstrel, labourer, glutton and hypocrite and very much a man involved in the world. In short he poses again the question "what is Dowel among the people?". His cloak is a symbol for his manner, or self-presentation; as his external covering and an artefact it represents the face prepared to meet the faces that he meets.

Yet this fabrication is intended to conceal rather than mislead; there is no malicious intent and indeed it is affected by and in part betrays the very personality it is meant to cover. Just as his cloak is stained by the marks of his way of life, so his true nature gradually becomes apparent behind the front of the minstrel and the streaks and blots on his character are revealed. So it is clear that he fails, as he does not to live up to the expectations of goodness which were created by his declaration that he is a follower of Piers. Yet this failure is mitigated to some extent by the external signs of his contrition – the tear-stains on his cloak.

It is significant that it is Wil who sees Haukyn's flaws and that he sees them for himself, rather than having them pointed out to him. This is an indication that he is applying the knowledge so lately gained. By using his dreamer in this way Langland is able to demonstrate that those who have sought to understand the processes which lie behind what they are learning and have made themselves aware of the possible uses and abuses of the system, are in a stronger, more secure position, since they are more able to judge the source of their information and so are less likely to be misled or confused.

Haukyn's introduction of himself unmistakably asserts a link with the active life:

> 'I am a mynstral,' quod that man, 'my name is *Activa Vita*.
> Al ydel ich hatie, for of Actif is my name'. (B.XIII.224–25)

This appears to be unequivocal, but it is an assertion which Hussey finds impossible to accept:

> . . . if Haukyn is to represent active life, even a lower type of active life, and if active life equals Dowel, it seems strange that he should be guilty of all the sins in the calendar – after all, most writers (including Hilton and Langland . . .) regarded it as sufficient for salvation – and that Haukyn himself after his confession wishes that he 'hadde ben ded and doluen for Doweles sake'. (B.XIV.321)[1]

He goes on to suggest that Langland is not using 'Activa Vita' as a technical term, noting that the assertion that Haukyn hates idleness 'seems to savour more of etymology than of mysticism', although adding that he would 'not insist upon this'. The etymological link is obviously valid, but etymology and mysticism are not mutually exclusive, since an awareness of the effects of terminology are as much a part of the affective discourse as of Langland's vocabulary. One has only to reflect on the richness of the mystic writers who exploit the connotations of the language they use in order to achieve

---

1 Hussey, 'Lives', p. 138.

specific effects (disorientation in the case of the cloud image; stress on light in Hilton's phrase 'lightsome dark' and above all the taste metaphor used to explain the root of *sapor*) to accept that the mystics were well aware of the effect such a term as 'active life' would create. This is further supported by the emphasis placed on the assertion that the exercise and effort necessary to follow a contemplative life make it a far from easy option: an attitude reflected in Langland's assertion that it is a type of work, (B.VI.247–49) and also found in Rolle:

> . . . it es swa harde to com to, for þe freelte of oure flesch and þe many temptacions þat we er unsett with, þat lettes us nyght and day.[2]

Such emphasis is necessary in order to avoid the assumption that if one life is active it obviously involves action and effort, whereas its opposite is easy, demanding no physical effort or hardship merely the meditation its name suggests – contemplation. The above quotation from Rolle is clearly a case in point, as it follows immediately after a description of the difficulties which beset an active life:

> Actife lufe es mykel owteward, and in mare travel, and in mare peryle for þe temptacions þat er in þe worlde. Contemplatyfe lyfe es mykel inwarde; and forþi it es lastandar and sykeror, restfuller, delitabiler, luflyer, and mare medeful.[3]

It is not surprising that Rolle felt it necessary to balance the descriptions of the two lives given the bleak outlook he gives here for the likelihood of leading a blameless active life.

Precisely the same acknowledgement of the virtual impossibility of leading an active life without sinning is evident in Wyclif, Hilton and Langland, and has been encountered already in the course of this exploration of the approach to knowledge beyond reason. So Hussey's objection can be answered by agreeing that active life is sufficient for salvation, but by admitting that it is also accepted that a follower of this life is bound to be stained by sin; hence the low place in heaven ascribed to such people. It is this very paradox of a life sufficient for salvation also being one in which sin is regarded as practically unavoidable that Langland tackles in the figure of Haukyn.

By the time Haukyn enters the poem in the second dream of the Vita, Wil has passed through the rather bemusing experience of attempting to assimilate and understand all the different ways of knowing and attitudes

---

2   Richard Rolle, 'The Form of Living', ch. XII in *The English Writings of Richard Rolle*, ed. Hope E. Allen (Oxford, 1931), p. 117.
3   Rolle, *ibid.*

towards knowledge presented to him in the previous passus. His encounter with the various personifications of academic knowledge has been counter-balanced by the vision of Middelerthe and debate with Ymaginatif which showed him the convincing force of experience and the power of emotive rather than deductive persuasion. His ensuing meeting with the Doctor of Divinity has shown that he now holds the attitude to knowledge expressed by Roger Bacon in his section 'On Experimental Science' in his *Opus Majus:*

> Duo enim sunt modi cognoscendi, scilicet per argumentum et experimentum. Argumentum concludit et facit nos concedere conclusionem sed non certificat neque removet dubitationem ut quiescat animus in intuitu veritatis, nisi eam inveniat via experientiae; . . . Ergo argumentum non sufficit, sed experientia.
>
> (For there are two modes of acquiring knowledge, namely, by reasoning and experience. Reasoning draws a conclusion and makes us grant the conclusion, but does not make the conclusion certain, nor does it remove doubts so that the mind may rest on the intuition of truth, unless the mind discovers it by the path of experience, . . . Therefore reasoning does not suffice, but experience does.)[4]

Wil's reaction to the personification of scholastic misuse, if not abuse, of the desire to reach conclusions through reasoning has been to realise its flaws and reject them, preferring to follow the internal attributes of Conscience and Pacience, who may be regarded as intuitions of truth. This decision indicates a break away from the deductive learning of *scientia* into a more thorough exploration of the emotive path to *sapientia*. This break is particularly evident in the C-Text with the sudden decisive movement of Resoun as he leaps out of the poem, never to return, leaving Wil to choose between conscience and learning:

> And whan he hadde yworded thus, wiste no man aftur
> Where Peres the plogman bycam, so priueyliche he wente.
> And Resoun ran aftur and riht with hym ȝede;
> Saue Concience and Clergie y couthe no mo aspye.   (C.XV.149–53)

Significantly, Resoun runs after Peres in order to go with him. This action indicates that Resoun is no longer presented as a guide, instead he has become a follower of Peres, who has just asserted the value of emotive understanding. However, by emphasizing that Resoun accompanies Peres ('and riht with hym ȝede') Langland is demonstrating that one does not abandon rationality by chosing to follow the search for *sapientia* rather than

---

4 Roger Bacon, *The 'Opus Majus' of Roger Bacon,* Part VI, 'On Experimental Science', ch. 1, ed. J.H. Bridges (Frankfurt/Main, 1964), 2, 167–68. Translated by R. Belle Burke, *Roger Bacon 'Opus Majus'* (New York, 1928), p. 583.

scientia. Resoun no longer takes the lead, but he is not entirely deserted either.

In this dramatic way Langland has in effect removed the possibility of a third, intermediate, option which would allow Wit to continue along a course which would combine the deductive and emotive routes. Reason, like imagination, is necessary to both the deductive and the affective discourses, but with differing emphases; once he has disappeared, and so can no longer act as an independent guide, Wil must decide to follow either the figure whose limitations he has just seen exposed in the Doctor's example and stay with Clergie, or cast in his lot with the figure whom he has just encountered and whose limitations he has yet to discover – Pacience. He chooses to follow Pacience, and so embarks on an investigation of the approach to knowledge as *sapientia* which surpasses the limitations of reason. Again the C-Text is more dramatic, as it is made clear that in choosing this course Wil has gone beyond the point where academic learning has a place in the affective quest:

> 'By Crist,' quod Consience, 'Clergie, y wol nat lye,
> Me were leuere, by oure lorde, and y leue sholde,
> Haue pacience parfitlyche then half thy pak of bokes!
> Lettrure and longe studie letteth fol monye,
> That they knoweth nat,' quod Concience, 'what is kynde Pacience.
> Forthy,' quod Concience, 'Crist y the byteche,
> With Pacience wol y passe, parfitnesse to fynde.'   (C.XV.178–84)

The C-Text does not offer the comforting possibility, which seems to exist in the B-Text, of combining reason and experience, to give, in Bacon's phrase 'an unassailable unity'. In this the C-Text agrees with *The Book of Priuy Counselling* which reveals that, although reason is essential for the lower stages of contemplation, as soon as the soul has an intimation of true contemplation, reason no longer has a part to play:

> ... & as sone as a soule is touchid wiþ verrey contemplacioun, as it is in þis noble nouȝtnyng of it-self, & þis hiȝe allyng of God, scherly & verrely þan dieþ alle mans reson.[5]

It is a view echoed in the Middle English *Beniamyn*, where the affective, emotional side of the experience is emphasised in the use of 'ravished' to describe the action by which one attains this state:

> For whi in what tym þat a soule is rauischid abouen hymself by habundaunce of desires & a greet multytude of loue, so þat it is enflawmyd with þe liȝt of þe Godheed, sikirly þan dyȝeþ al mans reson.[6]

5 *The Book of Priuy Counselling*, ed. P. Hodgson, p. 85.
6 *Beniamyn*, ed. P. Hodgson, p. 144.

So, Reson is no longer the guiding light as Pacience takes over the role and we enter the part of the poem which explores, examines and queries affective ideology. Yet this examination is not carried out by confronting the emotive way with the other, deductive, tradition in debate or contest, but by presenting it with an embodiment of one of its inevitable results and points of anxiety in the figure of Haukyn and his relation to the world.

In effect Haukyn represents the result of misunderstanding the affective definitions of life. He introduces himself as the 'actif-man': 'Al ydel ich hatie, for of Actif is my name,' (B.XII.225). It soon transpires that he has woefully misunderstood his name: he has, understandably, assumed that avoiding idleness entails great busyness and so he is involved in everything – but to the wrong end. Like the Doctor he has misdirected his energies and his skills, and so again the result is hypocrisy. The comparison may be taken further: just as the Doctor was rendered suspect from the first by being a friar and master, so the figure of Haukyn is rendered problematic by being connected with another, equally suspect, section of society, the minstrels (B.XIII.221), whose credentials are queried in the poem.

According to Langland there are two distinct types of minstrel: those who tell true stories and are termed God's minstrels, and those who tell tall tales and sing immoral songs, the janglers. At first Haukyn appears to be one of God's minstrels because his comments on those he serves and the treatment he receives from them implies that he is disliked because he offers his audiences Holy Writ rather than ribald tales. In addition his trade is making communion wafers and his dress is plain, indicating that he is not as well-off as he would be if he told entertaining stories (the 'didos' referred to by the Doctor in B.XIII.172), or could provide music to his audience's taste, rather than the blessings and prayers he is accustomed to offer:

> A wafrer, wol ye wite, and serve manye lordes –
> And fewe robes I fonge or furrede gownes.
> Couthe I lye and do men laughe, thanne lacchen I sholde
> Outher mantel or moneie amonges lordes mynstrals.
> Ac for I kan neither taboure ne trompe ne telle no gestes,
> Farten ne fithelen at festes, ne harpen,
> Jape ne jogele ne gentilliche pipe,
> Ne neither saille ne sautrie ne synge with the gyterne,
> I have no goode giftes of thise grete lordes
> For no breed that I brynge forth – save a benyson on the Sonday,
> Whan the preest preieth the peple hir Paternoster to bidde
> For Piers the Plowman and that hym profit waiten –
> And that am I, Actif, that ydelnesse hatie.   (B.XIII.226–38)

His portrayal of all the ways he is rewarded, as opposed to the ways he could be rewarded, by his temporal masters echoes the description of the true minstrels whom Studie clearly supports as virtuous, but acknowledges are neglected in Passus X:

> Harlotes for hir harlotrie may have of hir goodes,
> And japeris and jogelours and jangleris of gestes;
> Ac he that hath Holy Writ ay in his mouthe
> And kan telle of Tobye and of the twelve Apostles
> Or prechen of the penaunce that Pilat wroghte
> To Jesu the gentile, that Jewes todrowe –
> Litel is he loved that swich a lesson sheweth,
> Or daunted or drawe forth – I do it on God hymselve!
> . . .
> Ac murthe and mynstralcie amonges men is nouthe
> Lecherie, losengerye and losels tales –
> Glotonye and grete othes, this game they lovyeth. (B.X.30–37; 48–50)

The fact that Haukyn's description of his treatment complies with that of Scripture predisposes his audience of Conscience, Pacience and Wil in his favour, as well as the reader. This inclination is further supported by the implication that he is also fulfilling his role in life according to the description of how each member of the commonwealth ought to behave, as given by Piers in Passus VI.

Haukyn's claim to provide the bread for the lords is an echo of Piers' promise to supply enough food for all (B.VI.17–20) and reminds us of the value attached to the life of the labourer. However, there is a vital difference between Piers' initial statement and Haukyn's later reference to the same view. Throughout the Prologue and up to the end of Passus IV, and again in Passsus VI, we have been shown how the creation and maintenance of a perfect commonwealth can be thwarted by the forces of covetousness and greed; these forces were externalised and personified in the King's court by Mede and represented in the half-acre by the wasters. Haukyn has no such clear-cut adversary, for he is battling with the combined forces of his own character and the indifference, if not actual corruption, of society around him. Langland has altered his use of allegory in order to emphasize that Mede is not a purely external force but also an internal characteristic, hence Haukyn's complaint revolves around his own position and has a smack of greed in the desire for the 'goode giftes' which he clearly feels are his due. There is no sign of the sort of mentality which resulted in the agreement between Piers and the Knight (B.VI.24–36) where each agreed to fulfil his role to the best of his ability without any mention of the direct payment that Haukyn seems to be seeking here.

As a result of this change Haukyn is a more fully developed figure – is indeed a character rather than a figure – and as such presents a more immediate picture of grievance. His opening speech paints a picture of himself as a man who tries to live according to the laws of active life, but who is so little rewarded for this, and so ignored by the very people he serves, that life itself is impossible. At the same time, he accepts that some responsibility for a peaceful society rests with him, and that man must strive to make himself worthy of God's blessing:

> Ac if myght of myracle hym faille, it is for men ben noght worthi
> To have the grace of God, and no gilt of the Pope.
> For may no blessynge doon us boote but if we wile amende,
> Ne mannes masse make pees among Cristene peple,
> Til pride be pureliche fordo, and that thorugh payn defaute.
> For er I have breed of mele, ofte moot I swete,
> And er the commune have corn ynough many a cold morwenyng;
> So, er my wafres be ywrought, muche wo I tholye.   (B.XIII.255–62)

Yet the fact remains that those in the cities, those better off, for whom the labour of life is at one remove, do not sufficiently repay the labours of those who provide for them, despite the lessons of history, which show that if the labourers fail, so does the food supply. Haukyn presents an impossible situation – his hypocrisy seems to spring from force of circumstance rather than a personal flaw; a contrast to the Doctor's intellectual pride.

The external sign of this hypocrisy is the coat Haukyn wears. The harsh interpretation of this coat which follows in the poem is Wil's, who sees the stains and patches, the pride, scorn and scoffing, and comes to the conclusion that Haukyn's deliberate policy is that 'alle men wende he were that he is noght' (B.XIII.279). There is no mention of the contrition which becomes evident after the interchange with Pacience; instead Wil's closer inspection reveals still more marks of sin, for 'It was fouler bi fele fold than it first semed.' (B.XIII.319). Wil is clearly critical, but Conscience, who could be expected to be critical likewise, does not rebuke Haukyn. Instead he merely comments that his coat is stained:

> 'By Crist!' quod Conscience tho, 'thi beste cote, Haukyn,
> Hath manye moles and spottes – it moste ben ywasshe!'
> (B.XIII.313–14)

This receives a ready admission from Haukyn, followed by a long detailed explanation of how it is that, despite his claim to lead an unsullied active life, he still sins so much.

It is this section which seems to have puzzled Hussey and made him decide that Haukyn could not be a representation of the mystic notion of active life; however a solution may be found when we realise that the highly critical reactions are all filtered through Wil and are not supported by the conduct of his two companions Conscience and Pacience. Here Wil is ignoring one of the fundamental attitudes of mysticism as set out by Hilton in that he is judging his fellow man.[7] This in itself is as much an indication of Wil's failure to understand and follow the emotive path as of Haukyn's failure to lead a perfect active life. Under Wil's critical gaze and with the attention of both Conscience and Pacience focused upon him, Haukyn expands upon his original role and gradually seems to become the embodiment of sin in every walk of life, confessing freely to malpractice, greed, and coveteousness until he succumbs to wanhope. Yet the very fact that he can become the victim of such despair is an indication that he is not irredeemable; he is aware of the magnitude of his sins, admitting both his actions and his culpability, but cannot see any alternative, hence the despair, which is itself a sin. His reaction is a response to the influence of Conscience and Pacience, two of the most necessary attributes for progression towards contemplative life, but also requirements for a properly conducted active life. In terms of the latter Haukyn could be regarded as progressing from attrition, through contrition to confession as his speech progresses and he responds to the effects of Conscience and Pacience, as first one and then the other detects more marks on his garment (B.XIII. 313ff and 354ff).

Yet, despite the long catalogue of sin, the opening of Passus XIV returns us to the theme of Haukyn as a man whose place is in the world, and so is fraught with difficulties and pitfalls. Conscience's question about why Haukyn does not clean his coat prefaces a return to Haukyn as a real person rather than the canvas for sins he has become by the end of Passus XIII. This in turn opens the way for a discussion of how one may escape from this paradox of how to live sinlessly in a sinful world and still make enough of a living to survive. The change of tone is signalled by the phrasing of Conscience's reported question:

> Thus Haukyn the actif man hadde ysoiled his cote,
> Til Conscience acouped hym therof in a curteis manere,
> Why he ne hadde wasshen it or wiped it with a brusshe.
>
> (B.XIII.457–59)

It may be an accusation, but it is a gentle and polite one delivered in a courteous manner, designed to elicit a felt response rather than a defence.

The ensuing conversation with Conscience amounts to a true cry for help, and wish to reform, rather than the impulsive self-denigration of Passus XIII. After this the exchange with Pacience reveals a Haukyn who seems to understand the philosophy being presented to him rather than just hearing it and following its letter. He even demands that Pacience explain the meaning of poverty in English so that he can understand it properly. Given all this one would expect some kind of assurance of his redemption, but despite his penitential tears, which wake the Dreamer, the final impression

---

7 Hilton, *Scale*, Book 1, ch. 17, p. 112.

is far from simple. Rather than expressing thanks for salvation, or even renewed hope, he seems to feel that he has lost his chance of redemption:

> 'Allas,' quod Haukyn the Actif Man tho, 'that after my
>   cristendom
> I ne hadde be deed and dolven for Dowelis sake!
> So hard it is,' quod Haukyn, 'to lyve and to do synne.
> Synne seweth us evere,' quod he, and sory gan wexe,
> And wepte water with hise eighen and weyled the tyme
> That evere he dide dede that deere God displeased –
> Swouned and sobbed and siked ful ofte
> That evere he hadde lond or lordshipe, lasse other more,
> Or maistrie over any man mo than of hymselve.
> 'I were noght worthi, woot God,' quod Haukyn, 'to werien
>   any clothes,
> Ne neither sherte ne shoon, save for shame one
> To covere my careyne,' quod he, and cride mercy faste,
> And wepte and wailede – and therwith I awakede.   (B.XIV.320–332)

Such grief could be construed as the outward signs of penitence, contrition and so a step towards salvation, but after the previous mention of wanhope (B.XIII.406) there is an ambiguous note to these lines.

This ambiguity springs from two sources. The first is his reiteration of the fact that life entails sin, which is unavoidable:

> 'So hard it is,' quod Haukyn, 'to lyve and to do synne.
> Synne seweth us evere.'

This brings on his sorrow, the cause of which reminds us that one remaining problem has not been answered by Pacience, one which Haukyn clearly feels still operates as he bewails

> That evere he hadde londe or lordshipe, lasse or more,
> Or maistre over any man mo than of hymselve.

He is well aware that it is impossible for an active man, necessarily bound up with responsibilities and dependants, to live a sinless life, still less one of poverty, without becoming guilty of inflicting hardship upon those dependent upon him. It is a paradox admitted by the mystics themselves – and one which they could resolve only by encouraging such men of the world to do the best they could and allotting a suitable, low, place in heaven for them. If Haukyn accepts these words he is debarred from following the life recommended by Pacience. Even his consolation that salvation is possible provided he uses his wealth properly has been severely shaken by Pacience's reply:

> Though men rede of richesse right to the worldes ende,
> I wiste nevere renk that riche was, that whan he rekene sholde,

> Whan he drogh to his deeth day, that he ne dredde hym soore,
> And that at the rekenyng in arrerage fel, rather than out of dette.
> Ther the poore dar plede, and preve by pure reson
> To have allowaunce of his lord; by the lawe he it cleymeth:
>
> (B.XIV.104–109)

It appears that whatever course he chooses Haukyn cannot make himself worthy of redemption.

Although Wil must be able to see Haukyn clearly we are uncertain of his physical position in the scene (at least in the B-Text) as he seems to have become an observer of the action rather than a partaker in it. He watched Pacience and Conscience leave the banquet ('And as thei wente') and is not included in exchanges between Conscience, Pacience and Haukyn in any way. This leaves open the choice of paths offered – Wil has followed Pacience but not yet joined him and so finally sided with neither Clergie nor Pacience – and also serves to draw the reader out of the dream world by creating a distance between it and us. In the C-Text this is altered to show Wil following Pacience and Conscience 'with grete wille', which is a nice, even self-ironic, pun, but he takes no more active part in the ensuing scene than his B-Text counterpart. The distance Langland creates by using Wil in this way is important because it has become gradually more obvious that it is impossible even to attempt to understand and judge all the possible ways of approaching knowledge when one is surrounded with people and involved in the world. This is because the character and charisma of those surrounding us influence our choices, as was illustrated in the episode in the Land of Longyng (B.XI). In the same way we are hampered by our obligations to fulfil our position in society and duty to dependants, as Piers and Haukyn have demonstrated. In other words, Langland gives Wil and, through him, the readers the very lack of involvement which Haukyn has shown he needed but did not get.

This need for independence is the same as the need Reson had for distance and disinterest to ensure he was able to judge fairly. For Haukyn has done his best to be reasonable in the world's eyes while following the Active Life to the utmost of his ability without becoming corrupt, and yet when he renounces the world, in a fit of contrition and enthusiasm for Pacience's teaching, he suddenly swings to an extreme:

> Iwere noght worthi, woot God . . . to werin any clothes,
> Ne neither sherte ne shoon, save for shame one
> To covere my careyne . . . (B.XIV.329–331)

A cool, dispassionate decision is impossible for one caught up in the world, for the affairs of this world hamper any attempt at disinterested action. The only hope seems to be to leave all previous concerns behind, much as Wil removed himself from the norms of his society when he tried to come to an understanding of this world and its problems in his dream. Paradoxically, once this decision to distance oneself from the world has been made one must also leave behind the dependence on deduction and reason as the only reliable methods of reaching understanding. This paradox is illustrated in *Piers Plowman* as Haukyn's reaction comes at a point where the poem has revealed how callous and unsatisfactory the involved theorising of the intellectuals can be and how moving and effective (as well as affective) the more emotive persuasion of Pacience is.

The paradox is maintained when the dreamer wakes, leaving Haukyn weeping and wailing because he sees no solution to the problem of meriting salvation and yet leading the active life demanded by his responsibility to society and his dependants:

> 'Allas,' quod Haukyn the Actif Man tho, 'that after my cristendom
> I ne hadde be deed and dolven for Dowelis sake!
> So hard it is,' quod Haukyn, 'to lyve and to do synne.
> Synne seweth us evere,' quod he, and sory gan wexe,
> And wepte water with hise eighen and weyled the tyme
> That evere he dide dede that deere God displesed –
> Swouned and sobbed and siked ful ofte
> That evere he hadde lond or lordshipe, lasse other more,
> Or maistrie over any man mo than of hymselve. (B.XIV.320–28)

The problem Haukyn poses remains unresolved – how can anyone simultaneously fulfil their part in society, which necessarily involves active participation in potentially corrupting systems, and still live a life worthy of the name 'Dowel'? It is apparent from Haukyn's example that Dowel, when defined as Active Life, includes sin; this brings us again to John Wyclif:

> impossible est hominem vitam activam ducere nisi peccet venialiter.
>
> (It is impossible for a man to lead an active life without venial sin.)[8]

It would appear that the only solution to the question of how to live as sinlessly as possible is to retreat from the Active Life, which is the route Haukyn seems to be taking at the end of Passus XIV when he declares himself unworthy of even wearing clothes, except for a simple garment for decency.

Yet in the terms of the poem this response, too, is unsatisfactory, as such a swing to the opposite extreme necessitates deserting one's place in the commonwealth. As he has made clear at several stages in the poem – particularly the half-acre episode – Langland distrusts those who do not contribute in some way to society in general. It is doubtless because of this

---

8 John Wyclif, 'Super Evangelia de Sanctis XX', printed in *Johannis Wyclif Sermones*, ed. J. Loserth, vol. 2, p. 147.

considerable reservation that we do not see Haukyn actually change his identity from 'Active Man' to 'Contemplative Man'; indeed, in the C-Text even the suggestion of taking this course of action is abandoned altogether. Activa Vita offers no response to Pacience's exposition; instead Haukyn's speech describing his life and part of the description of his coat, which in the B-Text precedes his repentance, is moved forward to form part of Pride's confession (C.VI.30–60), while the actual speech of repentance is omitted. Activa Vita himself is left in silent opposition to Pacience's words and the Contemplative Life.

Langland has presented this paradox before, as Haukyn's state at the end of B.XIV echoes Wil's reaction to Scripture's text of B.XI.3. In each case it suddenly seems impossible for anyone to merit salvation, unless they withdraw totally from the world, and even then salvation is not assured: the result is despair. Such a reaction is the affective counterpart of the mistaken self-assurance of the Doctor. Each is the result of taking the theories of their particular school to the extreme. Both Wil's reaction and Haukyn's illustrate the power of an emotive response, but also its dangers; and in each instance it leaves a highly complex and perturbed reaction, which Langland recognises and portrays in each of Wil's confused awakings from the dreams which deal with this topic. The first description is 'And I awaked therwith, witlees nerhande' (B.XIII.1); the second is similar in its evocation of craziness:

> Ac after my wakynge it was wonder longe
> Er I koude kyndely knowe what was Dowel.
> And so my wit weex and wanyed til I a fool weere;
> . . . folk helden me a fool; and in that folie I raved.   (B.XV.1–3; 10)

It is possibly in order to avoid this confusion and the attendant possibility of despair that Langland changed Haukyn into the much-simplified and cut down version of the C-Text.

Activa Vita is still a minstrel and as such retains the opening speech criticising the rich who prefer to give their money to the janglers of this world rather than God's minstrels. Like Haukyn, Activa Vita clearly begrudges the fact that he works to provide food for others and gets little reward, but his tone seems to be of resigned dissatisfaction rather than the more forceful complaint of Haukyn. He regards his position in the world as being more central than Haukyn, for he declares that he provides food for all levels of society, not just the lords, and does not complain that he receives no payment apart from their prayers:

> Y am sory þat y sowe or sette but for mysulue,
> Ac þe prest and oþere peple preyeth for Peres þe plouheman

And for me, Actyf, his man, þat ydelnesse hate;
Lordes and lorelles, luther and gode,
Fro Mihel-masse to Mihel-masse y fynde mete and drynke.

(C.XV.212–16)

He is also more aware of his role as provider, for he expresses his regret if he sows only for himself. This echoes Piers' stance of B.VI and links him to the ploughman of *The Canterbury Tales* who

wolde thresshe, and thereto dyke and delve,
For cristes sake, for every poore wight,
Withouten hire, if it lay in his might.   (Prol. 536–39)

So, Activa Vita presents a complete picture of the active life being lived successfully in the world.

Yet he is altogether a flatter character, being portrayed through his words only; gone are the descriptions of his appearance and his cloak, so vital to Haukyn's characterisation, and with them much of the ambiguity and complexity which made Haukyn more than a mere figure or simple personification. He has been cut down to a simple, two-dimensional illustration of active life, no longer vividly a man involved with the world, burdened by a household and sharply aware that his way of life is far from sufficient for salvation. Thus it is only his words that Pacience can respond to, which he does in a rather tangential manner, suddenly interrupting with:

'Pees!' quod Pacience, 'Y preye ȝow, sire Actyf!
For þoȝ nere payn ne plouh ne potage were,
Pruyde wolde potte hymsulf forth thogh no plough erye.
Hit am y þat fynde alle folke and fram hunger saue
Thorw the helpe of hym þat me hyder sente.'   (C.XV.233–37)

The effect on the reader is to look for the pride in Actyf's words, a search which results in the realisation of how sure of his own position Actyf is. However, this hardly justifies the long drawn out speech which Pacience proceeds to deliver as he anatomises the virtue and power of patience and poverty, going through each of the sins in turn. This passage, which in the B-Text was clearly a full answer to Haukyn, taking into account his character as well as his words, becomes in the C-Text revision an over-long response which makes Pacience sound like a moraliser on his favourite hobby-horse. Actyf intercedes once more to act as a prompt for the explanation of poverty, after which he speaks no more. Unlike Haukyn, he does not leave a faint uneasiness with the audience, a feeling of a point unanswered, but simply fades from the mind and the poem, the victim of a C-Text revision.

So, Actyf disappears from the poem, having served his purpose, whereas Haukyn is left as an unresolved paradox whose pragmatic knowledge of the world has not been fully reconciled with the exacting yet comforting teachings of Pacience. It is ironic that it is the power of experience that undermines the mystic philosophy, as the problem of what Dowel, Dobet and Dobest are in this world is once again left unanswered, and another possible source of authority, that of the man who declares knowledge based on personal experience, is shown to be flawed. Ironic, because the emotive path placed great store by the force and persuasive power of experience. The standing of the speaker was not as important as whether or not the hearer felt the words to be true. Langland does not allow the apparent victory of Pacience and Conscience to go unchallenged. Had he done so it would have been possible to dismiss the whole of the scholastic section, with its careful exploration of the approach through reason, as a totally mistaken and misleading red herring. This in turn would actually have undermined both Pacience's attitude at the banquet, where he insists on allowing the Doctor to speak and on allowing learning its place, and Ymaginatif's advice:

> Forthi I conseille alle creatures no clergie to dispise,
> Ne sette short by hir science, whatso thei don hemselve.
>
> (B.XII.121–122)

Instead, by presenting Haukyn as the true mirror-image of the Doctor, he has shown that just as intellectual knowledge without faith is doomed to failure, so faith without understanding will go astray. Thus he does not advocate the blind pursuit of any particular path to, or interpretation of, the Do-triad, but rather balances various ways and definitions so that they mitigate each other and show that a considered combination of methods is better than the use of any one in a purist form. Wil's progress bears this out. He has shown himself more aware of the pitfalls and so better equipped to avoid them by seeing the faults of both Doctor and Haukyn without having to rely on a guide-figure. Above all he finally has knowledge, and further-more understands what knowledge is and the effect it ought to have, as his ability to challenge the Doctor of Divinity and to notice the state of Hau-kyn's coat show. This may lead to the need to differentiate between knowl-edge and wisdom, as it did for Alexander and Bonaventure, but it also leads to a recognition that the sort of knowledge the Doctor has, personified by Clergie, may not lead to the kind of understanding Wil seeks, which Pacience seems to possess. As *The Book of Vices and Virtues* puts it when discussing the Active and Contemplative Lives:

> Þe ȝifte of vnderstondyng ledeþ to parfiȝtnesse of riȝtful knowynge. Þe ȝifte of wisdom ledeþ to parfiȝtnesse.[9]

---

9   *The Book of Vices and Virtues*, ed. W. Nelson Francis, EETS o.s. 217 (London, 1942), p. 221.

The power of such teaching, which is not only based on experience but also aims to elicit an affective response from its listeners, has already been exploited in the poem by Ymaginatif in the service of Reson and the deductive approach to knowledge. However, the moment when the power of emotive language and emotional response is given the freest reign is in the inner dream of Passus XI.

13

The First Inner Dream
and the Force of Experience

The vision of Middelerthe is the point at which the A-Text ends, halted by what Pearsall terms a 'crisis of intellect' which in the B-Text is written through 'in a series of turbulent and eddying developments'.[1] The progress of the inner dream is indeed turbulent and even bewildering as Langland shifts the tenor and pace of his poem in a sudden contrast to the more considered mode of the exchanges with the previous personifications of the mental faculties. Wil has brought this change upon himself, however, by citing examples of how the learned are easily led astray, while the uneducated are less likely to fall into sin (B.X.466–72a); the confusion and whirling events which catch up with him in the Lond of Longynge are illustrations of the likely consequences of rejecting learning completely.

The shift from the intellectual sphere to the realm of emotive experience is indicated by the terminology: 'For I was ravysshed right there' (B.XI.7). As previously demonstrated, 'ravysshed' is a recurrent word in mystic texts used by such different writers as Hilton and Rolle to indicate the highly-charged moments when the soul is lifted beyond the body into communion with God. It is thus imbued with strong, positive, affective connotations which are simultaneously intensely spiritual and intensely sensuous. However, the allusion to this state here is paradoxical, if not ironic, for although Scripture induces this state, it is Fortune who conducts Wil through the Lond of Longynge. According to Boethius in Book II of his *Consolation of Philosophy*, Fortune is the ruling power for those who are so caught up in this world that they ignore God, or any higher truth, so were this a purely religious experience, Fortune would not be acting as Wil's guide. If one takes up with Fortune, one must be prepared to accept all that she brings, but if one renounces her then she can have no jurisdiction:

---

1   D. Pearsall, *Piers Plowman C-Text*, p. 201, nn. 163–68.

Thus, at the laste, it byhoveth the to suffren wyth evene wil in pacience al that is doon inwith the floor of Fortune (that is to seyn, in this world), syn thou hast oonys put thy nekke undir the yoke of hir. For yf thow wilt writen a lawe of wendynge and of duellynge to Fortune, which that thow hast chosen frely to ben thi lady, artow nat wrongful in that, and makest Fortune wroth and aspre by thyn impacience? And yit thow mayst nat chaungen hir. . . . Thou hast bytaken thiself to the goveraunce of Fortune and forthi it byhoveth the to ben obeisaunt to the maneris of thi lady.[2]

This is far removed from the apprehension of God which the word 'ravysshed' seemed to indicate. On the contrary it becomes apparent that the more earthly connotations of the word are the ones which control the inner dream into which Wil is thrown. The thwarted possibilites of enlightenment played out in the exploitation of the two very different potential meanings of this one word mirror the action of the poem here, as the high-minded discussion with Scripture is displaced by the maelstrom of the inner dream. So the time in the Lond of Longynge can be seen to be an illustration of the fate in store for Wil if he renounces his quest at this point and follows the way of the world and Fortune, its governing power.

It is a nice irony that Wil is 'ravysshed' into the world of physical desires and sensations just after he has declared to Scripture that it is the learned men who are most likely to be 'yravysshed fro the righte bileve' (B.X.454). His glib dismissal of learning turns sour as he discovers how easily the ignorant can be led astray by their desires and lack of education, which allows them to be misled by influences like Rechelesnesse. For, as Boethius points out, theological expertise has no place in the domain of Fortune. Not only is any attempt at dispassionate knowledge ousted from the Lond of Longynge, but also the measured pace of Wil's investigations up to this point is overthrown and he finds himself in the middle of a crowd of figures and opinions. After the slower tempo of Passus VIII–X, where Wil has passed from one figure to the next with usually one and never more than two interlocutors at a time, he is suddenly surrounded in, Passus XI, by all sorts of characters, each pressing a reaction, a point of view, a way of life upon him. The effect is bewildering. Such a concentration of characters, some more fully rounded than others, has not occurred since the description of the field of folk and the King's court and trial of Mede. We are presented with similar half-realised personifications with similar names, *Concupiscencia Carnis*, Coveitise of Eighes, Faunteltee, their names are their character, just as they were for False-Fikel-tonge, Symonye and Trewe-tonge. These figures form a backdrop for the minority of more rounded characters such as Rechelesnesse.

---

2 Chaucer, *Boece*, Book 2, prose 1, p. 408.

Knowledge Beyond Reason:

In the midst of this whirlwind Wil suddenly finds himself confronted by Elde who warns him of the future consequences of trusting Fortune:

'Man,' quod he, 'if I mete with thee, by Marie of hevene
Thow shalt fynde Fortune thee faille at thi mooste nede,
And *Concupiscencia Carnis* clene thee forsake.
Bittrely shaltow banne thenne, bothe dayes and nyghtes,
Coveitise of Eighe, that evere thow hir knewe;
And Pride of Parfit Lyvynge to muche peril thee brynge.'

(B.XI.28–33)

These gloomy warnings strike a discordant note with the care-free attitude pressed upon him by Fortune and gaily recommended by Rechelesnesse (XI.34–41). Needless to say, both Elde and Holynesse, who joins him in bewailing Wil's choice (XI.44–45), go unheeded as Wil is 'conforted' by Coveitise of Eighes, who keeps him company for the ensuing forty-five years covered in this dream. All thoughts of Dowel and Dobet are swept aside by the multitude of experiences offered to him until, suddenly, he finds himself in the very situation Elde foresaw:

And thanne was Fortune my foo, for al hir faire biheste,
And poverte pursued me and putte me lowe. (B.XI.61–62)

Wil discovers that Fortune is not the only one to desert him when, despite their former readiness to absolve and bury Wil, the friars, so highly recommended by Rechelesnesse, are less willing to help him when he is poor. The matter is somewhat complicated by Wil's sudden recollection of his duty to be buried in his own parish church, giving his parish what little funds he has:

And tho fond I the frere afered and flittynge bothe
Ayeins oure firste forward, for I seide I nolde
Be buried at hire hous but at me parisshe chirche
(For I herde ones how Conscience it tolde
That there a man were cristned, by kynde he sholde be buryed).
And for I seide thus to the freres, a fool thei me helden,
And loved me the lasse for my lele speche. (B.XI.63–69)

The friars attempt to dissuade him, considering him a fool for insisting on burial at his own church rather than in one of theirs as a member of their order, which, it was believed, was all but a guarantee of eventual salvation because of the reserves of prayers for the dead and good works a friary could supposedly call upon to aid their members' souls. Their disparagement incenses Wil, who gives voice to an indictment of the friars' preference for burial (which brings with it the possibility of funds from the deceased's estate) to the less lucrative ceremony of baptism.

170

Fortune has indeed abandoned him, but this proves to be beneficial to Wil, for, once the physical temptations of the secular world are removed, he can again give consideration to his previous concerns of salvation and right living. Yet this resurfacing of earlier preoccupations does not bring with it a return to the forms of dispute he was using before he entered the inner dream. He still challenges the 'lettred men' (B.XI.83) but he does not resume the kind of theological argument he left behind in the outer dream, even though Lewte seems to recommend that he enters the academic fray once more and attempt to 'reden in retorik' his anger against the friars and the reason for it (101–2). Lewte's advice may be an attempt to free Wil from Fortune's sway, as it echoes Philosophy's recommendation to Boethius at the beginning of Book II that he should turn to rhetoric and forget Fortune:

> But now is tyme that thou drynke and ataste some softe and delitable thynges, so that whanne thei ben entred withynne the, it mowe maken wey to strengere drynkes of medycines. Com now forth, therfore, the suasyoun of swetnesse rethorien, which that goth oonly the righte wey while sche forsaketh nat myn estatutz. And with Rethorice com forth Musice, a damoysele of our hous, that syngeth now lightere moedes or prolacions, now hevyere.[3]

This is not unlike the defence for verse-making that Wil later uses to Ymaginatif (B.XII.23–24), but at this stage he rejects this option and instead points out that the friars will be able to cite texts to support their arguments and also quote the injunction *Nolite iudicare quemquam* (Matt. 7:1) at him as a reminder that he ought to refrain from judgment (B.XI.89–90). Obviously he does not wish to escape from the frying-pan of the desires endemic in the Lond of Longynge merely to find himself back in the fire of scholastic dispute. The fact that he neither wishes to pass judgement on the friars nor to follow Lewte's advice indicates that he has learned something from his experience. He has in fact acquired a little of the self-knowledge that Scripture accused him of lacking immediately prior to the inner dream.

When Scripture responds to Wil's attack on clerics with the pseudo-Bernardine Latin tag '*Multi multa sciunt et seipsos nesciunt*' she is showing her scorn for Wil's recently acquired learning, which has brought him no nearer the true knowledge which he ostensibly seeks than he was at the beginning of Passus VII. He has directed his energies outward into finding definitions of Dowel, Dobet and Dobest from which to deduce knowledge and in doing so has ignored the possibility of internal seeking. He has gathered debating skills and collected many interpretations of Dowel, but he does not know himself. The shock of this realisation, driven home by Scripture's sudden rage and citation of the Latin text, throws him into the

3 *Ibid.*

deeper consciousness of the inner dream where he meets all the impulses that drive mankind, and so is forced to recognise their existence. Yet it transpires that simply acknowledging them is not enough; he must learn to overcome them if he is to continue his search for truth and the life which leads to salvation. For this inner dream not only impresses on Wil how powerful arguments can be when they are shaped in order to appeal to the emotions, but also how dangerous they may prove if the wrong sort of emotional responses are allowed to take over entirely.

The text which Scripture uses to such effect is taken from pseudo-Bernard's *Meditations* and forms part of a discourse on the mistaken search for knowledge outside the self:

> Multi multa sciunt et seipsos nesciunt. Alios inspiciunt, et se ipsos deserunt. Deum quaerunt per ista exteriora deserentes sua interiora, quibus interior est Deus. Idcirco ab extorioribus redeam ad interiora, et ab inferioribus ad superiora ascendam: ut possim cognoscere unde venio, aut quo vado; quid sum, vel unde sum; et ita per cogitionem mei valeam pervenire ad cogitationem Dei.
>
> (Many people know many things but do not know themselves. They scrutinise others, but ignore themselves. They seek God through these external things, ignoring the things within themselves, although God is internal. Therefore I will return from the external things to the internal, and ascend from the inferior to the superior: so that I may know whence I come or where I am going; what I am or from what I come; and so through contemplation of myself I may come to contemplation of God.)[4]

Knowledge of this type is the wisdom of *sapientia* as opposed to the learning of *scientia*. It is more innate and far less deductive, relying on the senses rather than the mind. Self-knowledge is thus not only a knowledge of one's character acquired by introspection, but also a recognition of the mass of desires and emotions, weaknesses and possible strengths which make up humanity. Far from seeing oneself as removed from the rest of the human race, one has to apply a knowledge of human life and behaviour to oneself, and then humbly attempt to overcome whichever aspects block the way to God. Rolle presents such self-knowledge as a pre-requisite for wisdom, which is knowledge of God:

> And þat ledys a man theder, es þys;
> þe way of mekenes pricipaly,
> And of drede, and luf of God almyghty,
> þat may be cald þe way of wisdom:
> In-tyl whilk way na man may com
> Wyth-outen knowyng of God here,

[4] St Bernard (attrib.), *Meditationes piisimae de cognitione humanae conditionis*, PL, 184, col. 485; quoted in Wittig, p. 214.

. . .
Hym byhoves knaw him-self withinne,
Elles may he haf na knowing to come
In-til þe forsyade way of wisdome.[5]

Meekness, dread and love of God will come with the acquisition of proper self-knowledge.

Although both the deductive and affective approach acknowledged the need for self-knowledge, it was possible to go far along the deductive route without it. This is not the case for the affective, for without proper knowledge of oneself it is impossible to procede to the higher stages of contemplation. Moreover, acquiring such proper self-knowledge enables the contemplative to reject the kind of misleading advice offered to Wil in the Lond of Longynge. As the Middle English *Beniamyn* puts it:

. . . by þis ilke Joseph he [the contemplative] is not only lernyd to eschewe þe deceyte of his enemyes, bot also oft a man is led by hym to þe parfite knowyng of hymself. . . .
    Bot longe aftyr Joseph is Beniamyn borne; for whi trewly bot ȝif it so be þat we vse us besyly & longe in goostly trauayles, wiþ þe whiche we ben lernid to knowe oureself, we mowen not be reisyd to þe knowyng contemplacioun of God. He doþ for nouȝt þat liftyþ up his iȝe to þe siȝt of God, þat is not ȝit able to see hymself.[6]

There is a long time between the birth of Joseph (self-knowledge) and of Benjamin (contemplation) during which the acolytes must come to an understanding of the spiritual aspects of their own identity.

Since the affective path places great emphasis on individual response and seeks to convince its followers by evoking powerful emotional reactions, it is clearly crucial that the emotions to which it appeals and the responses it gets are of the right sort. Both Hilton and the *Cloud* author warn their audiences against the wrong sort of reaction by making it clear that the correct emotions are felt only when one has severed links with all worldly concerns. Hilton links this relinquishing of earthly desires with the acquisition of self-knowledge as he stresses that a soul which has achieved a degree of self-recognition has 'departid from beholdynge of alle erþly þinges & from þe vse of bodily wittes, þat is feliþ itself as it is in þe owne kynde withouten a body'.[7] The *Cloud* author asserts the importance of distancing oneself from worldly pleasures by describing the cloud of forgetting

---

5 Rolle (attrib.), *The Pricke of Conscience*, ed. R. Morris (1863: rpt. Amsterdam, Paris and New York, 1973), pp. 140–45 and 148–50.
6 'Beniamyn', p. 143.
7 Hilton, *Scale*, Book 1, ch. 30, pp. 122–23.

which develops between the true contemplative and the world, blanking out all connection with earthly feelings.[8] Langland presents a different way of driving home the same point in the episode of the Lond of Longynge where he provides the readers with a vivid picture of the likely result of heeding the wrong sort of emotional responses by plunging Wil into his bewildering experience and reveals how easily the unwary are led astray. Thus making use of the very kind of imagery that the treatise writers tended to avoid.

This use of dramatic verse to present negative examples as warnings is counter-balanced by the second section of Wil's visit to the Lond of Longynge, in which Langland reveals how vivid language and the force of experience can be used in an affirmative and positive way.

---

[8] *Cloud*, ch. 5, pp. 13–14.

14

Trajan

The attempt to find an alternative to the deductive discourse seems to have failed, as the type of experience Wil gained in the Lond of Longynge. It bound him closer to worldly pleasures rather than releasing him from them. Nevertheless, the result was not wholly negative, as Wil and the reader have certainly been reminded of the power of distractions offered by Fortune, and have found that the end result is far from desirable. The force of experience and emotional response have been illustrated, but its potential for positive encouragement to the good has yet to be exploited. The fact that Scripture's words once again have a deep effect on Wil (B.XI.112–18) indicates that the emotive discourse is still in play and may yet prove a positive force. For, although Wil's initial reaction to Scripture's words is fear, he finds solace in the promises of welcome for the faithful which he cites from Isaiah 55:1 (B.XI.120a) and Mark 16:16 (B.XI.124a) and in the action of Mercy, which he acknowledges may be summoned to the aid of the sinner at the request of Contrition. Scripture affirms the power of Mercy to redeem all, but in doing so she invokes the authority of books – 'as oure bokes telleth' (B.XI.138). It appears that Wil has been returned to depending on books to validate any opinion he may have. However, the power of personal experience is once again made apparent with the entrance of Trajan.

Trajan bursts in and brushes aside the appeal to written authorities, which Wil and Scripture have just made, and asserts that salvation can be gained through living a good life. Learning and knowledge of the law is not necessary, because living by the precepts of law and justice suffice. He sums up this claim in two forceful lines:

'Lawe withouten love,' quod Troianus, 'ley ther a bene –
Or any science under sonne, the sevene arts and alle!' (B.XI.170–71)

His impact is all the greater because he is an historical figure and also the first person from the waking world to enter the poem since the two friars at the beginning of Passus VIII. He enters the dream as neither personification

175

nor allegory, but he is representative. Thus from the moment of his entry both the content and the mode of presentation of this section form a contrast with the previous passus. Trajan picks up the theme of the intellectually ignorant but spiritually experienced and knowledgable guide, last seen when Piers offers a powerful alternative to the priest at the end of Passus VII. It is perhaps indicative of this similarity between Piers and Trajan that each of them makes a dramatic entrance into the poem by suddenly coming in unannounced: Piers popping up in the crowd (B.V.537), Trajan from Hell, (according to his introduction as 'oon was broken out of helle' (B.XI.140)). The knowledge possessed by these figures has been culled from their understanding of the world in which they find themselves, a method which Fortune has offered to Wil by showing him the mirror of Middelerthe and which is repeated when Kynde takes him up the mountain of Middelerthe and shows him the workings of the natural world below (B.XI.318ff).

Such 'kynde knowyng' is gained from experience and may be passed on through teaching 'by ensaumples'. Trajan himself is one such *exemplum* and a favourite one at that, whose legend is preserved in the compendium of saints' lives to which he himself refers, the *Legenda Aurea* of Jacob de Voraigne (Jacobus a Voragine, 1230–98). Here the story of Trajan's miraculous redemption from Hell is told as part of the legend of Saint Gregory in which we are told how Gregory was reminded of the Roman Emperor Trajan by his monument and recollected that Trajan was renown for his justice and mercy, exemplified by the tale of how he delayed his departure for war in order to grant the request of a poor widow who wished her dead husband to have a proper burial. The Pope was moved to tears at the thought that this just man must be damned, despite his merits and worthy life, simply because he was a pagan, and prayed that Trajan's soul might be redeemed. Gregory's prayer was answered and Trajan's position as the prime example of the Saved Heathen assured.

Since it was his reputation for justice and good deeds which moved Gregory to intercede on his behalf, Trajan is a fitting figure to have as an advocate of the possibility of salvation through good deeds. For not only was he a pagan but also, as he lived from 53 to 117 AD, a pagan in Christian times, which means that he could have been baptized into the faith, but was not. Yet despite this, the power of God's mercy and the action of His justice is such that even a pagan living after Christ can be saved, provided he merits salvation through worthy deeds and a blameless life. In this instance, then, mercy allows the law of just rewards to act where otherwise it would be prevented by Trajan's lack of faith. Thus Trajan is a perfect illustration of Scripture's tag, '*Misericordia eius super omnia opera eius*' (B.XI.139a) and his entry at this point in the poem brings the debate alive rather than destroying it.

By introducing the figure of Trajan himself into the text, rather than merely alluding to him, Langland is continuing the method of the inner dream which has been to demonstrate the power of argument based on empirical evidence rather than on the theoretical abstractions. This exploits the force of visual impact when seeking to substantiate an opinion: it is difficult to deny something when incontrovertible proof literally stands before you. The persuasive power of what one sees, as opposed to what one hears and is told, forms the basis for Nicholas of Cusa's metaphorical description of the ascent of the uneducated believer to a direct experience of God in his treaty *De Docta Ignorantia*:

> Deinde ardentiori desiderio fideles continuo ascendentes ad intellectualitatem simplicem rapiuntur, omnia sensibilia transilientes, quasi de somno ad vigiliam, de audita ad visum pergentes, ubi ea videntur, quae revelari non possunt; quoniam supra omnem auditum sunt et vocis doctrinam.

> (Thereupon the believers, who continue to ascend with more ardent desire are caught up unto simple intellectuality; and leaping beyond all perceptible things, they pass as if from sleeping to waking, from hearing to seeing. There they see things which, because they are things beyond all hearing and all vocal instruction, cannot be revealed.)[1]

Although this text post-dates *Piers Plowman* by sixty years (Nicholas of Cusa lived from 1401 to 1464), it expresses the attitude behind such works contemporary with *Piers* as *The Cloud of Unknowyng*, Rolle's *Incendium Amoris* and Hilton's *Scale of Perfection*, i.e. that direct apprehension of the divine cannot be communicated verbally and that path that leads to such moments of apprehension is best described figurally rather than abstractly. This preference in style of language clearly reflects the belief that the higher levels of spiritual awareness cannot be taught but must be experienced directly. This does not rule out attempts to give some intimation of these heights of understanding, but it does mean that those who try to describe them are more likely to use images, metaphors and allegories which have a more direct effect on the audience, for a powerful figure gives an audience something or someone with which to sympathize. The persuasive effect of such devices lies in the fact that the audience is led to believe that its vicarious experience is very like the actual experience of (in this case) reaching a direct apprehension of the divine. Langland's use of Trajan as an actual character in his text reflects this recognition of the advantage of sight over words for Trajan has a striking visual impact and carries more conviction than any reference to him could, even if the character making that reference were Gregory, who perhaps would have been a more suitable figure to present the ensuing resumé of Christian doctrine. The power of having Trajan himself speak is that he knows that right living alone, with-

---

1 Nicholas of Cusa, *De Docta Ignorantia*, ed. Paolo Rotta (Bari, 1913), Book 3, ch. 11, p. 156. Tr. J. Bruce Ross, *Nicholas of Cusa, On Learned Ignorance*, in *Late Medieval Mysticism*, ed. R.C. Petry, The Library of Christian Classics XII (Philadelphia and London, 1957), p. 365.

out knowledge of theology, can merit salvation and presents himself as a case in point. Yet inevitably Trajan is not without his ambiguities, most of which spring from the tensions between what he says, the way he presents it, and his own place in the very books he seems to despise.

Trajan's opening cry dismisses not only books and references to *auctores*, but also the whole world of the intellect. He builds on his declaration by asserting the precedence and sufficiency of love alone (B.XI.170–71) and then forcing the *intellectus* to admit the power of the *affectus*:

> ... clerkes wite the sothe –
> That al the clergie under Crist ne myghte me cracche fro helle
> But oonliche love and leautee and my laweful domes. (B.XI.144–45)

It is a startling and powerful entry, yet gradually the autonomy of this figure is undermined as he uses the academic habit of reinforcing assertion with suitable *auctoritates*:

> For Seint Johan seide it, and sothe arn hise wordes:
> *Qui non diligit manet in morte.* (B.XI.175)

Similarly at B.XI.189–95, 203–203a and so on throughout the remainder of his speech.

These citations serve a purpose as they mean that his words cannot be dismissed as an emotional outburst, since he is able to support them by Biblical texts and references, thereby illustrating that his claims rest on impeccable foundations. Given this it may seem that Trajan's use of texts and authorities reveals an inclination to the deductive approach to knowledge after all, but this is not the case. For the deductive discourse dissects and debates its authorities in order to prove an argument whereas in the emotive language used by Trajan, they serve to put the final seal of approval on a view which he considers he has already proved by his own history. However, there is a problem: Trajan's own authority comes from the fact that he has been recorded in books, a fact he acknowledges when he refers his audience to the major source of his own legend. 'The *Legenda Sanctorum* yow lereth more largere than I yow telle.' (B.XI.160) Later he appeals to its content to support his argument:

> Thanne is bileve a lele help, above logyk or lawe.
> Of logyk ne of lawe in *Legenda Sanctorum*
> Is litel alowaunce maad, but if bileve hem helpe. (B.XI.219–21)

Trajan owes his very survival to the power of books, and furthermore is willing to refer to the same volume which has assured his continued existence, to clinch his own argument.

Clearly, then, if Trajan's integrity is to be maintained we cannot take his opening exclamation literally, we cannot dismiss books ignoring their contents utterly, for they contain things other than scholastic arguments. Furthermore Trajan's own use of *auctoritates* undermines any interpretation which rules out the appeal to established authorities in favour of faith and personal experience of God alone. Yet, despite these complexities, there must be a valid case to be made for Trajan's central claim that a life lived as well as possible will merit salvation, because Langland neither undermines Trajan's standing, and so queries his words, nor shows him to be dangerously misleading, both of which he does with the Doctor. On the contrary much of what Trajan stands for is endorsed by Ymaginatif and borne out in the rest of the poem, as demonstrated by Wil's choice to follow Pacience, rather than Clergie.

Yet there is another paradoxical aspect to Trajan's speech in that we are presented with a long treatise on the virtues of poverty delivered by a Roman Emperor. This paradox may be resolved by recalling that the act for which Gregory remembered and honoured him was that of delaying his departure for war in order to see justice done to a poor woman.[2] So, by being convinced by the widow's arguments and taking pity on her plight, Trajan became an *exemplum* of humility and mercy, especially for the prosperous, and therefore is qualified to present a speech whose theme appears to be so removed from its speaker's actual circumstances. His own act forms the basis of his speech, as all his examples are of acts of mercy done towards those in great need by those who are comparatively affluent: the exhortation to invite those in need to a feast rather than one's prosperous friends (B.XI.189–95), the story of Cleophas (230–40), and his interpretation of the Martha and Mary episode (B.XI.248–56; Luke 10:42). The content of the speech thus returns us to the character of Trajan himself and the reputation which has endowed him with so much authority.

Unfortunately on closer inspection this character cannot offer much comfort for the disconcerting effects of Scripture's text, *Multi multa sciunt et seipsos nesciunt*. Ever since Scripture uttered this text which induced this inner dream the theme of self-knowledge has recurred as a vital concept. If it is important that the questioner should have some degree of self-knowledge, then surely this must be indispensable in any guiding figure, and it is precisely in this that Trajan fails. He seems to misunderstand wilfully his own salvation, crediting it to his own justice and good works rather than to Gregory's petitions and prayers and Divine mercy. It is undoubtedly true that had it not been for Gregory's recognition of Trajan's deeds, his pity for his damnation and his subsequent prayers, Trajan would

---

2 Jacobus de Voragine, *Legenda Aurea*, ch. 46: De Sancto Gregorio, ed. T. Graese (Osnabrück, 1969), p. 196.

never have been redeemed. Yet Trajan has the effrontery to deny the need for and, by implication the power of, prayer:

> That al the clergie under Crist ne myghte me cracche fro helle
> But oonliche love and leautee and my laweful domes.
>   Gregorie wiste this wel, and wilned to my soule
> Savacion for soothnesse that he seigh in my werkes.
> And after that he wepte and wilned me were graunted grace,
> Withouten any bede biddyng his boone was underfongen,
> And I saved, as ye may see, withouten syngynge of masses,
> By love and by lernyng of my lyvynge in truthe,
> Broughte me fro bitter peyne ther no biddyng myghte.
>
> (B.XI.144–152)

Although it is true that no formal commemorative prayers or masses were said for Trajan, the earnestness and strength of Gregory's desire for Trajan to be saved, a desire which almost amounts to willing him into heaven ('wilned'), must be seen as a kind of prayer. It is certainly regarded as such by the compiler of the *Legenda Aurea*, Jacobus de Voragine, for in his text the divine voice which responds to Gregory's tears calls his request a *'petitio'* and, more explicitly, warns him against thinking he can redeem other souls through praying for them. Here the word is *'preces'* (prayer), an unambiguous sign that this weeping and petitioning is a form of prayer.

The fact that Trajan chooses not to term Gregory's desire a prayer seems to indicate a gross lack of humility and self-knowledge in a figure brought in specifically as an *exemplum* of these virtues. It is true that Trajan's deeds had the power to move Gregory to his petition that Trajan be redeemed, but it is ungracious, to say the least, to claim that it was the value of his life alone that saved him. It would be possible to resolve this apparent *impasse* were Gregory regarded as the immediate cause and Trajan's justice as the final, yet such a resolution is not even suggested, neither by Trajan nor by Ymaginatif in the following passus. By ignoring this option, however, Langland is able to stress the infinite power of God's mercy here, as declared by Ymaginatif later:

> . . . *Salvabitur vix iustus in die iudicii;*
> *Ergo – salvabitur!* (B.XII.279–80)

According to this text, to require a direct cause for salvation (such as Gregory's petition) is to limit God's power as it would imply that all God's ways were easily comprehensible to man. Clearly an all-powerful deity would be capable of redeeming Trajan without requiring the intercession of even so good a man as Gregory; if one gives too much emphasis to Gregory's role one questions the power of the Almighty. Nevertheless the apparent pride and assurance with which Trajan speaks rather undermines his authority, for the Trajan Langland uses is the product of books (as opposed to the historical Trajan, who clearly was not). This fact and his denial of the need for books and learning generally, lends a certain irony to his warning to other 'lordes':

> Wel oughte ye lordes that lawes kepe this lesson to have in mynde,
> And on Troianus truthe to thenke, and do truthe to the peple.

(B.XI.157–58)

Trajan's 'truthe' in justice and deeds remains intact, but his truthfulness as a character has suffered a blow.

Although closer inspection of the literary figure of Trajan casts a shadow of doubt over what he advocates (i.e. that salvation may be merited through good deeds alone), the role Gregory plays in the legend and the hope of redemption through faith and the power of prayer it presents seems to remain intact. For it was Gregory's compassion and faith that led him to intercede for Trajan's soul and it was his prayer that freed Trajan from hell. However, closer examination reveals that Gregory's prayer may not have had quite as powerful an effect as Trajan leads us to believe. Moreover, the *Legenda Aurea* not only records that Gregory was warned not to pray for any more pagans, but also includes a version of the end of the tale which relates how Gregory paid for his presumption of desiring the redemption of one already damned.

To begin with Trajan's fate; it transpires that there is no absolute assurance about that. Ymaginatif's claim that 'he is saaf, so saith the book, and his soule in hevene' (B.XII.282) is right, but misleading, for 'the book' also says that there are several different opinions about the eventual fate of Trajan's soul; the view that it is in heaven is only one of many:

> Alii dixerunt, quod anima Trajani non fuit simpliciter a reatu poenae aeternae absoluta, sed ejus poena usque ad tempus, scilicet usque ad diem judicii fuit suspensa. Alii, quod poena quo ad locum vel modum aliquem tormenti sub conditione fuit taxata, donec orante Gregorio per Christi gratiam locus vel modus aliquis mutaretur. Alii ut Johannes dyaconus, . . . quod ejus anima non est ab inferno liberata et in paradiso reposita, sed simpliciter ab inferni cruciatibus liberata. Valet enim (ut dicit) anima et in inferno exsistere et inferni cruciatus per Dei misericordiam non sentire. Alii, quod poena aeterna consistit in duobus, scilicet in poena sensus et in poena damni, quod est carentia visionis divinae. Poena igitur aeterna quantum ad primum est sibi dimissa, sed quantum ad secundum retenta.

> (Others say that Trajan's soul was not directly freed from the state of one accused in eternal torment, but that his punishment was suspended for a time, namely, until the day of the Last Judgement. Others that the place and manner of punishment was estimated conditionally until it was changed to another place and manner as a result of Gregory's prayer through the mercy of Christ. Others, such

181

as John the Deacon, . . . [say] that his soul was not freed from hell and placed in heaven, but simply freed from the torments of hell. For (he says) that a soul has the power to exist in hell but, through the mercy of God, not feel the torments of hell. Others that eternal punishment consists of two things, namely the punishment of the senses and punishment of loss, which is deprivation of the sight of God. Therefore his eternal punishment was cancelled as far as the first was concerned, but retained as far as the second.)[3]

Ymaginatif is technically correct in his version of events, but he is also selective. He refers to the story of Trajan in order to support his statement that the just will be saved on the Day of Judgement, regardless of whether or not they were Christians. According to Ymaginatif, those who have fulfilled the precepts of the best law they knew and who would have changed their conduct had they become aware of a better law, have great hope of salvation. He ignores the opinion that the salvation accorded to non-Christians may not be of the same order as that awarded a Christian, as the passage from the *Legenda* above illustrates. The word *'vix'* which Ymaginatif uses (B.XII.279) hints at the possibility of such discrimination, but it is only when reference is made to the *Legenda Aurea* itself that the full force of this hint becomes clear. More disconcertingly, Ymaginatif ignores the point that since Trajan lived after Christ, and so was aware of a better law, the fact that he did not alter his beliefs accordingly, means he fails to fulfil Ymaginatif's paranthetical caveat for the salvation of pagans. For Ymaginatif is quite clear that the one who merits redemption –

> . . . lyveth as his lawe techeth and leveth ther be no bettre,
> (And if ther were, he wolde amende) and in swich wille deieth.
>
> (B.XII.286–87)

If we accept Ymaginatif's explanation of how a heathen may merit salvation we can no longer believe that Trajan's conduct was his major redeeming factor. It helped him only insofar as it inspired pity in a saint.

This leaves us with the view that Trajan's salvation was made possible through the efficacy of faithful and fervent prayer. Yet the evidence that Gregory, a saint and a pope, was severely reprimanded for presuming to pray for a soul in Hell destroys any trust in the power of prayer to redeem those whose righteous living apparently makes them candidates for retrospective salvation:

Tunc sibi divinitus est responsum: ecce, petitionem tuam complevi et Trajano poenam aeternam peperci, de caetero autem diligentissime caveas, ne pro damnato aliquo preces fundas.

[3] *Legenda Aurea*, ch. 46, p. 197.

(Then through divine power he received this reply: Behold, I have fulfilled your petition and have spared Trajan eternal punishment, but take the utmost care about others, lest you pour forth prayers for others who are damned.)[4]

It is made very clear that this is to be an unique event. Furthermore, the *Legenda Aurea* records that in some versions of the tale Gregory had to suffer some severe punishment himself because he dared to pray for a pagan. According to this tradition Gregory was offered the choice between spending two days in Hell after his death or the rest of his life in ill-heath and infirmity. He apparently chose the latter, and Jacobus de Voragine lends weight to this account by adding quotations from Gregory's letters in which he complains of his continuous illnesses.[5]

It seems that later accounts and re-tellings of the Trajan legend regarded Gregory's affliction as a vital part of the tale, for even in Etienne de Besançon's *Alphabetum Narrationum*, where Trajan is used as an instance of the redemptive power of prayer, the caution issued to Gregory is included, despite the fact that this would appear to detract from the very thing it seeks to illustrate. The detail is retained in the fifteenth-century translation of the *Alphabetum*, the *Alphabet of Tales*, where the warning against presumption is presented as the unchallenged ending to the tale:

> We rede in 'Gestis Beati Gregory' how on a tyme as Saynt Gregor walkid befor þe palace of Traian and vnthought myn of his mekenes, he began to fall opon a sore wepyng. And he prayed hym so long for hym as Saynt Petur altar, wepyng & makyng sorow, vnto a voyce spak vnto hym & sayd. þat Traiayn þurgh his prayers was delyverd oute of þe payn of hell; bot it bad hym þat fro thens furth he sulde bewar, & not presume hym to prey fro none vncristend man þat was dampned.[6]

This version of the legend is presented explicitly as an illustration of the saving power of prayer; it appears under the heading *Oracione reuocatur ab infernis dampnatus* and no mention is made of Trajan's actual deeds, which might be regarded as meriting salvation, only of his general meekness. This makes the warning Gregory receives all the more striking, for it is clearly regarded as important enough to be included even in such an abridged version of the legend intended to demonstrate how a soul can be redeemed through prayer. The audience of this text is prevented from putting any kind of final trust in prayer and faith alone, for the warning is a caution against presuming too much on God's mercy in the hope of mitigating the operation of His justice.

4 *Legenda Aurea*, ch. 46, p. 196.
5 *Legenda Aurea*, ch. 46, p. 197.
6 *An Alphabet of Tales: A Fifteenth Century Translation of the 'Alphabetum Narrationum' once attributed to Etienne de Besançon*, ed. Mary McLeod Banks, EETS o.s. 126–27 (1905), p. 393.

The final result of this exploration of Trajan's appearance in *Piers Plowman* is not the certainty which Trajan's own assurance seemed to promise, but more misgivings about the wisdom of putting trust in any one interpretation of an authority, particularly a written one. The more one seeks for concrete guidance, the more elusive it becomes and the more disconcerted the seeker becomes too. Nevertheless, despite the paradoxes surrounding Trajan's refutation of books and book-learning, his impact in the poem is unimpaired. His entrance is dramatic and entirely in keeping with the highly visual and emotive atmosphere of the inner dream of Passus XI and the fact that he gives Wil and the reader of *Piers Plowman* cause to think is in itself a demonstration of the methods of the emotive discourse. So Trajan may still be regarded as a successful component of the inner dream's bid to present a viable alternative discourse to the language and approach of the deductive route to knowledge. Yet in the C-Text revision Langland reduced Trajan's role to a cameo part, presenting the possibility of salvation through righteous works alone. The rest of the passage is given to Rechelesnesse, whose part is greatly expanded in the C-Text and whose obviously dubious character, indicated by his name, greatly affects the interpretation of the attitudes presented.

The expansion of the fleeting B-Text figure of Rechelesnesse into the larger character of the C-Text has been discussed at length by E.T. Donaldson[7] who puts the case for Rechelesnesse as a neutral figure. He makes the point that not worrying about the future or about one's own place in society can be positive attributes, as they may be the result of utter trust in God and a lack of concern about earthly matters. This type of carelessness is encouraged by the examples of the birds of the air and lilies of the field cited in Matthew 6:25–34 and is endorsed by the *Cloud* author in Chapter 42 of *The Cloud of Vnknowyng* where the writer rejects the notion of adopting strict rules for eating and drinking in favour of cultivating a lack of regard about such things:

> & I miȝt gete a wakyng & a besi beholdyng to þis goostly werk wiþinne in my soule, I wolde þan haue a rechelesnes in etyng & in drynkyng, in sleping & in spekyng & in alle myn outward doynges. For sekirly I trowe I schuld raþer com to discrecion in hem by soche a rechelenes þan by any besy beholding to þe same þinges, as I wolde bi þat beholdyng set a merke a mesure in hem.[8]

It is, therefore, a mistake to translate 'Rechelesnesse' as 'Recklessness' as this word has predominantly negative connotations in Modern English.

---

7 E. Talbot Donaldson, *The C-Text and Its Poet*, Yale Studies in English 113 (New Haven, 1966), p. 172.
8 *Cloud*, ch. 42, p. 45.

Donaldson's case can certainly hold true for the B-Text Rechelesnesse, as it is possible to regard him as thoughtless and foolhardy but not actually sinful, his ragged clothes being a sign of praiseworthy disregard for the things of this world, a view embraced by Piers at the end of B.VII. However, this is not possible for his C-Text counterpart, whose care-free attitude is culpably careless. This presentation is closer to that given in Chapter 11 of the *Cloud*, where the author is adamant that carelessness, especially concerning apparently trivial lapses, will lead to deadly sin:

> For o þing I telle þe: þat who chargeþ not, or setteþ litil bi þe first þou3t – ye, þou3 al it be no sinne vnto him. he, þat whosoeuer þat he be, schal not eschewe rechelesnes in venial sinne. Venial synne schal no man vtterly eschue in þis deedly liif. Bot rechelesnes in venial synne schuld alweis be eschewed of all þe trewe dissiples of perfeccion; & elles I haue no wonder þof þei sone sinne deedly.[9]

Langland makes it obvious that he is using 'rechelesnes' in this negative, if not actually pejorative, way in the C-Text by explicitly linking Rechelesnesse with Wanhope:

> Sir Wanhope was sib to hym as som men me told. (C.XI.199)

At this point Langland seems to be at pains to present Rechelesnesse in a bad light and so avoid any interpretation that could lend credence to his words.

This change has a marked effect on the issues raised by Rechelesnesse, for, having rendered his speaker suspect by linking him with Wanhope, Langland goes on to undermine points that in the earlier version were regarded as valid. Thus the challenge to the upholders of learning, which seriously queried the amount of trust one could place in these figures, is presented in such a way as to render the argument untenable. Rechelesnesse exploits a possible abuse of the creed of predestination, which he presents in C.XI.204–211, to declare that, since the fate of one's soul has already been determined, there is no reason to try to be worthy of salvation. This, coupled with the notion that riches hinder entrance into heaven, to which he refers by quoting Matthew 19:23–24 (C.XI.204a), results in the heedlessness personified by this C-Text Rechelesnesse, which is a travesty of unworldliness. He is, therefore, an illustration of the effect the character and standing of a speaker have over his words, regardless of which path to knowledge one follows. Belief and respect for the source of a doctrine are as important for the affective way as for the deductive – Augustine's words of *De Doctrina Christiana* hold true for both:

---

[9] *Cloud*, ch. 11, p. 21.

... titubabit autem fides, si divinarum scripturarum vacillat auctoritas. Porro fide titubante caritas etiam ipsa languescit. Nam si a fide quisque ceciderit, a caritate etiam necesse est ut cadat. Non enim potes diligere quod esse non credit.

(... for faith will waver if the authority of the holy scriptures totters. Indeed once faith wavers charity itself weakens. For if one falls from faith then he must fall from charity. For it is not possible to love what one does not believe to be.)[10]

This statement is particularly pertinent to the search for *sapientia* which, as we have seen, places great emphasis on the power of example and the importance of faith.

Rechelesnesse's words are perfectly sound theologically and so ought to present an opposite view to that put forward by Scripture and Clergie. However, by taking over Wil's speeches and those of Ymaginatif, as well as Trajan's, he in effect discredits their arguments for the salvation of the right living but theologically ignorant. In the B-Text Wil uses the examples of Noah and the Redeemed Thief to illustrate his case that it is faith, not knowledge or even works, which merit salvation. By choosing such reliable, unexceptionable instances and by raising the problems attending the characters and fates of Solomon and Aristotle, Wil shows that he is able to evaluate theological arguments and see flaws in them. Theoretically the points remain as sound in the C-Text, but, as in the case of the Doctor of Divinity, his evident abuse of the opinions he voices means that his character subverts his words: the speaker has no credibility so the opinions become shallow.

Yet, despite the use of Rechelesnesse as the main proponent of the views put forwards in the inner dream, the final impression left by the C-Text is not one of bolstering the deductive approach to knowledge. As in the B-Text, the experience of the inner dream alerts the reader and Wil to the fact that the speaker's character must be taken into account before his ideas are accepted. Here, by picking out the 'wel ywitted men and wel ylettred clerkes' for criticism because 'seldom ar they seyn so lyue as they lere' (C.XI236–37), Rechelesnesse actually puts us on guard against his own views and prevents us from embarking on the life illustrated in the Lond of Longyng. However, Langland alters his (and our) attitude towards Rechelesnesse at the beginning of C.XII and goes on to give him perfectly orthodox views in Passus XIII. This essential shift in attitude is effected by Couetyse-of-yes's words to Wil:

> ... Rechlesnesse, reche the neuere; by so thow riche were,
> Haue no consience how þou comst to good – confesse the to
> > som frere;
> > (C.XII.4–5)

[10] Augustine, *De Doctrina Christiana*, 1.37, *CCSL*, 32, p. 30; tr. Roberston, p. 41.

Couetyse-of-yes is obviously to be regarded with deep suspicion, a suspicion which is justified when she recommends that Wil does not worry about what Rechelesnesse has said, nor about how he may become good, for all will be well as long as he has money enough and a friar to whom to confess. This means that any attempt on her part to pour contempt upon another character has the opposite effect: if one figure is called into question by another who is clearly suspect, the result is to increase the authority or standing of the first figure.

By these means Rechelesnesse becomes a figure to be taken seriously. One may still be faintly worried by the extreme nature of his assertion of the preferential treatment given to the poor, but overall his arguments are far more reasoned in the C-Text than in the B-Text. He admits that riches are not bad *per se*, but points out that having them makes living a righteous life more difficult: a view he illustrates by comparing the delays attendant on a merchant's business with the speed of a messenger, who may even cut across fields of corn without fear of reprimand because his office is recognised as being of vital importance. The rich are like the merchant; they will reach their journey's end but with many delays and having had to pay out a great deal of their riches on the way to alleviate the condition of those less fortunate than themselves. The poor beggars and mendicants, however, have no such responsibilities to discharge and travel light. As long as they love and have faith and acknowledge themselves to be Christian, they are assured of salvation (C.XIII.25–97a). This concurs with Pacience's words to Haukyn at B.XIV.104–109:

> Though men rede of richesse right to the worldes ende,
> I wiste nevere renk that riche was, that whan he rekene sholde,
> Whan he drogh to his deeth day, that he ne dredde hym soore,
> And that at the rekenyng in arrerage fel, rather than out of dette.
> Ther the poore dar plede, and preve by pure reson
> To have allowaunce of his lord; by the lawe he it cleymeth.

If such a reliable figure as Pacience supports the argument, then clearly it is trustworthy.

The fact that Rechelesnesse sometimes voices an opinion which is later espoused by a more credible figure (such as Pacience) means that we must admit that he is not always wrong in what he says. The case is even stronger when his views are echoed by a reliable figure later in the same version of the poem, as this removes any possibility of Langland having changed the impression he wishes to give between revisions. An instance of Rechelesnesse's words being paralleled later in the text is the declaration that he would rather have a touch of grace than all the learning Clergie and Scripture can offer:

Ac me were leuere, by oure lord, a lyppe of goddes grace
Thenne al þe kynde wyt þat ȝe can bothe and kunnyng of ȝoure bokes.

(C.XI.227–28)

This is very similar to Conscience's assertion at the end of Clergie's banquet, that he would rather follow Pacience than have half of Clergie's books (C.XV.178–81); in each case the pronouncement is laudable.

Yet Langland does not relinquish the suspect side of his C-Text Rechelesnesse figure altogether. We are reminded of his ambivalence by the summary of Rechelesness's words which is provided at the end of his speech:

Thus Rechelesnesse in a rage aresenede Clergie
And Scripture scornede þat many skilles shewede,
Til þat Kynde cam Clergie to helpe.   (C.XIII.128–30)

His case against Clergie has been convincing, but we are alerted by the words 'in a rage' to the fact that it should be read carefully. This wariness is further increased by his scorn for Scripture since the scriptures must be accepted as the ultimate authority; only a very reckless man indeed scorns them. His only vindication is that he is attacking a Scripture that 'many skilles shewede', which could be regarded as an abuse of Holy Writ, but considering we have already seen how Scripture is necessary to any approach to God, this is a dubious defence.

This attack on Scripture is reminiscent of Trajan's interruption and apparent refutation of Scripture in the B-Text (B.XI.140). This is not the only way these two figures are alike, for, although the use of Rechelesnesse in the C-Text clearly alters the tenor of much of what Trajan says in the B-Text, each character has a salutary effect on both Wil and the reader. For Rechelesnesse does not render the affective discourse entirely suspect and so subvert it and make it useless, nor does a greater knowledge of Trajan's background render all he says null and void. Instead they are both warnings against placing too much trust in unguided faith, just as the Doctor of Divinity is a caution against trusting to theological expertise. So the whole sojourn in the Lond of Longynge is a demonstration of how blind trust can lead to misunderstanding and error as easily as over-cleverness can. This is an unsurprising conclusion given that Wil is thrown into this inner dream by an enraged Scripture. However, having issued his warnings, Langland proceeds to show that the proper kind of faith can be achieved by the unlearned by taking lessons from the natural world. It is a question of having the correct disposition and seeking the right kind of knowledge in a humble way. It is this type of affective understanding, learnt from experience, which Kynde offers Wil in the final section of the inner dream.

15

Wit Through Wonders

Kynde's revelation of Middelerthe is very different from that instigated by Scripture's derision. The knowledge required to interpret Scripture's world has been gathered from Thoght, Studie and Clergie; Kynde demands a recognition of an affinity between the individual and the world in which they find themselves. Kynde does not display a land of longing in which human desires are paramount; instead we are reminded of the larger natural world beyond the human race which is also a mirror in which the wonders of God can be regarded. This shift of plane is signalled by the re-assertion of the Dreamer's presence and the call to take an active part in his own vision:

> . . . and sithen cam Kynde
> And nempned me by my name, and bad me nymen hede,
> And thorugh the wondres of this world wit for to take.
> (B.XI.320–322)

The action of calling Wil by his name recalls him to himself, setting aside the projection of how he could be which has occupied the sojourn in the Lond of Longynge. Kynde then proceeds to offer him an alternative view of the world, as seen from the mountain of Middelerthe.

By withdrawing to the mountain Kynde is removing Wil from the direct involvement with the world (as the Lond of Longynge), which has just proved to be such a bewildering experience. The distance provided by this vantage point enables Wil to survey the world with clearer sight and so allows him to perceive that there is an underlying law, that of nature as put into effect by reason. The precedence of image over deduction is asserted by the explicit statement that Wil has all this revealed 'by ensaumples' (B.XI.324), which reinforces Kynde's instruction to Wil to learn by means of the marvels the world displays:

> . . . and bad me nymen hede,
> And thorugh the wondres of this world wit for to take.
> (B.XI.321–22)

Kynde's lessons are learnt from observation of the surrounding world rather than from studying discussions and theories about authorities. Wil is physically removed from the sort of all-embracing contact with the world provided by Fortune, by being placed on a mountain-top, but since the understanding offered by Kynde is empirically based, he must retain some level of involvement with the world he views. Were it otherwise he would not be struck by the wonders in it, nor angered by Reson's apparent lack of concern about mankind.

In fact Wil's reaction to the spectacle of Middlelerthe is profoundly emotional. As he looks down from his vantage point, the emphasis is on wonder, the inexplicable and hence on those things which are beyond comprehension. Langland repeats such words as 'wondres', 'merveiled', 'selkouthes' as he reinforces the impression of the intellect defeated and a proper sense of wonderment, if not indeed awe, taking its place. It is at this point, when Wil is in a position really to look at and appreciate the world around him, that he has the opportunity to learn 'thorough ech a creature, Kynde my creatour to lovye' (B.XI.325). This recalls Holi Chirche's words of combined explanation and rebuke in Passus I:

> It is a kynde knowyng that kenneth in thyn herte
> For to loven this Lord levere than thiselve. (B.I.142–43)

Significantly, it also prefigures Kynde's final advice to Wil, which is given when Wil actually meets Elde in Passus XX (as opposed to his encounter with him in the inner dream of the Lond of Longynge). Here, in response to Wil's question about which skill is the best to learn to become a member of Unitee, Kynde tells him 'Lerne to love . . . ane leef all othere' (B.XX.207).

However, although Wil seems to have an inkling of this craft of love as he stands next to Kynde in his inner dream and is moved by the panorama below, he does not maintain this new-found level of understanding. As he looks he sees that he is not surveying an ideal society, for out of all the species before him only mankind is not governed by Reson. As soon as he realises this, his mood changes and he turns to Reson demanding an explanation. The response he gets is not only a reprimand but also indicates that the understanding Wil momentarily achieved through Kynde is no more able to answer all Wil's questions than the knowledge he was offered by Clergie:

> Recche thee nevere
> Why I suffre or noght suffre – thiself has noght to doone.
>
> (B.XI.375–76)

Furthermore there are some things that just do not concern Wil, and wondering why people are not created incapable of wrong-doing is clearly one of them.

Wil's desire to know the reasons and causes for the way the world works is very similar to the process of investigation described by Boethius of Dacia in his treatise *On The Supreme Good*:

> ... by studying the caused beings which are in the world and their natures and relationships to one another, the philosopher is led to consider the highest causes of things. For a knowledge of effects leads to a knowledge of the cause. And in noting that higher causes and their natures are such that they must have another cause, he is led to a knowledge of the first cause.[1]

Although the spur for enquiry may be affective, the method described here by Boethius is deductive as it advocates a structured, rational process of discovery based on working out each cause and effect. This method of enquiry is very like that of the deductive discourse; seeking to deduce knowledge rather than attempting to experience it. Wil tends to look for answers in this structured way, for by the time Wil is arguing with Reson he has really left the emotive realm which taught him to love Kynde through the feeling of wonder inspired by his view of Middelerthe, and drifted back to the deductive discourse which held sway before this inner dream intruded. The fact that Wil's fleeting sense of unity with the world is shattered when Reson is introduced, indicates that the two discourses, deductive and affective, do not mix easily. Yet this does not mean that one is necessarily better than the other; they are different, and there is something to be said for them both. Ymaginatif declares the need for both:

> Clergie and kynde wit cometh of sighte and techyng,
> As the Book bereth witnesse to burnes that kan rede:
> *Quod scimus loquimur, quod vidimus testamur.*
> Of *quod scimus* cometh clergie, a konnynge of hevene,
> And of *quod vidimus* cometh kynde wit, of sighte of diverse peple.
> (B.XII.64–68)

However, Ymaginatif is not as neutral as this initial summing up implies; in his next two sentences he reveals a decided preference for clergie:

> Ac yet is clergie to comende, and kynde wit bothe,
> And namely clergie for Cristes love, that of clergie is roote.
> (B.XI.70–71)

He has moved on from a defence of Reson, which is to be expected from a faculty who is a helper of reason, through an appreciation of both learning

---

1 Boethius of Dacia, *On the Supreme Good*, tr. J.F. Wippel, Medieval Sources in Translation 30 (Toronto, 1987), p. 33.

and intuition to a unequivocal preference for learning. The addition of 'And namely clergie' is tantamount to saying 'learning and innate knowledge are both good – especially learning'. It is a preference which is given great support as Ymaginatif enlarges on the value and necessity for learning, warning Wil against arguing with 'clerkes' and imparting the rather disturbing view that the 'kynde witted man' is at the mercy of the learned who hold the keys to not knowledge alone but, through that, to salvation:

> And as a blynd man in bataille bereth wepne to fighte,
> And hath noon hap with his ax his enemy to hitte,
> Na moore kan a kynde witted man, but clerkes hym teche,
> Come, for al his kynde wit, to Cristendom and be saved –
> Which is the cofre of Cristes tresor, and clerkes kepe the keyes,
> To unloken it at his likyng . . . (B.XII.105–110)

Ymaginatif himself is clearly well informed, as he goes on to deal with several of the points Wil has argued about in his inner dream, offering resolutions of a sort to each query and finally leaving the poem, proclaiming the high esteem in which 'wit and wisdom' were once held, clearly implying that Wil ought to value them properly.

Langland himself seems to have been less convinced by the merits of seeking salvation through learning and trust in authorities and the deductive route to knowledge. It is significant that this striking and remarkably knowledgable figure of Ymaginatif has been following Wil for forty-five years in vain, but is able to address him only when he has been shocked out of his dependence on the written word into an awareness of the role the senses and affective learning play in spiritual progression. Yet the affective path as presented by the inner dream is no more satisfactory than the deductive, as the variety of stimuli and responses it offered bewilder Wil, first leading him astray and then drawing him into fruitless questioning. The fact that Langland includes reservations about the approach to understanding based on affective discourse indicates that, unlike the *Cloud* author, he is not convinced that 'felyng may not begile'.[2]

The single unit comprising the third and fourth visions is the place where Langland explores the possibilites and difficulties of different forms of language and knowledge most rigorously, precisely because he places the alternatives in one and the same framework. Thus, the encounter with the friars will yield interpretations to both the deductive and the affective approaches, and Haukyn can be seen to present the shortcomings of both attitudes when applied to the case of an earnest but ill-educated man for whom seclusion is an impossiblilty. The intertwining of the two discourses

---

2 *Priuy Counselling*, p. 98.

is also evident in the figures of the Doctor of Divinity and Haukyn, whom Langland presents as examples of how following either route can lead to a way of life and understanding which is clearly mistaken, but from which the figures themselves cannot see a way out, even if, like Haukyn, they wish to relinquish it for something better.

The third vision of *Piers Plowman* has been described by John Burrow as displaying

> Langland's sense of the inadequacy and untrustworthiness of words, of neat formulations and improving sentiments.[3]

Yet it is not just words which can be inadequate: Wil's experience in the Land of Longyng and Trajan's assertions have shown that images and emotional responses, too, can be misinterpreted or misused. What is required is a state of apprehension which acknowledges how things are, without feeling the need to be able to understand and explain them all rationally. Wil briefly achieved this state when he gazed at the world revealed to him by Kynde, but he loses it as soon as he seeks to know the reason for mankind's apparently perverse nature. The appeal to Reson fragments the moment of insight Wil had gained and he does not regain it even when Ymaginatif, who is both the faculty which provides the images as raw material for Reson to work with and also offers interpretation of the phenomenal world,[4] attempts to explain the working of the understanding to Wil.

The sequence of events demonstrates that if one is to gain a fairly high degree of affective knowledge or understanding one must be predisposed to receive the insights one seeks. In fact one must be prepared to believe without necessarily being able to provide a rational reason for belief. Yet, while not requiring rational explanations, one must be able to interpret any moments of insight properly in order to avoid being misled or falling into error. Wil achieved his fleeting moment of insight because Kynde called him by his name (B.XI.320–21), thereby appealing to Wil both as an individual and as a personification of the faculty of the will. The will, not the intellect, is called into play and Wil is able to receive a hint of enlightenment which is akin to that which Beryl Smalley describes when discussing the notion of revelation:

> The fideist holds that God has revealed certain truths which a Christian must believe even if or because he cannot understand them by use of

---

3 J. Burrow, 'Words, Works, and Will: Theme and Structure in *Piers Plowman*', in *'Piers Plowman', Critical Approaches*, ed. S.S. Hussey (London, 1969), p. 120.

4 See B. J. Harwood, 'Imaginative in *Piers Plowman*', *Medium Aevum*, 44 (1975), 251–52, and H. White, 'Langland's Ymaginatif, Kynde Wit and the *Benjamin Minor*', *Medium Aevum*, 55 (1986), 241–42, for detailed discussions of this aspect of Ymaginatif.

reason. It follows from this position that the truths must have been revealed at a given time. Eternally present to God, they are only temporally present to man. They remained out of man's reach before God revealed them, because they were inaccessible to human reason.[5]

This ability to recognise something as important and true without feeling the need to dissect it through definition or explanation is precisely the 'will to abide in hope before what is worthy of thought' which Heidegger regarded as a crucial element to a 'thinking enquiry'.[6]

It is significant that as Wil relinquishes his desire to know everything through deduction and definition, the forms of his visions change. The constant redefinitions of Dowel, Dobet and Dobest disappear and the action of the poem progresses in increasingly more dramatic terms, more reminiscent of the form of the visions preceding the Pardon and the creation of the concept of 'Dowel'. The characters and events of the later visions require prior knowledge to understand them as the episodes become more like parables, which require some knowledge of what they mean before they can be interpreted. Thus the Tree of Charity combines aspects of the Garden of Eden with doctrine about the relative merits of the states of virginity, marriage and widowhood. So, too, Abraham is both the patriarch of the Old Testament and the embodiment of the Old Law of the Ten Commandments, and the jousting scenes are allegories for the Crucifixion. These visions rely so heavily on Biblical events that without knowledge of the stories they allegorise they would be utterly incomprehensible. Yet despite this, the actual method of communicating the ideas is more immediate than the dry discussion and debate which form so large a part of Passus VIII–XIV. Thus Abraham is a vivid character as well as the representative of the Old Testament laws and the battle for the souls of mankind holds the attention as the joust and its aftermath are played out.

Yet the fact remains that one must have knowledge in order to realise that the joust and subsequent events are more than just descriptions of courtly entertainments; they are also allegories of the crucifixion and the Harrowing of Hell. In the same way Abraham is both the patriarch and the representative of the Ten Commandments, just as Spes is both the personification of Hope, specifically the hope of redemption brought by Christ's life and crucifixion, and also the representative of the New Commandments to love God and neighbours. Only such awareness of the metaphorical aspect of all around them will enable the followers of the affective path to accept and understand whatever revelations or states of apprehension are proffered or

---

[5] Beryl Smalley, 'The Bible and Eternity: John Wyclif's Dilemma', *Studies in Medieval Thought and Learning* (London, 1981), p. 399.
[6] Martin Heidegger, 'A Dialogue on Language', *On the Way to Language*, tr. P.D. Hertz (London, 1971), p. 13.

described: for the vast majority such knowledge comes from learning. Richard Rolle was very decided on this point:

> Truly if þou despise techynge of doctours, & trow þi-selfe better may fynde, þen þu tech þe in þer writynge, knaw itt forsoith, cristis lufe þou sal not taste. ffond sayinge truly it is: god taght þame, qwhy þerfore sal he not tech me? I answere þe, for þou art not slike as þa were. þou art prowd & sturdy, & þa wer lawly & meek, & þu presumand of god askyd no-þyng, bot þame-self vndyr all mekand toke conynge of sayntis. Þerfore he taght þame þat we in þer bokes suld be taght.[7]

Only a few are granted direct instruction; for the rest it must suffice to learn from books written by the fortunate few. To demand that it be otherwise is to display pride which immediately precludes one from being one of those selected for direct instruction or enlightenment. Once again the need for a combination of clergie and kynde is recognised.

In *Piers Plowman* Langland demonstrates that not only are both the deductive and the affective approaches necessary if one is to achieve some apprehension of the divine, but also that they must mutually modify each other if such understanding is to be accessible to ordinary people. Without this modification the approach to knowledge as *scientia* unavailable to the majority of laymen and the path to understanding as *sapientia* seclusion from society that is impossible for those who have responsibilities to others. In a similar way, without some restraining factor to prevent the extremes of either approach from dominating their respective discourses, each route to knowledge is in danger of corruption (intentional or otherwise) or is liable to be misinterpreted. By illustrating this difficulty by such figures as the Doctor of Divinity and Haukyn and also through the repeated questioning and bewilderment of Wil, Langland demonstrates how crucial the role of interpretation is and alerts his audience to the fact that the responsibility for correct interpretation and communication of knowledge must be shared by teacher and pupil. Both must be aware that ambiguities can easily creep in on either side and so each side must not only be alert but also constantly re-examine the information they receive or pass on. However, the very fact that language is a rich and potentially creative medium makes it a force to be reckoned with and at the same time delighted in. Both approaches to understanding have their merits, the trick is learning how to manage them; how to attain some level of control and ability to interpret language without sacrificing too much of its essential, creative and inspirational quality.

---

7 Rolle, *De Emendacione Vitae*, ch. 7, tr. R. Misgn in 1434 as *The Mending of Life, or The Rule of Living*, ed. R. Harvey, EETS o.s. 106 (London, 1896), p. 120.

Part Four

MANAGING LANGUAGE

Reden ist Übersetzen – aus einer Engelsprache in eine Menschensprache.

To speak is to translate – from a language of angels into a language of men.[1]

[1] Johan Georg Haman, 'Aesthetica in Nuce' (1762), in *Johan Haman: Sämtliche Werke, historisch-kritische Ausgabe*, ed. Josef Nedler (Vienna, 1949–57), vol. 2, 199.

16

Naming and Interpretation

The exploration of the paths to *scientia* and *sapientia* has exposed the limitations of each and the problems which confront a moderately well educated layman when seeking guidance on how to live a life worthy of salvation. It appears that either route can lead all too easily to an extreme which by its very nature is exclusive and esoteric, whether because it demands heights of learning open to only a few, or extremes of exclusion and introspection which can be achieved only through withdrawing fully from society and dissolving any ties with dependants. Yet without this high level of education or seclusion which bring an awareness of the pitfalls attendant upon each approach and also how to avoid them, it is all too easy to be led astray by the power of the discourses themselves and come to rely too much on either the processes of deduction or the power of emotion and blind faith. The result is error, misunderstanding and possible corruption. Not only must one be able to use the appropriate methods and discourses, but also be able to use them properly, to manage them so that they do indeed lead to the insight or knowledge which is their aim. Any hope of a balance between the two extremes must lie in a middle way which will acknowledge the existence of both forms of knowledge and their respective emphases on deduction and revelation; such an approach would be open to the majority of people. Yet, if the two forms of knowing are to be reconciled, or at least brought into some kind of dialogue, their discourses must also be able to speak to one another. As the conversation between Holi Chirche and Wil in the Prologue revealed, the two discourses do not easily communicate, for their expectation of language and use of it differ. In order for there to be any dialogue there must also be interpretation and translation.

This need for translation returns us to the definition of Christ, the Word Incarnate as the mediator, for, as the *Catholicon* states, a translator is a mediator:

> qui unam linguam exponit per aliam, vel unam linguam transfert per aliam. Et dicitur sic quia mediator est inter unam linguam seu loquelam et alium.

199

(One who explains one language by another, or one who translates one language by another. And he is so called because he is a mediator between one language or discourse and another.)[2]

As Balbus' definition makes clear, translation involves explanation, in other words, a translator is also an interpreter. It is no surprise then, that this definition of a translator is to be found under the entry *'interpres'* (interpreter) as the acts of translation and interpretation are inextricably linked.

Every act of translation must also include interpretation since it is one's own reading which determines the choice of words. Equally every act of interpretation is a translation – a carrying over of what the translator believes to be the meaning from one language or discourse into another. The connection between these two functions comes to the fore in discussions and defences of translations of the Bible. Here one is dealing with the difficulty of translating a text which was written under divine inspiration, and so is an authoritative text, yet recorded by human amanuenses who are naturally fallible. Furthermore, language itself is ambiguous which increases the difficulty of producing an accurate translation, since almost every Hebrew or Latin word will have several possible counterparts in other languages. These problems are acknowledged and a solution proposed in the prologue to the Wycliffite Bible.

> Wel y woot defaute may be in vntrewe translating, as my3ten haue be many defautis in turnyng fro . . . o langage into anoþer. But lyue men good lif, and studie many persones Goddis lawe, and whanne chaungyng of wit is foundun, amende þey it as resoun wole.[3]

The right use of reason and study will enable a translator to understand his text and so render it faithfully; but translators must also lead the sort of life which fits them for proper understanding, since intellectual skill and learning alone will not suffice.

So there is a fundamental paradox at work in the constant attempt to define or translate in approximate language. The result is a perpetual circling around a central perception of the *logos* as the definitive Word; this is the region of interpretation – the hermeneutic circle – the space within which interpretation, reading and understanding move. This space has as its centre-point the particular concept being explored and the investigator, who is the interpreter, the reader, moves constantly and freely around this point, within the area of interpretation. Hence the circle is essentially the area of dialogue between the interpreter and the interpreted.

There are various possible reactions to, and ways of dealing with, this

2   Balbus, *Catholicon*, s.v. 'interpres'.
3   John Wyclif, *De Officio Pastorali*, ch. 15, printed in *Fourteenth Century Verse and Prose*, ed. K. Sisam (Oxford, 1982), p. 118.

circle: one can engage with it in a way which seeks to find an answer, a single, definitive reading, which will offer a way out of the circle, an end of the constant movement and a final achievement of, or at least perceptible progression towards, the fixed point which, it is assumed, is at the epicentre of the circle. Once this point is attained all circling can cease as the concept has been pinned down and finally defined and the whole area of interpretation and understanding in its various forms can be viewed in triumph from the central vantage point. Alternatively, one can move within the circle, accept its confines and choose to explore its limits in a constant process of questioning and redefinition which does not expect to arrive at a finite explanation, hoping by so doing to come to a greater appreciation of the central concept. This method cannot offer the security of a definitive answer, or even the promise of one, for it recognises the ambiguous and even arbitrary nature of language which must mean that even at its most accurate, language is approximate and any attempt at exact translation is therefore doomed to some degree of failure. This does not mean that this approach must deny the existence of a definitive Truth (although that is an option), but it does mean that it admits that such a Truth cannot be expressed fully and unambiguously in the forms of language at our disposal. For Langland, then, the problem of the existence of the definitive Truth, the transcendental signifier, does not arise, for this Truth is synonymous with the *logos* which itself is simultaneously Christ as Word Incarnate and the mysterious creative power of the original word. This provides the central point around which *Piers Plowman* as a whole moves; the problem is how to address it in a way that reflects, however dimly, the complexities and potential of the power of language.

In a work which accepts the value and existence of this central point, as *Piers Plowman* does, and also accepts the approximate nature of language, the latter course of remaining within the circle in the hope of communicating some notion of its potential and even of approaching some kind of understanding of the *logos* itself, is both more honest and more fruitful. More honest because it rejects the possibility of coming to a fixed, final interpretation which would in effect limit the *logos*; more fruitful because this rejection allows for several approaches to be taken to a text which in turn may lead to a wider range of interpretations. It is this course that is exemplified in *Piers Plowman* as Langland investigates various types of language and knowledge and their extremes; at which point he undermines them, thus preventing his audience from settling on one as the predominant and authoritative form. Hence the major pre-occupation of the poem is not the attempt to overcome the approximate nature of language and so arrive at a definitive answer or stance, instead it is a presentation of, and movement within, the difficulties and play of language or discourses which arise when one is confronted with desire for authoritative renderings and interpretation.

It may seem that such an enterprise will not only be confusing but, perforce, must also result in confusion, yet this is not the case. What is required is a shift in expectation. There is a tendency to assume that when presented with a text, and especially a questing text, the most important thing is to discover its meaning, the transcendent signifier, or Truth, with the underlying presumption that that Truth will be single and undivided.[4] However when this transcendent signifier is already acknowledged, as it is in a Christian text by the faith which inspires it, then both reader and writer are free to look at the complex of significations which combine to make up Faith, Text and Meaning; to look at the fabric of the text – what Barthes terms the 'tissue' – and so approach the work in a very different way:

> Text means Tissue; but whereas hitherto we have always taken this tissue as a product, a ready-made veil, behind which lies, more or less hidden, meaning (truth), we are now emphasising, in the tissue, the generative idea that the text is made, is worked out in a perpetual interweaving; lost in this tissue – this texture – the subject unmakes himself, like a spider dissolving in the constructive secretions of its web.[5]

Here Barthes is really dismissing the need for any concrete meaning or truth, an attitude which, it is safe to say, Langland would not endorse. However, Langland does sink his representations of Truth into his text and out of sight in order to concentrate on the 'tissue', the way the edicts of Truth and even Truth itself, can be expressed, communicated and finally put into action.

Truth is initially represented in *Piers Plowman* by the solid Tower of Truth which stands on a knoll, significantly raised above and so removed from, the field of folk below. Such detachment is crucial for impartiality, and as Truth must be impartial, this position on a hill is essential to Wil's and the audience's perception of Truth. This tower, or castle, is a concrete object that, theoretically, could be reached; one could go to it and so find Truth. Yet it is also a fortress and as such is not only the tower of Truth but also the tower which contains Truth. So it is possible that even if one arrived at the tower one would not after all have achieved one's goal, for Truth would be inside, hidden from view and unattainable; nevertheless one would be nearer. However, this representation changes as Truth becomes a shrine, the

---

4 The shift suggested here is akin to the distinctions drawn by James Simpson and Mary Carruthers in their respective ways when they deal with the question of the kind of truth sought in the text. James Simpson distinguishes between general good and piety ('The Role of *Scientia* in *Piers Plowman*', p. 60) whereas Mary Carruthers develops the consequences of dividing the spirit and letter when she discusses the different ways that Piers and the priest react to the Pardon (*The Search for St. Truth*, pp. 77–80).
5 Roland Barthes, 'Theory', *The Pleasure of the Text*, tr. R. Miller (1975: rpt. New York, 1988), p. 64.

object of a pilgrimage to be reached through penance, right-living and a journey of commitment. Despite this shift in image, the essentials remain the same, for it is still a place to go, the end of a journey. The final and most disconcerting shift in representation comes when Truth is presented as the shadowy originator of the pardon sent to Piers, for at this point Truth is no longer a firm, static entity which can be sought, travelled towards and even perhaps reached, but is a vague presence which requires understanding and need not be fixed in one place. This Truth is no longer secure. Furthermore the edicts issued by Truth are contained within a text, the pardon, which is sent without explanatory gloss or interpreter. So the text becomes the bearer of truth, and in containing truth in a way becomes Truth, and yet clearly is not Truth in its entirety in the same way as the tower was, for the physical entity of the pardon can be ripped and discarded, but this action does not affect the truth it represents, whereas if one could reach and enter the Tower one would have acquired perfect understanding.

The metaphor of Truth as the tower or shrine is thus displaced by Truth the figure, for whom Piers has worked (B.V.537–555) and who issues the pardon. Yet this figure never actually appears in the text for Langland has submerged him in a text, the Pardon. By making the Pardon the centre of debate rather than Truth himself, Langland removes the possibility of arriving at Truth, at a definitive meaning, and instead focuses on the text, the tissue. Moreover, just as Truth, the initiator of the pardon, offers no key to a sure interpretation, so Langland does not embark on a treatise intended to describe a sure road to knowledge or understanding. Instead he presents an investigation of how different approaches may be taken and where they might lead and, by intertwining their disparate elements in the same text, he reveals how they are inter-related.

So, we are left with a plurality of meanings, a variety of ways and a great potential for knowledge and understanding, which together may serve to bring us to a greater appreciation of the end, but each of which is inadequate and approximate. The emphasis is not so much on what is sought, be it Truth, Dowel or Piers, but on the act of seeking – process not stasis. We must discard the notion of language as solid, secure and completely transparent and come to terms with it as at best a fruitful and creative approximating force. This of course is the result of language as a human construct only, i.e. a necessary consequence of the discourse of *verbum*. Such consequences might be avoided could we use the pure language of the *logos* since it alone can be utterly accurate. For the *logos* is the Word incarnate, without which nothing could be made and without which all signification would in fact be impossible; for if we did not believe that some approach to accurate communication could be made we would be forced to relinquish the unequal struggle altogether. Yet, as the exchange between Wil and Holi Chirche showed, the *logos* redefines words in such a way that they can be understood only if all the users of this discourse already know what is being said:

had Wil been aware the 'tresor' signified divine love and understanding of God he would have been able to join Holi Chirche in her discourse. However, without such previous insight into the meaning of what is being said, the traces of the discourse of the *logos* must be translated to some extent and partake of the human discourse in order to be comprehensible. This indeed was the case for the Divine Word itself, for in order to enter the world it had to become incarnate and take on a human form – a metamorphosis echoed in *Piers Plowman* where Christ must become a knight in order to enter the jousting metaphor of B.XVIII and so take part in the action of the poem.

The view of text as tissue offered by Barthes in *The Pleasure of the Text* is one idea of what a text is which is applicable to *Piers Plowman*, but there is another notion, also presented by Barthes, which concentrates on the practice of interpretation rather than articulation, linking the text with the society which produces it:

> The notion of the text is historically linked to a whole world of institutions: the law, the Church, literature, education. The text is a moral object: it is written in so far as the written participates in the social contract. It subjects us, and demands that we observe and respect it, but in return it marks language with an inestimable attribute which it does not possess in its essence: security.[6]

This, too, may be of assistance for a reading of *Piers Plowman*, as there can be no doubt that Langland produced a text which is concerned with law, Church and education, yet is also notorious for its constantly shifting language and fragmented format. Nevertheless, although *Piers Plowman* is a text which is connected most obviously with the 'world of institutions' it queries the right of those institutions to be the sole source of interpretation and instruction within the poem. For it presents a ploughman as better informed and more fitted than the priest to be an interpreter and mediator between the mass of common people and the pardon, the text within the poem, despite the fact that the priest's office indicates that he is trained to be just such an interpreter. The question of the articulation and interpretation of a text lies at the heart of Langland's poem. It is a question which neither the deductive nor the affective approach has been able to answer satisfactorily, for Langland has shown how both of these approaches are open to misinterpretation, ambiguity and abuse. Nevertheless the very process of his investigations into where an ordinary person may find reliable guidance on how to merit salvation has provided a greater understanding of how language and knowledge interact and interrelate. So it is that we are better equipped to enter upon a reading of the text whose interpretations lie at the very root of the entire poem.

---

[6]   R. Barthes, 'Theory of the Text', in *Untying the Text*, ed. P. Young (Oxford, 1982), p. 32.

It may seem perverse to come to a reading of the pardon scene after exploring the later sections of the poem, but Langland himself sends his readers back into the text at the end of the poem, so it is surely worthwhile to bring the light of the investigations of the later passus to bear on this crucial passage. However, it is to be remembered that the issue being explored in *Piers Plowman* is that of interpretation, not truth, and so it is not the pardon itself, nor its tearing, which commands attention, but the conflict between the Priest and the Ploughman.

As soon as Truth's pardon is sent to Piers the priest offers his services as translator and interpreter (the two functions being connected, as has been established). He does so in the belief that he is the only person qualified to read the Latin document since the rest of the assembled company is 'lewed', ignorant of the ways of the Church as well as of the Latin language. He is then doubly disconcerted when first the pardon turns out to be no pardon in the usual sense of the word (since it is not a formal church document and has no obvious mention of granting absolution from sins committed or to be committed in the future) and then, worse still, the ignorant ploughman turns out to have a fair command of Latin himself. This last draws comment from the chagrined priest:

> "What!", quod the preest to Perkyn, "Peter! as me thinketh,
> Thow art lettred a litel – who lerned thee on boke?"
> "Abstynence the Abbesse," quod Piers, "myn a.b.c. me taughte
> And Conscience cam afterward and kenned me muche moore."
> "Were thow a preest, Piers," quod he, "thow myghtest preche
> where thow sholdest
> As divinour in divinite, with *Dixit insipiens* to thi teme."
> (B.VII.131–136.)

The priest is understandably surprised to discover that a ploughman can not only cite texts but can even do so in a way that indicates a thorough understanding of them. His immediate response is to assume that Piers has received some kind of basic education, for it is inconceivable to him that understanding could come from any source other than formal learning. For him the deductive route to knowledge is the only route.

The priest here stands as a representative of the Church establishment, one of the most powerful of those institutions which seeks to give meaning to language. As such he could be regarded as one who at least ought to be able to recognize the difference between the figurative language used to give some intimation of the *logos* and the utilitarian contract of the *verbum*. Moreover, it would be reasonable to assume that, as a trained priest, he is accustomed to explaining the more metaphorical language of the *logos* to congregations who have not had the benefit of his education and are used to using language only as a human contract. Indeed, his presentation of himself as a translator and interpreter is based on this very assumption. However, although he has put himself forward solely in order to construe and teach a text (the pardon) – a process which has involved translation and attempts at interpretation – he has failed and been replaced, even displaced, by a ploughman. Piers' opposition to the priest is in fact an indication that there is another type of language that could be used here. His use of Abstinence as a personification as well as an abstract concept indicates a shift from literal to allegorical language, for his Abstinence is clearly more than a nun who taught Piers. Yet she cannot be a symbolic figure in the way Piers and the priest are, because she is the personification of an inner quality rather than representative of a type. In view of this, Piers' Latin may be regarded as a sign of his ability to move freely between different levels of language in a way that allows them to interact rather than cancel each other out. For his usage allows his own discourse to co-exist with the discourse of the establishment, the defining institution, without being over-laid and defined by it. This ability to make use of the Church establishment's language (Latin) does not mean that Piers breaks away from the defining power of the Church. For, just before we can embrace enthusiastically the notion of the unlearned having greater spiritual insights than those who form part of the defining institutions, we are told that Piers, too, has been taught by one whose position is inextricably linked with the Church on earth. Abstinence may well be an inner attribute whose lessons come from hard experience rather than schooling, but she is also an abbess and that one word keeps us within the Church's discourse, making it clear that Piers has learnt his interpretative skills from the same general source as the priest. Piers' choice of allegory reveals that the Church, the defining institution, has influenced his knowledge and his way of thinking and so has left its mark on his language. His training has been very different from the priest's, but he is not free from the defining power of the priest's church.

This change in the level of language is emphasised by A.V.C. Schmidt, who observes that Piers speaks in more abstract, metaphorical terms than the priest, but, as the terminology of Schmidt's own comments reveals, the ruling discourse is still that of the Church:

> it was not a literal nun who instructed him in a literal alphabet but a virtuous mode of *life* . . . that grounded him in the elements of religion and a progressively developed moral *habitus* that widened his grasp of its *grammatica*.[7]

Regardless of whether 'abstinence' or 'abbess' is stressed, it remains true that while Piers' statement is an assertion of his ability to read in an appropriate and fitting manner (and so seems to challenge the need for the elitist

---

[7] A.V.C. Schmidt, *The Clerkly Maker* (Woodbridge, 1987), p. 87.

discourse and training of the priest) it is also an admission and reinforce-ment of the Church's appropriation of the discourse. For it is the Church who provides the tools of interpretation, whether they be the skills of the Latinist priest or the 'elements of religion and progressively developed moral *habitus*' which enable Piers to understand the pardon. Piers' words thus exemplify Foucault's claim that

> Any system of education is a political way of maintaining or modifying the appropriation of discourses, along with the knowledges and powers they carry.[8]

In this case as the system of education is directed by the Church, and as even those who received no formal education at all will have attended church services and been instructed in the main tenets of the Christian faith, it is inevitable that the discourse of deduction and *scientia* will prevail. Piers, however, represents an alternative, in that he understands how the docu-ment sent by Truth can be a pardon, despite not being the expected certifi-cate. He thus offers a different type of understanding, that of *sapientia* and is seen to be qualified to do so because of his evident comprehension of the meaning of the text and also because of his formal education, revealed in his ability to speak and understand Latin and his reference to Abstinence, which indicates a connection with the faith of the Christian Church rather than with its establishment only. Hence, when Piers first appears he does not represent the rejection of the Church institution. It is only when he realises the priest's inability to respond affectively and so effectively, to the pardon that he rejects this world and takes the decision to reform, or re-write, himself and his identity.

So, this interchange between priest and ploughman presents a confronta-tion between two different sources of supposedly authoritative interpreta-tion: the priest who has the trappings and status which go with authority, and the ploughman who has been shown to be the type of the right living man who has enough education from the right sources to understand the text appropriately. The matching of the appropriate form of knowledge and discourse with the text to be interpreted in Piers' reading results in an interpretation which is a proper translation, i.e. one that is understood. Crucially, it also results in action, itself a kind of translation, as words become works and true understanding of the type described by St Bernard and quoted by Anima comes into play:

> "*Beatus est,*" seith Seint Bernard, "*qui scripturas legit*
> *Et verba vertit in opera* fulliche to his power." (B.XV.60–61)

---

8   M. Foucault, 'The Order of Discourse', in *Untying the Text*, p. 64.

Knowledge is useful only if it is regarded as a means to an end, not an end in itself, otherwise it can become the sort of knowledge that put Adam and Eve out of Eden.

Action has been one of Piers' strengths in the poem – he is essentially a doer, one involved in the society around him, whose knowledge in general, and of St Truth in particular, comes from experience, not theory:

> I have ben his folwere al this fourty wynter –
> Bothe ysowen his seed and suwed hise beestes,
> Withinne and withouten waited his profit,
> Idyked and idolved, ido that he hoteth.   (B.V.542–45)

Just as it is his active experience as one of Truth's followers that means he knows the way to Truth, so the respect he commands from the pilgrims is based, at least in part, on his active involvement with those he guides. His position as both an exceptional man because he is a servant of Truth, and yet one of the commonalty because he is a ploughman, means that he commands the power of knowledge and a degree of *auctoritas* as well as the emotive force of an *exemplum*. The potential he has for affective persuasion based on his standing as a type of Common Man, predisposes an audience in his favour, and this, combined with his role as guide and his apparent ability to understand the pardon and its place without needing to read it, may lead to an inclination to regard Piers as authoritative and to reject the priest as superfluous. Yet Piers' ability to understand, interpret and even operate on the same level as Truth's pardon and recognize that words can be used figuratively as well as part of a contract, has been furnished by the very institution the priest represents. For the Church itself made great use of figurative language as it glossed and interpreted the Bible through the use of allegory in its sermons and treatises (the works of Nicholas of Lyre and Richard of St Victor are cases in point). It would appear that there is no escape from the interpretative power of the Church, no way out of the paradox that in order to acquire enough knowledge to assess whether or not the Church's representatives can be trusted to give correct interpretation and guidance, one must learn the tools of the trade at their hands. Yet Langland does provide a way out of this vicious circle in the shift to the alternative discourse and route to understanding which occurs with Piers' subsequent action.

Piers renames his tools and by doing so divests himself of his initial role of untaught but godly man whose humble knowledge is sufficient to make him both guide and attainable ideal, and becomes instead a privileged user of code systems – that is, one who not only understands but also makes use of other discourses. By quoting Latin texts and citing Scriptural examples Piers shows himself capable of using the same language-system as the priest, but he uses it to free himself from the priest's discourse, which has failed to interpret the pardon and sought to relegate Piers to the ranks of the foolish ignoramus, and define his own signs to create a new code of signification:

> 'I shal cessen of my sowyng,' quod Piers, 'and swynke
> noght so harde,
> Ne aboute my bely joye so bisy be na moore;
> Of preieres and of penaunce my plough shal be herafter,
> And wepen whan I sholde slepe, though whete breed me faille.'
>
> (B.VII.118–121.)

Piers' plough thus becomes purely allegorical; it is to be a mark of the life he embraces hereafter, an external sign of internal qualities rather than an attribute which shows him to be a member of a particular class of society. It is still the symbol of his means of livelihood, but that livelihood is seen now in spiritual rather than corporal terms. So Piers' attributes change from being badges of his social standing to indicators of the type of interpreter he is, showing him to be as well-fitted for a religious life and as capable of reading a religious text as the priest, whose position and function in society rest on skills considered as the province of an elite few only, that is, the ability to translate and interpret.[9]

Yet, Langland does not remove Piers from the realms of the common man – his terminology is still immediate, the language of the 'lewed' not the learned, as 'swynke' and 'bely joye' maintain his identity as an everyman-figure. Furthermore, his choice of parable retains a link with his persona of ploughman as Piers talks about the 'foweles in the feld, who fynt hem mete at wynter?' (B.VII.129). The imagery is still that of agriculture and the production of the basic necessities of life – food. He could have used the lilies of the field and referred to the need for clothing, to convey the same point, but this would have put a distance between him and his previous role and so severed all links with the half-acre which is still the setting for the action of the poem.

Surprising as this act of renaming is, it is not the first that Piers has performed, for when the structure of the half-acre was originally laid down Piers enacted a similar process of redefinition:

> 'And I shal apparaille me,' quod Perkyn, 'in pilgrimes wise,
> And wende with 30w I wil til we fynde Treuthe;
> And caste on me my clothes, yclouted and hole,
> My cokeres and my coffes for cold of my nailles,
> And hange myn hoper at myn hals in stede of a scrippe;
> A busshel of bredcorn brynge me þerinne,

---

[9] For an alternative reading of Piers' actions here see Malcom Godden, 'Plowmen and Hermits in Langland's *Piers Plowman*', *RES*, 35 (1984) pp. 129–63.

For I wil sowe it myself, and sitthenes wil I wende
To pylgrymage as palmers don, pardoun forto haue.

(B.VI.59–66, Bennett)[10]

By explicitly using his hopper instead of a scrip Piers is making the pilgrimage a way of life which is as much involved with the world as his former occupation as a ploughman was. Obviously there are allegorical allusions in the use of bread-corn and sowing, but he is preparing himself for a day's work, not for a journey or standard pilgrimage. The difference is made clearer by the tacit contrast with the appearance of the palmer of the previous passus who with bowl, bag, shells and souvenirs, is also said to be 'apparailled . . . in pilgrymes wise' (B.V.516ff). So in this first instance of definition we have pilgrimage re-defined as a way of life, whereas in the later one, at the end of Passus VII, we have life re-defined as pilgrimage: where the hopper becomes the scrip, the plough becomes prayers and penance.

Crucially this second act of renaming transforms the plough, the object which has given Piers his identity in the poem up to this point. He initially entered the poem as a Plowman, without any other name (B.V.537), and is not called 'Piers' until nineteen lines later (B.V.556) when it is the name given to him by the would-be pilgrims. By renaming the plough Piers thus leaves behind his previous identity as one who labours in the fields, with all the Biblical overtones that entails, and takes up the position of the 'lewed' yet knowledgable representative of the commune with the name that the people gave him. He does not appear as an actual ploughman again in the poem. although he is still referred to as one by being called 'Piers Plowman'. He is now an ideal to be sought but never attained, a fleeting figure whose exact appearance changes according to context and collocation but who nevertheless exerts great affective influence as he is invoked and sought throughout the remainder of the poem. Indeed his power as an emotive authority is so great that Wil swoons at the mere mention of his name in B.XVI.18.

This shift in identity is an important one as it legitimises the use of plural interpretations of the same sign without necessarily undermining or rendering suspect either the signified or the signifier. In other words we do not find ourselves doubting that the Piers figure is a reliable one or having to find justifications for his changing roles and actions when considering his words – which could imply a fallibility and lack of integrity in the figure. Rather Langland reinforces our trust in this figure by ensuring that Piers' integrity is not destroyed by an insistence on one narrow form of interpretation

---

10 The Bennett edition is quoted here (equivalent to Schmidt B.VI.57–64) as it avoids the rather clumsy change of speaker which Schmidt's reconstruction presents. The speech is clearly a complete unit; to divide it betweeen Piers and the dreamer seems unnecessary.

which must be accepted as right. By giving us an assessment of the second vision which is explicitly the dreamer's, rather than an authoritative writer's, and so preventing any particular interpretation being put forward as superior, Langland foregrounds the process of interpretation and reading without forcing us to accept any single set of premisses or conclusions.[11]

Upon waking Wil begins to assess his dream experiences. Before he can embark on the process of analysing them and attempting to draw conclusions he must first decide whether or not to accord status to his dreams, that is whether or not to regard them as discourses embodying Truth and therefore worth interpreting. His first reaction shows an inclination to regard his visions as texts to be interpreted, to be dwelt upon and weighed up, but also to be treated with caution:

> Many tyme this metels hath maked me to studie
> Of that I seigh slepyng – if it so be myghte.   (B.VII.144–45)

But the recollection of the priest's actions brings him to a halt and forces him to examine the notion of dream-interpretation and consider its supporters and detractors, and so to consider his own position as interpreter as well:

> . . . how the priest inpugned it with two propre wordes.
>   Ac I have no savour in songewarie, for I se it ofte faille;
> Caton and canonistres counseillen us to leve
> To sette sadnesse in songewarie – for *sompnia ne cures.*
>   Ac for the book Bible bereth witnesse
> How Daniel divined the dremes of a kyng
> That was Nabugodonosor nempned of clerkes . . .
>   . . .
>   Al this maketh me on metels to thynke –   (B.VII.148–54; 168)

If he follows the advice of Cato and the church authorities he will bear in mind the Latin tag he quotes and place no trust in what he sees while asleep. In which case he would presumably discount Piers' actions as wishful dreaming and return to a blind, if uneasy, trust in the guidance of the ministers of the Church. On the other hand the Bible itself provides

---

11 If Simpson is right in suggesting that Langland is careful to keep within the bounds of ecclesiastical legislation, than this passage could be counted as an example of his caution. Nonetheless the theological and poetic considerations alone, with their desire to avoid one single and apparently trustworthy doctrine seem to be powerful enough to explain the deliberate multiplicity of this passage. See J. Simpson, 'The Constraints of Satire', in *Langland, The Mystics and The Medieval English Religious Tradition*, ed. H. Phillips (Cambridge, 1990), pp. 11–30.

examples of prophetic dreams and, in the case of Nebuchanezzar's dream, even recounts an instance when a seeming nobody correctly interpreted the vision of a member of the ruling class.

Wil returns to his process of weighing up, eventually deciding in favour of Piers' reaction to the pardon, but at the same time making it clear that this decision does not mean that the priest was wholly wrong:

> And so I leve leely (Lord forbede ellis!)
> That pardon and penaunce and preieres doon save
> Soules that have synned seven sithes dedly.
> Ac to trust on thise triennals – trewely, me thynketh,
> It is noght so siker for the soule, certes, as is Dowel.   (B.VII.177–81)

Wil is careful, perhaps over-careful, to state that pardons and commemorative prayers must save souls because the Church says so, 'And so I leve leely (Lord forbede ellis!)'. Yet at the same time he is clearly inclined to trust more fully in Piers' example, which does not rely on such forms and certificates, but instead aims to merit salvation by the life led in this world: 'trewely, me thynketh,/ It is noght so siker for the soule, certes, as is Dowel'.

Here, then, is an instance of plural interpretation: both interpreters of the pardon are admitted to be right to some degree, and although Wil has a preference it is only a preference; it does not require the other reading to be dismissed as wrong. However, the dreamer himself is also an interpreter, even though he appears to be simply assessing the case before him. In fact his act of reading or interpretation is the most radical of them all, since he actually rewrites the terms of the text under consideration. For it is Wil who changes the imperative 'Do well' into a noun 'Dowel' (B.VII.169) and by so doing creates the opportunity of approaching the issue from a different angle. Without this crucial act the quest for Dowel could not take place, or at least not in the form which it takes in this poem. Yet Wil has not misinterpreted the text, not altered it beyond recognition, but he has read it in a very different way, which is another kind of translation.

So the pardon scene and Wil's subsequent recollection of it results in an increased awareness of the signifying processes and also with a sense of freedom to interpret the same signs in totally differently ways, according to the approach adopted by the interpreter. A plough may be an essential agricultural tool, a metonym for the socio-religious implications of the themes of ploughing and pilgrimage which have gone before, but it may also be an implement of prayer, and so become a sign of its wielder's faith and understanding, manifested in action, rather than in words alone. Equally, the terms used in a text may be read and interpreted in vitally different ways without rendering the whole nonsensical, or querying its original integrity. In each case the change is a shift of angle rather than a total destruction of the text. By the simple but radical action of re-naming, Piers frees himself from being bound and defined by his external attributes and instead defines them. In the same way Wil's rewriting of his dream changes his relationship to it and so enables him to explore it more fully.

17

Dixit Insipiens

Disconcerting as this process of exploration is, it has not been sprung upon the readers unawares. The priest's suggestion of a theme that Piers could elaborate were he to preach, and indeed the very notion that Piers could be a priest himself, however sarcastically intended – 'Were thow a preest, Piers' – prepare the way for an overturn of the status quo. *Dixit insipiens* – the unwise, the fool spoke. Yet in any society the voice of the fool is necessarily beyond the circle of 'normal' discourse – hence its madness, its folly, and hence also its privileged position. For fools, like seers, may be regarded as having some kind of direct communication with the divine. They are under the protection of a benign divinity whose children they are, and as such are removed from the normal sphere of human experience and understanding. Furthermore, the fool's detached position could be seen as similar to the distance required for those who wish to pronounce judgments on society as a whole. So the fool can be regarded, paradoxically, as being in the same position as Reson in the Prologue, or as Wil on the mountain of Middelerthe; in each case the detached stance allows for a panoramic view of society.

The first appearance of an actual fool in *Piers Plowman* exploits this strange possibility of having a fool give a penetrating opinion of the society whose margins he inhabits. This fool is the lunatic who addresses the King in the B-Text prologue:

> Thanne loked up a lunatik, a leene thyng withalle,
> And knelynge to the Kyng clergially he seide,
> 'Crist kepe thee, sire Kyng, and thi kynryche,
> And lene thee lede thi lond so leaute thee lovye,
> And for thi rightful rulyng be rewarded in hevene!'
>
> (B. Prologue 123–27)

Langland immediately presents the picture of a lunatic speaking with learning, 'clergially', which Margaret Goldsmith calls 'the paradox that we may hear wisdom from a fool [which] is at the heart of the poem'.[1] This paradox is a familiar one exploited by, amongst others, Augustine, and before him by St Paul (in 1 Cor. 1:25), to emphasize the infinity of God's wisdom by comparing divine folly with mortal wisdom to the detriment of the latter. In *De Doctrina Christiana* Augustine cites St Paul in showing how this inversion works in terms of the movement between God and man:

> Sed quia nos, cum ad illam uenimus, sapienter facimus, ipsa, cum ad nos uenit, ab hominibus superbis quasi stulte fecisse putata est. Et quoniam nos cum ad illam uenimus, conualecscimus, ipsa, cum ad nos uenit, quasi inferma existimata est. Sed quod stultum est dei, sapientius est hominibus, et quod infirmam est dei, fortius est hominibus.
>
> (Since we do wisely when we come to Him, he was thought by proud men to do foolishly when He came to us. And since when we come to Him we grow strong, he was thought to be weak when He came to us. But 'the foolishness of God is wiser than men; and the weakness of God is stronger than men.')[2]

Here wisdom is still preferred to foolishness, but the wisdom of God is so great that even His folly is wiser than the wisdom that mankind can achieve. It is a comparison of degree which does not actually challenge the assumption that wisdom is better than folly. However St Paul does challenge this supposition in 1 Corinthians 3:18–19 where he revises the defining characteristics of wisdom and folly so that apparent folly becomes actual wisdom and so the desired state:

> Let no one deceive himself. If any one among you thinks that he is wise in this age, let him become a fool that he may become wise. For the wisdom of this world is folly with God.

Not only is the wisdom of his world folly with God, but the state termed folly by the world is to be preferred. The use of the relation of the binary opposition wisdom/folly has gone beyond comparison and seeks to redefine the terms of the opposition itself.

In different ways and to different extents these writers are reversing the norm, deliberately using the fool, the mad, to define what they wish to regard as the preferred discourse. Yet this is not a collapsing of the binary system of difference which requires that the 'mad' be defined and placed outside the 'normal' in order for the normal to have an identity; rather it is a direct inversion which allows the system, the technique of definition through opposition, to remain the same, while the terms are simply reversed. The basic premises are not challenged – knowledge and wisdom

---

1 M. Goldsmith, 'Wil's Pilgrimage in *Piers Plowman* B', in *Medieval Literature and Antiquities: Studies in Honour of Basil Cottle*, ed. M. Stokes and T.L. Burton (Woodbridge, 1987), p. 119.
2 Augustine, *De Doctrina Christiana*, I.xi.11, *CCSL*, 32, p. 12; tr. p. 13.

are still desired and, once achieved, bestow strength in the form of power and a place in the privileged society. It is simply that what was previously regarded as folly is now regarded as wisdom.

St Paul and Augustine can only propose such an inversion because they have an alternative system within which to operate, whose structure is a mirror image of the system they are re-working. It is a part of both systems that fools and madmen are the opposites of learned and wise men; that lunatics are not kings but yet co-exist with them, and in fact are necessary to the court and sane society in general, as the notion of wisdom cannot exist without the idea of folly. As wisdom is the absence of folly, it becomes impossible to describe wisdom without having some notion of folly to act as an opposite. Therefore, if one removes the concept of madness it becomes impossible to define wisdom. This mutual dependence of the sane and the mad is articulated in the morality play *Mundus et Infans*:

> For folly is fellow with the world
> And if you put me out of your world
> Your World right wrath will be.[3]

Folly is not only fellow with the world but also necessary to it.

In the Prologue the lunatic's presence at the King's investiture is not challenged, implying that he is an accepted member of society and even of the court, too, since he is permitted to address the King directly whereas the commune have to have someone else to speak for them (in this case the angel). The lunatic's prayer (B.Prol.125–27) is a serious one and it is only we, the readers, the outsiders, who are disturbed by the fact that it is a lunatic who speaks. The words embody rational sense and yet are being spoken by a madman: at once the suspicion of irony enters – could it be that only a madman would really believe that the fulfillment of this prayer is possible? If so, then by admitting the rationality of his speech we are in danger of putting ourselves in his position – we, too, become mad. It is only the tradition of the fool being wise in the eyes of God which saves us from this fate and which allows us to accept the possibility of a lunatic uttering perceptive and pertinent comments, in other words speaking 'clergially' (B.Prol.124). It is this tradition too, which allows us to accept the notion of a learned ploughman as socially representative.[4] In each case we are tacitly acknowledging the need for some system which will allow that the ignorant

---

3 'Mundus et Infans', lines 619–21, *Three Late Medieval Morality Plays*, ed. G.A. Lester (London, 1981), p. 141.
4 See Kathryn Kerby-Fulton, 'The Voice of Honest Indignation: A Study of Reformist Apoclyptism in Relation to *Piers Plowman*' (D.Phil. York, 1985), pp. 68–69 and M. Bloomfield, *'Piers Plowman' as a Fourteenth-Century Apocalypse* (New Brunswicks, 1961), p. 27, who both discuss the linked topoi of the ignorant but blessed rustic and the mad in relation to the figure of Piers.

and the half-witted must be able to achieve salvation. It is this which Wil cites in his defence in Passus X:

> The doughtieste doctour and devinour of the Trinitee,
> Was Austyn the olde, and heighest of the foure,
> Seide thus in a sermon – I seigh it writen ones –
> *"Ecce ipsi idiote rapiunt celum ubi nos sapientes in inferno mergimur"* –
> And is to mene to Englissh men, moore ne lesse,
> Arn none rather yravysshed fro the righte bileve
> Than are thise konnynge clerkes that konne manye bokes,
> Ne none sonner saved, ne sadder of bileve
> Than plowmen and pastours and povere commune laborers,
> Souteres and shepherdes – swiche lewed juttes
> Percen with a Paternoster the paleys of hevene
> And passen purgatorie penauncelees at hir hennes partyng
> Into the blisse of paradis for his pure bileve,
> That inparfitly here knewe and ek lyvede. (B.X.450–60)

Here, Wil is asserting the claim that simple ignorant souls win a place in heaven because of their very simplicity, whereas those who are more educated have more opportunity to go astray, with less excuse. Yet, although the opposition set up here appears to be that of educated clerk/ignorant layman, it is significant that the word 'yravysshed', with its affective connotations, is used to describe the way the intelligentsia could be drawn away from their proper belief. There is a suggestion that the oppositions need not be so rigid as they appear; but this is only a suggestion, for clearly this passage is based on the assumption that the language of the fool and the unlearned will differ from that of the learned and wise.

Reflecting this presumed opposition, the lunatic of the Prologue is answered, not by the King whom he addresses, but by the angel who 'lowed to speke in Latyn' (B.Prol.129). This angel is removed from the immediate society he addresses just as the lunatic is, and furthermore he speaks for the very section of that society which is incapable of understanding him – the 'lewed men [who] ne koude/ Jangle ne jugge that justifie hem sholde' (129–30). The angel's words echo the lunatic's; they both present maxims of how a king ought to behave if he is to be a responsible and benign ruler. The ignorant, however, cannot understand what is said on their behalf, so their attempt to use the discourse of the angel by chanting the Latin tag 'Precepta Regis sunt nobis vincula legis!' (B.Prol.145) results in revealing their vulnerability rather than including them in the discourse which the angel uses. This results in an affirmation of the system which accords knowledge power, a point which A.V.C. Schmidt explains:

> The irony of their own utterance of a "vers of Latyn" affirming implicit obedience to royal edict (Pr.143, 145) is thus pointed up by the parenthesis "construe whoso wolde" (Pr.144) with its dual implication that the lewed

cannot interpret the maxims they mouth and therefore become vulnerable to the "will" of those who can: ignorance is weakness because knowledge is power.[5]

It does not matter whether it is the learning of the clerics or the understanding of the 'lewed' which is regarded as knowledge; knowledge itself will always be aligned with power and authority, and the alternative looked upon as an opposite and regarded as weakness.

It is indicative of the force of the prevailing system that the only figure who is able to move between both discourses is the goliard. This strange figure suddenly appears in the poem; he is a combination of rogue, travelling minstrel and educated man, and as such occupies a middle ground between the Latin-speaking angel and the inarticulate commune. The fact that as a goliard he is necessarily a wanderer places him on the margins of society, and so he is not part of the defining norm; yet he is not quite an outsider either, for he belongs to and operates within the same type of reality as the King and his court. This marginal position means he occupies a mid-point between the mainstream of society and its concepts of normality and reality, and the lunatic whose insanity removes from the accepted norms and indicates that he operates within a different concept of reality, or perhaps even without any notion of reality at all. In a similar way the goliard is both linked to and separate from the commune, for he wields no actual power within society, but unlike the people, he is educated and can use the discourse of the privileged classes with understanding. Bronistav Geremet provides evidence that the term 'goliard' was often used to refer to the 'many common robbers [who] came from the ranks of the tonsured' even if they had long since ceased to work as clerics.[6] This can only add further layers of ambiguity to this figure whose social position links him with the ignorant, while his language connects him with the learned, who have the power to define words and meanings. This latter ability is demonstrated by his speech in which he re-inforces the need for learning by asserting the etymological link of *rex* with *regere*: if the linguistic connection is abused so is the position of ruler, which becomes a mere hollowness – a *nomen sine re*.

The truth of the goliard's speech cannot be denied – it has been illustrated in the Prologue in the case of the King and his advisers, and reappears throughout the poem, particularly in the scene of the half-acre. Langland consistently castigates those who do not fulfil the obligations of their position, especially false beggars and charlatans – these are wastrels, whether of material or intellectual resources. Yet the goliard himself

---

5 Schmidt, *Clerkly Maker*, p. 81.
6 Bronistav Geremet, *The Margins of Society in Late Medieval Paris*, tr. J. Birrell (Cambridge, 1987), pp. 141–43.

becomes a suspect figure: as a 'gloton of wordes' he is tacitly accused of loving words more than sense, itself a form of *nomen sine re*. As Proverbs says:

> A fool takes no pleasure in understanding, but only in expressing his opinion. (Proverbs 18:2)

Furthermore he undeniably falls into the category summarily dismissed in lines 35–39 of the Prologue:

> Ac japeres and jangeleres, Judas children,
> Feynen hem fantasies, and fooles hem maketh –
> And han wit at wille to werken if they wolde,
> That Poule preceth of hem I wool nat preve it here:
> *Qui loquitur turpiloquium* is Luciferes hyne.

So the goliard must be accepted as part of society but he must also be treated warily as he is potentially, if not actually, a disruptive element and so cannot to be regarded as a reliable representative of the general mass. His ability to manage words and discourses, to move between them and combine them, correlates with this ambiguous position of being recognised as being part of society and yet having no fixed position or status in it. He is, in every sense, unstable. Thus although the goliard's learning and competence in Latin enable him to speak the same language as the angel, it is in fact the lunatic, who has no such learning, who articulates the angel's meaning. The lunatic's words show that his understanding of how a king ought to act is close to the view expressed in the angel's verse. That is, that a king has a duty to rule righteously, without letting the power of his position corrupt him or prevent him from mitigating the laws with mercy. In other words the ruler must be worthy of his position; it is not enough, despite what the goliard says, to act only as an enforcer of laws.

The contrast between the unreasoned comprehension of the ignorant lunatic and the clever, analytical definition put forward by the learned goliard is similiar to the contrast between the affective and deductive discourses. Each is offering an interpretation of the angel's speech which, like the *logos*, is incomprehensible to the 'lewed' mass and so must be translated for them in some way. Of the two speakers available, the goliard seems to be the best qualified to act as a mediator and translator for the commune, but his connection with the janglers and the suggestion that he could be counted as one of 'Judas Children' disqualifies him. So, in the end, it is the understanding and language of the lunatic which is preferred to the unreliable and uneasy combination of discourses seen in the goliard.

However if the alternative system of discourse represented by the lunatic is to be adopted, the defining limits of mad and normal must be abandoned and the speech of the mad must become the words of the sane. Furthermore, the logical links of language must be left behind, since despite the fact that *rex* is linked to *regere* the best king is not one who rules strictly according to the rules of justice alone – mercy must be allowed to temper justice and grace must be given space to operate. This need for ameliorating factors in any process which involves decision-making has already been discussed in relation to the Four Daughters of God, but it is more clearly demonstrated in the trial of Mede where Reson and Conscience act as mutually mitigating factors in the judgement of the case. Yet even at this early point in the poem the system of definition, upon which the goliard's discourse is based, is undermined as the whole framework of the society of the 'feld ful of folk' fragments. The very system of signification is rendered unreliable as etymological links are left behind, and madmen speak a language more understandable than that of either angels or minstrels.

It is at this point of apparent collapse that Langland abandons the allegorical system that has dominated so far by suddenly introducing the rat parliament. It is as if the only refuge available to the poem is to shift abruptly into another sphere and a different image, relying on the continued use of the theme of government to sustain some form of coherence. Yet, although this sudden appearance of a clearly political allegory seems to rescue the poem from the immanent breakdown of fragmenting language and meaning by asserting that representation is possible and can be understood and interpreted reliably, the rat fable has more than simply the theme of government in common with the preceeding allegory. For the point of the fable is that there must be some form of authority, or defining body, in order for any society to exist without being destroyed by its components. Were it not for the cat, the rats and mice would wreak havoc, even to the extent of destroying the society which provides their habitat. For the rats are governable only because there is an external controlling force; without it they would be incapable of ruling themselves. Or such is the case as presented by the mouse, who, according to Wil, speaks sense.

It is certainly true that the mouse's reasoning seems faultless, but its aim is perhaps dubious. For this mouse is not only advocating that the cat should be free because without it there would be chaos, but also because with the system as it is, everyone knows how it works and can survive within it, albeit at others' cost. The mice and the rats can exploit this system they can live in the unremarked corners, just as the goliard can make a living by exploiting the boundaries of his system. Corruption of society and language is possible and also can be profitable. In such a society the wise man is the one who can survive – 'wit wel his owene' (B.Prol.209).

So the mouse's native wit could be seen to be a form of low cunning and once again Langland demonstrates that any system which is allowed to operate unchallenged can be corrupted even by the very elements it seeks to control. The ones who suffer most are the majority of innocent people who do not know or cannot understand what is going on and have no power to affect the situation either way. These people are caught between the en-forcers of the system and the corrupters: the humans of the rat fable.

Langland returns to the theme of powerlessness in the face of confusion by refusing to offer an interpretation of this part of the dream and indeed making it clear that any interpretation is beyond Wil's capabilities. As with the commune when faced with the angel's Latin, any system runs the risk of incomprehensibility if there is no common ground between the two halves of an opposition. At this point in the poem Langland does not offer any obvious hope of resolution. Instead he embarks on an investigation of the way authority in society works by presenting the visions of Mede's mar-riage and trial, and of Piers and his half acre. It is only at the end of Passus VII that there is a comparable challenge to its whole system of meaning, where again a shift occurs as the whole system of signification seems to be about to collapse.

The pardon and its text resurrect the issue of interpretation and authority and who has the right or the capability to define language and knowledge. Once again the oppositions are those of knowledge/ignorance, power/ weakness, but this time the result of breaking down the oppositions is fundamentally different, for the priest's choice of theme for Piers has the opposite effect from that he intended. Far from leaving Piers outside the establishment by labelling him as a fool, unqualified to speak, it actually awards him a privileged position within it. He is one of the 'lewed' who merit salvation by their virtuous life, and yet he is also able to speak Latin, the language of the Pardon and the angel. The priest's final gibe of implying he is a fool by suggesting he is well qualified to use the text 'the fool said' becomes ironic. It serves to place Piers in the position of the lunatic, and to allot him the language of the mad, which is what the priest intended but, contrary to his aim, this identification is complimentary to Piers, since the episode of the lunatic and the goliard has shown this position to be one of insight and his discourse to be the one which was preferred. For in rejecting the prevailing system of oppositions and moving to turn away from the type of knowledge represented by the priest, Piers becomes a personifica-tion of the combination of learning and understanding as he puts the par-don's words into action. Yet, crucially, his reformation is a self-reformation, for if both sides of the oppositional system are brought together there is no need for an external force. In effect Piers removes himself from the debate by incorporating both sides of it. This is made evident by the fact that he disappears from the poem at this point and does not reappear until the banquet scene, when he is not one of the disputants, but a representation of the right combination of learning and understanding; the embodiment of an alternative.

So, at the end of Passus VII, Piers' discourse is awarded the position of the fool/mad – the Other – which must exist in order for the Self to define itself, to create and maintain an identity. Yet in this case the fool, the ignorant ploughman, the Other, speaks the language of the Self, the Normal, and furthermore is understood and seen to be right, thus ousting the previous upholder of the normative, defining discourse and interpretation, the priest, and so forcing the circle of interpretation to be re-drawn. This fool speaks reason and, unlike the lunatic of the Prologue, does so from a position of power, for he has been governing and defining the society of the half-acre and he was the one to whom Truth sent the Pardon. Hence the priest's attempt to call Piers a fool backfires; it collapses the oppositions of fool/wise man, reason/madness that he wishes to operate, and so his structure of evaluation and definition of what constitutes knowledge must collapse too. For falsehood can no longer be equated with fool and truth no longer with wise man, or reason, which is the element in the opposition the priest considers he represents. Piers' actions of rejection and re-definition thus form part of the general process that has already begun; discourse itself is redefined as the pilgrimage to Truth becomes unnecessary in the terms originally proposed and the debate moves temporarily from the realms of verbal language into those of visual signs.

In allegorical writing the attributes connected with a figure are an essential part of the reading process since these visual signs act as keys to possible interpretations. The presentation of a character or figure guides our reactions to them. Holi Church is simply dressed, Mede richly; the palmer is decked with shells, carries a staff and other external signs of pilgrimage 'for men sholde knowe/ And se bi hise signes whom he sought hadde.' (B.V.523–524). Of all the various forms of language, allegory and iconography in particular rely upon the agreed use of such signs. They allow us to distinguish prophets from apostles and apostles from each other; they provide identity and limits of interpretation. When these tacit but agreed codes are broken the associations usually connected with specific attributes or figures must be abandoned as being no longer applicable. This can result simply in irony or satire – palmers in general become objects of suspicion, priests and friars regarded with caution – or it can disrupt the whole signifying process and require a shift in register. So it is that Piers' act of redefinition not only brings this particular vision to an end, but also throws open and fractures the closed system of signification which has been dominant (but not exclusive, as the fleeting appearance of the lunatic has shown) till now. Necessarily by so doing he also fragments his own identity – 'The subject unravells himself in the tissue of the text' – and so, in effect, the original Piers disappears. In order to even begin to fulfil his potential Piers must fragment or deconstruct and break down his identity into a plurality of possible identities. The same may be said of the language or poetic discourse of the poem itself. The search for the one transcendent signifier (Truth) in a fixed and readily defined form (the tower or shrine) is abandoned and instead a process of exploration is begun which investigates the way one's notion of what knowledge is, or ought to be, affects not only one's language but also the way one seeks to acquire such knowledge. This process of investigation demands re-assessment, re-definition and finally the abandonment of the term which at first is taken as the signpost or indicator of the way – Dowel.

A reading along the lines described above may seem to make *Piers Plowman* into a fundamently nihilistic text in which all terms are undermined, the processes of assessment, learning, preaching and reasoning are destroyed, and even the concept of knowledge itself is queried. Yet if a pluralistic approach of the kind taken here seems to deny any status to the text by opening it to many interpretations and so refusing it one authoritative reading, is not the opposite method open to the criticism of needlessly limiting the text? For *Piers Plowman* shows how the search for a definitive reading or meaning must be restrictive as it imposes upon the quest, the text, a fixed idea of what such a definitive interpretation must be like, and by so doing it curtails the interaction between dialogues, the play, within the text and denies the possibility of the co-existence of other equally correct meanings and interpretations. Some kind of synthesis is needed.

Paradoxically this is provided precisely by the acknowledged existence of a transcendental signifier, since this relieves the need or the call for a definition of such an ultimate 'truth' silently supporting or lying within the text, and allows the attention to shift to the text itself. The fundamental security a belief in such an ultimate provides is described by Foucault in 'The Order of Discourse':

> . . . in a philosophy of the founding subject, in a philosophy of originary experience, and in a philosophy of universal mediation alike, discourse is no more than a play, of writing in the first case, of reading in the second, and of exchange in the third, and this exchange, this reading, this writing never put anything at risk except signs.[7]

The 'founding subject' in a Christian text is the *logos* which provides the assurance of the existence of a final meaning, an ultimate Truth. The text and its audience are thus relieved from trying to discover or define this Truth. Any quest within the text is therefore a search for, or exploration of, the possible ways of expressing this Truth; the status of that Truth itself is not questioned. This means that the focus shifts from wishing to discover the underlying meaning to studying the fabric or tissue of the text. It is, therefore, only the signs, the modes of expression, which are under scrutiny or put at risk, not the meaning of the text itself. Moreover, when it is, deemed impossible to express that underlying truth in its entirety in human language (as is the case with the divine Word), it is clearly restrictive to limit

---

7 Foucault, 'The Order of Discourse', p. 66.

the approaches to interpretation, since plurality reflects the many ways the Word can express itself and be expressed. Hence the greater the number of readings the nearer one comes to an appreciation of the transcendent whole.

So it is in the play that the interest lies: it is this which is explored and exploited as the process of writing, reading and interaction or exchange are seen to operate. And Langland's text is surely one of the best to use as a locus for this type of exploration, since he offers in Wil a figure of this very process at work – the reader who is both interpreter and an integral part of the text, being character, personification and interpreting force. Further- more the text itself includes and takes its life from constant shifts and changes in mode, style, and even language. Even the personifications and figures do not necessarily retain their original signification, as a character who previously seemed to be a simple figure is gradually revealed to be far more complex than originally suspected – Mede, Haukyn and Piers himself being excellent examples of this process. In the case of Mede the shift is from a straightforward presentation of corrupting lucre to a necessity of any earthly society, which is open and even liable to abuse. Mede is certainly not an unbiased source, but what she says is pragmatically true:

> Beggeres for hir biddynge bidden men mede.
> Mynstrales for hir myrthe mede thei aske.
> The Kyng hath mede of his men to make pees in londe.
> Men that kenne clerkes craven of hem mede.
> Preestes that prechen the peple to goode
> Asken mede and massepens amd hire mete also.
> Alle kyn crafty men craven mede for hir prentices.
> Marchaundise and mede mote nede go togideres:
> No wight, as I wene, withouten Mede may libbe! (B.III.219–227)

Conscience heavily modifies this presentation of the central role of money and worldly goods to remind his audience that although such things may be necessary in context, any undue attachment to them constitutes the love which is the root of all evil. However, he does not deny that money in some form is a requirement of a sophisticated society; just reward is one thing, simple profit another:

> Ther are two manere of medes, my lord, by youre leve.
> That oon God of his grace graunteth in his blisse
> To tho that wel werchen while thei ben here.
> . . .
> 'Ther is another mede mesurelees, that maistres desireth:
> To mayntene mysdoers mede thei take. (B.III.230–233; 246–247)

Mede to some extent represents both these kinds of meed; the use of such a complex figure allows Langland to acknowledge the necessity for some kind of meed, but yet show that the likelihood is that the corrupt form will dominate.

The demonstration of this type of play is possible precisely because the final meaning of the text is never in doubt and indeed is provided by another supreme text or Word – *logos*. This brings problems of its own as writers and readers engage with the recurrent difficulties raised by the approximate nature of language and concomitant problems of expressing anything, least of all the Divine, truthfully and completely. The preferred stance must be that offered by Augustine:

> . . . qui nostram istam rationem libefactet dicendo apostolis non uerborum, sed rerum auctoritatem esse tribuendam.
>
> (we must attribute to the Apostle authority in the matter of realities, but not in the use of words.)[8]

The point is that by according the Apostle's meaning (*sententia*) authority we are liberated from having to retain his exact words. There is also the admission that words are not 'realities', but merely ways of articulating them. As such one particular way may be preferred to another, but there is no need for the words to remain the same. Meaning is not contained in the words but only indicated by them:

> Hacentus uerba ualuerunt, quibus ut plurimum tribuam, admonent tantum, ut quaeramus res, non exhibent, ut norimus.
>
> (The utmost value I can attribute to words is this. They bid us look for things, but they do not show them to us so that we may know them.)[9]

This notion is surely very similar to Barthes' text with its 'more or less hidden meaning (truth)'. It is indicative of a belief in the possibility of a definitive interpretation, and an admission that such an interpretation is a practical impossibility in this world: hence the impulse to look further than the words themselves and regard them as signs not as ends. And from this we move on to the process of definition itself by which many definitions may be given, all be correct and yet not all be the same. This is exactly the process that Langland presents in *Piers Plowman* and particularly in Passus VIII–XIV. Wil is given several definitions of Dowel, Dobet and Dobest, each different, although some may be related, and each correct. Yet all are limited and any of these taken in isolation may lead to error and is certainly unsatisfactory. This deductive approach to knowledge, this definition of what knowing is, must be replaced with a desire to understand the processes of knowing if we are to escape the limited circle of thought they describe.

As so often in *Piers Plowman* we are directed towards a scrutiny of

8 Augustine, *De Magistro*, V.15, *CCSL*, 29, p. 173; tr. Burleigh, p. 80.
9 Augustine, *De Magistro*, XI.36, *CCSL*, 29, p. 194; tr. Burleigh, p. 94.

language, to understand or at least explore its operations and learn from that how it may be possible to go beyond its limitations and achieve some kind of apprehension of the arch-signifier. This undermines any idea of language as static and reliable and replaces it with the recognition of its fundamental ambiguity. However, vitally, it also renders this ambiguity fruitful rather than threatening. The danger lies in taking words too literally and so regarding an ability to speak as an indication of having knowledge, authority and power. To recall Schmidt's phrase, 'ignorance is weakness *because* knowledge is power' (my emphasis); if power and knowledge are no longer regarded as synonymous, if the expected appearance and trappings of knowledge are re-examined and inverted, or if knowledge itself is redefined and the set of oppositions that regard knowledge and power as linked is collapsed, then ignorance can become strength and the ability to speak well need no longer be an indication of authority. As Augustine so appositely said,

> Sunt sane quidam, qui bene pronuntiare possunt, quid autem pronuntient, excogitare non possunt.
> (There are some who can speak well but who cannot think of anything to say.)[10]

The difficulty comes in working out if one is being convinced by the medium or the message.

The power of language need not be negative, the devices used to fragment language and so pass beyond the limitations of any single medium may themselves become ways of displaying the possibilities of language to suggest and even create for the reader the notion of some entity beyond the reaches of simple linguistic expression. The descriptions of the affective discourse demonstrated how the mystic writers, particularly the *Cloud* author and Meister Eckhart, exploit the affective powers of language as they seek to give their readers some intimation of the apprehension of God which defies precise description by using connotative words and images. Similar effects can be achieved through word-play and puns, as these demand that the reader and user acknowledge other possible readings and meanings of the words apart from the most obvious and so stretch language to its limits. This process is the one to which Morton Bloomfield refers when he is describing Langland's 'remarkable sense of the power of language':

> Thought, serious thought, must always struggle against its medium, words. In using several different languages or in writing acrostics, a poet is indicating his desire to pass beyond the limitations of his medium and

---

[10] Augustine, *De Doctrina Christiana*, IV.xxix. 62, *CCSL*, 32, p. 165; tr. Burleigh, p. 166.

at the same time indicating his belief, possibly subconscious, in the magic power, in a literal sense, of language.[11]

In *Piers Plowman* the desire and belief are linked as the endeavour to express in some way an approach to the *logos* must combine a desire to surpass the limits of the discourse of the *verbum* in order to communicate a notion of the creative power of the original Word.

Langland's use of different languages has been discussed in the context of the angel's words to the commune and of Piers' Latin at the end of Passus VII. In each case its introduction has been an indication of privileged communication with the transcendent and also proof of the speaker's qualification to speak. These uses of Latin and its translation remind us that translation is a process of interpretation which not only transmits sentences into another language or discourse but also invests them with an exalted position. For the very fact that something is considered worth translating indicates that it is regarded as important; hence the very act of translation invests the text being translated with a certain aura of authority:

> While content and language form a certain unity in the original, like a fruit and its skin, the language of the translation envelopes its content like a royal robe with ample folds. For it signifies a more exalted language than its own and thus remains unsuited to its content, overpowering and alien.[12]

A translation, then, both exalts and restricts its original. For in order to translate a piece one must interpret it and by dressing it in the 'ample folds' of a new language (or even by re-phrasing it in a different register of the same tongue) one is diverting attention from the content of the piece to its form. This makes the audience vulnerable to the danger of attributing authority to the medium rather than to the content. This can result in the translator's interpretation being regarded as the definitive reading and to the translation being treated as the original, which may in turn lead to later readers starting from a position of restricted, or possibly even wrong, understanding. Furthermore, if we agree that in effect all language is translation, since it is an approximation of meaning, then we are once again put on our guard against taking any one reading as the 'true' meaning.

It is vital to remember that texts and even short phrases and single words can be used and interpreted in widely different ways. Wil's misreading of Holi Chirche's use of 'tresor' is an example of how restricting it can be to assume that a word is always used in the same way by the same person. Words are not natural entities, they do not have an unchanging, unchangeable

11 Bloomfield, p. 37.
12 Walter Benjamin, 'The Task of the Translator', in *Illuminations*, ed. H. Arendt, tr. H. Zohn (London, 1973), p. 75.

essence, for they are always subject to changes in the human contract which is language. This impossibility of pure language, even for poetic use, is recognised and pin-pointed by Paul de Man in *The Rhetoric of Romanticism*:

> There can be flowers that 'are' and poetic words that 'originate', but no poetic words that 'originate' as if they 'were'.[13]

The pure, transparent language of the *logos* is beyond mortal reach and so to act as if any one locution was free from preceding influence and ambiguity is at best foolhardy, at worst a culpable error. It is by acting on the assumption that the influence of context is irrelevant that Mede is able to defend her actions with a Biblical quotation and it is the incompleteness of her reading that Conscience decries:

> Se what Salomon seith in Sapience bokes:
> That thei that yyven yiftes the victorie wynneth,
> And muche worshipe have therwith, as Holy Writ telleth –
> *Honorem adquiret qui dat munera, &c.*
> . . .
> This text that ye han told were tidy for lordes,
> Ac yow failed a konnynge clerk that kouthe the leef han torned.
> And if ye seche Sapience eft, fynde shul ye that foweth,
> A ful teneful text to hem that taketh mede:
> And that is *Animam autem aufert accipientium &c.*
> And that is the tail of the text of that tale ye shewed –
> That theigh we wynne worshipe and with mede have victorie,
> The soule that the soude taketh by so muche is bounde.
>
> (B.III.332–45)

It does not actually matter that any quotation or rendering of a text is incomplete as long as one acknowledges that this must be the case. It is when the fundamentally incomplete nature of any text is ignored that mistaken or misplaced trust in an *auctoritas* can occur.

A writer can try to prevent such misunderstanding by foregrounding the ambiguity of language and making the reader more aware of the responsibility of reading. This can be effected in several ways and the pun is one of them. For punning and word-play work by using the possibility of plural meanings and force the reader to hold the various interpretations in mind simultaneously without giving precedence to any one in particular. So it is that by recalling the Eucharist Langland is able to make the wafer that Pacience offers Haukyn both the bread, by which man does not live alone, and the Word, by which he does. This cannot solve anything, if by solve we

---

13 Paul de Man, *The Rhetoric of Romanticism* (New York, 1984), p. 7.

mean arrive at a single, unassailable and clear-cut truth, as this trick of language brings together the roles of Christ as Man and as Word but it does not make it any easier to express the *logos*. Yet, as Augustine indicates, this inability is itself appropriate, since it is a fundamental paradox that Christ is both eminently approachable and ultimately unattainable:

> In quantum enim homo, in tantum mediator, in quantum autem uerbum, non medius, quia aequalis deo et deus apud deus et simul unus deus.
>
> (For as a man, he [Jesus] is our Mediator; but as the Word of God, he is not an intermediary between God and man because he is equal with God, and God with God, and together with him one God.)[14]

By bringing us up against the limitation of language we are led to acknowledge both the existence of those limitations and the possibility of something beyond them that cannot be expressed.

So we are returned to the crux of the issue, the difficulty, the impossibility of expressing *logos*, and indeed the impossibility of pure language in any post-lapsarian circumstances. Our only hope must be to abandon the desire for a final authoritative and definitive reading and embrace the possibilities of plurality. One must acknowledge the 'very possibility of change' which Cixous has described as writing itself[15] and so re-interpret what Josipovici calls

> the tension that exists in each writer between the awareness of possibility and the necessity of choice, and which is resolved in the exploration, through art itself, of the dialectic between langue and parole, desire and reality.[16]

This is precisely what happens in *Piers Plowman*. In a single text Langland explores the possibilities of arriving at understanding through deduction, analysis, allegory and emotive language, and also queries the necessity of choice, of implying that one course is better than another, of justifying choice when it is made. The poem is an articulation of Josipovici's 'tension' which is further complicated by the pull towards authority, the desire for sure guidance and definitive readings – the medieval concern for support for what is said. So Langland not only strives to retain the *parole* (or *verbum*) of personal experience within the authoritative *langue* of the Church (the *logos*), but he also moves between different registers of *logos* and *verbum*, and, in an attempt to create and so reveal the tensions surrounding choice,

---

14 Augustine, *Confessiones*, X.xliii.68, *CCSL*, 32, p. 192; tr. R.S. Pine-Coffin, *Saint Augustine: Confessions* (Harmondsworth, 1961), p. 251.

15 Hélène Cixous, 'Le Rire de la Méduse', tr. K. Cohen and P. Cohen, 'The Laugh of the Medusa', in *New French Feminism*, ed. E. Marks and I. de Courtivron (Brighton, 1980), p. 254.

16 G. Josipovici, *The World and the Book* (London, 1979), p. 293.

includes reality as well as desire. Reality seems to demand that a choice be made in mode of expression in order to make communication possible, but desire reminds us constantly of other possible meanings and ways of communicating, and longs to include all those possibilities. In *Pearl* we see how resolution of the tension between the desire and reality may be achieved by giving one discourse precedence over another, in this case the *langue* of Church doctrine as presented by the Pearl-maiden suppresses the *parole* of the Jeweller as he is made to re-interpret his experience and renounce his discourse in an attempt to understand and achieve hers. But Langland rejects such a solution and shows by his constant revision, the cyclical format and the constant undermining and questioning of the figures and discourses within the poem, that it is a defeat of writing, not a victory, when the tension is denied. If any approach to wholeness and integrity is to be made by a text, that tension must be allowed to exist, and with it the constant flux and change of signification and meaning it entails.

The end result for Wil and for the audience of *Piers Plowman* must be a re-assessment of what reading and interpretation involve. It has become a cyclical process whose meaning is precisely that process, that movement, not a progression towards, or attempt to achieve, a static goal. Just as the pilgrimage for St Truth is changed into an attempt to live according to the Christian precepts so the type of reading which seeks a final, undisputed end – a definition of Dowel – is abandoned and the poem returns to the quest. The search continues, but with a wider notion of what seeking itself involves. This is reading as Paul de Man defines it:

> to read is to understand, to question, to know, to forget, to erase, to deface, to repeat . . .[17]

Langland leads us to understand the processes of reading by presenting us with a text which constantly undermines itself and yet adopts that very undermining as one of its strengths. We are shown in Wil how the act of questioning can be more fruitful than the act of defining and so we come to recognise that knowledge itself can be redefined. In the process we are encouraged to leave behind, to forget and erase the assumptions we have held previously and see that the desire to find a single transcendent answer can result in woefully narrow readings, if not actual misreadings. So now we are free to address the text in a totally different way, exploring its fabric rather than attempting to lift the veil – for we are no longer concerned to see the face beneath, even if we still believe that there is one. For this is not a circular text in the same way that *Pearl* is. The end of *Pearl* closes the circle and brings the text back to the beginning as a perfectly enclosed text. Yet in *Piers Plowman* all that this process does is to send us back again, endlessly,

---

[17] de Man, *Rhetoric*, p. 122.

upon the same quest, but entering this time in a different place to search from a different perspective. For at the end of the poem we, like Conscience, return to seek Piers the Plowman, and it is the Dreamer who finally escapes by leaving the sphere of his dream and waking for the last time.

This constant repetitive process is what de Man terms 'a madness of words' which 'no degree of knowledge can ever stop'.[18] For knowledge is a part of the madness, just as madness has been shown to be a type of wisdom, not a cure for it. What is left is the realisation that reading, like writing, is a strategy for dealing with what ultimately cannot be controlled and it must be treated as such if it is not to gain a false control over us. It is a means, or rather a variety of means, which have no value except those we choose to give them at any one time. Accordingly, Langland returns us to the poem to begin again the process of reading and interpretation, seeking a Piers who has long since ceased to be a ploughman, through a language which can no longer be regarded as secure.

[18] de Man, *Rhetoric*, p. 122.

BIBLIOGRAPHY

Editions of Piers Plowman

Bennett, J.A.W. *Langland, 'Piers Plowman'. The Prologue and Passus I–VII of the B Text*. Oxford, 1972.

Kane, G. and Donaldson, E.T. *Piers Plowman: The B Version. Will's Vision of Piers Plowman, Do-Wel, Do-Better and Do-Best*. London, 1975.

Pearsall, D. *'Piers Plowman' by William Langland: An Edition of the C-Text*. York Medieval Texts, 2nd series. London, 1981.

Schmidt, A.V.C. *The Vision of Piers Plowman: A Complete Edition of the B-Text*. London, Melbourne and Toronto, 1978.

Primary Sources

Abelard, *Sic et Non: A Critical Edition*. Ed. Boyer, B.B and McKeon, R. Chicago and London, 1976.

Alan of Lille (Alanus de Insulis). *Anticlaudianus*. Ed. Bossuat, R. Paris, 1955.

———. *Alan of Lille, Anticlaudianus*. Tr. Sheridan, J.J. Toronto, 1973.

———. *The Art of Preaching*. Tr. Evans G. Cistercian Studies, Series 23. Kalamazoo, Michigan, 1981.

Alexander of Hales. *Summa Theologica*. Quaracchi, 1924–48.

———. Tr. 'Sum of Theology', *Medieval Literary Theory and Criticism c.1100–c.1375: The Commentary Tradition*. Eds. Minnis, A.J. and Scott, A.B. Oxford, 1988.

An Alphabet of Tales: A Fifteenth-Century Translation of the 'Alphabetum Narrationum' Once Attributed to Etienne de Besançon. Ed. McLeod Banks, M. EETS o.s. 126–27, printed as one volume. London, 1905.

'The Annunciation and Visitation (The Spicers' Play)'. *York Plays*. Ed. Beadle, R. York Medieval Texts, 2nd series. London, 1982, pp. 110–17.

Anonymous of Bologna. *Rationes Dictandi* (1135). Tr. Murphy, J.J., *Three Medieval Rhetorical Arts*. Ed. Murphy, J.J. Berkeley, Los Angeles and London, 1971.

233

'Apocalypsis Goliae Episcopi'. *Latin Poems Commonly Attributed to Walter Mapes*. Ed. Wright, T. Camden Society, Old Series 16. London: Camden Society, 1841.

Aquinas, Thomas. *'De Regimine Principum'*, *'Commentum in X Libros Ethicorum'*. Ed. D'Entréves, A.P.; tr. Dawson, J.G., in *Aquinas' Selected Political Writings*. Oxford, 1959.

Augustine. *Confessiones. CCSL*, 28.

———. *Augustine: Confessions*. Tr. Pine-Coffin, R.S. Harmonsworth, 1961.

———. *De Dialecta*. Ed. Pinborg, J. Tr. Jackson, B.D. Dordrecht, 1975.

———. *De Doctrina Christiana. CCSL*, 32. Ed. Martin, J.

———. *On Christian Doctrine*. Tr. Robertson, D.W. Indianapolis, 1980.

———. *De Magistro. CCSL*, 29. Ed. Daur, K-D.

———. 'The Teacher', in *Augustine's Earlier Writings*. Tr. Burleigh, J.H.S. Library of Christian Classics 6. London, 1953.

———. *De Trinitate. CCSL*, 50. Eds. Mountain, W.J. and Fr. Glorie.

———. *The Trinity*. Tr. McKenna, The Fathers of the Christian Church vol. 45. Washington, 1963.

Bacon, F. 'Novum Organum', in *The Works of Francis Bacon Lord Chancellor of England: A New Edition*. Ed. and tr. Basil Montague. London, 1831. vol. 19.

Bacon, Roger. *The Opus Majus of Roger Bacon*. Ed. Bridges, J.H. 2 vols. Frankfurt, Main, 1964.

———. *Roger Bacon's 'Opus Majus'*. Tr. Burke, R.B. New York, 1962.

Balbus, Giovanni de. *Catholicon*. Mainz, 1460; rp. Aldershot, 1971.

Boethius of Dacia. 'On The Supreme Good', 'On Dreams', in *Boethius of Dacia*. Tr. Wippel, J.F. Medieval Sources in Translation 30. Toronto, 1987.

Bonaventure. *S. Bonaventurae Opera Omnia*. Quaracchi, 1882–1902.

———. *Breviloquium*. Tr. Nemmers, E.E. St Louis and London, 1946.

———. 'Commentary on Peter Lombard's Sentences'. Tr. in *Medieval Literary Theory and Criticism c.1100–c.1375: The Commentary Tradition*. Eds. Minnis, A.J. and Scott, A.B. Oxford, 1988.

———. *'Itinerarium Mentis in Deum': The Mind's Road to God*. Tr. Boas, G. Indianapolis, 1953.

'The Book of Privy Counselling', see under Hodgson, P.

The Book of Vices and Virtues. Ed. Holthausen, F. EETS o.s. 89, 159. London, 1888.

Charland, Th.-M. *Artes Praedicandi*, Publications de l'institut d'études medievales d'Ottawa. Paris and Ottawa, 1936.

Chaucer, Geoffrey. *The Riverside Chaucer*, 3rd edn. Ed. Benson, L.D. Oxford, 1987.

Cicero (attrib.). *Ad Herennium*. Ed. and tr. Caplan, H. Loeb Classics. London, 1954.

———. *De Inventione*. Ed. and tr. Hubbell, H.M. Loeb Classics. London, 1960.

'The Cloud of Unknowyng' see under Hodgson, P.

Le Débat Sur 'Le Roman de la Rose'. Ed. Hicks, E. Bibliothèque de XVe Siècle XLIII. Paris, 1977.

'Deonise Hid Divinite', see under Hodgson, P.

Eckhart, J. *Meister Eckhart Predigten*. Deutsche Werke I. Ed. Band, E. Stuttgart, Berlin, 1936–58.

———. *Master Eckhart: Teacher and Preacher*. Ed. McGinn, B. Classics of Western Spirituality. New York and Toronto, 1986.

Gallus, Thomas. 'Extractio on Dionysius' Celestial Hierarchy'. Tr. in *Medieval Literary Theory and Criticism c.1100–c.1375: The Commentary Tradition*. Eds. Minnis, A.J. and Scott, A.B. Oxford, 1988.

Geoffrey of Vinsauf. *Poetria Nova*. Ed. Gallo, E. *The Poetria Nova and its Sources in Early Rhetorical Doctrine*. Paris, 1971.

———. 'Poetria Nova'. Tr. Kopp, J.B., in *Three Medieval Rhetorical Arts*. Ed. Murphy, J.J. Berkeley, Los Angeles and London, 1971, pp. 29–108.

Giles of Rome. '*In Cantica Canticorum*', printed in *S. Aquinatis Opera Omnia*. Parma, 1852–72. XIV, 387–9.

———. 'Commentary of the Song of Songs'. Tr. *Medieval Literary Theory and Criticism c.1100–c.1375: The Commentary Tradition*. Eds. Minnis, A.J. and Scott, A.B. Oxford, 1988.

Glossa Ordinaria. See under Nicholas of Lyra.

Henry of Ghent. *Summa Quaestionum Ordinariarum*. Franciscan Institute, Text Series 5, vols. 1 and 2 of 5. Paris, 1520: rpt. New York, 1953.

Hilton, W. *The Scale of Perfection*, Book 1. Ed. Wykes, B.E. 1957, rpt; Michigan, 1984.

———. 'An Edition from the Manuscripts of Book 2 of Walter Hilton's *The Scale of Perfection*'. Ed. Hussey, S.S. Ph.D. thesis, University of London, 1962.

Hodgson, P. ed. 'Þe Book of Priuy Counseling', 'Þe Cloud of Vnknowyng', 'Deonise Hid Divinite', 'A Treatyse of Þe Stodye of Wysdome þat men clepen Beniamyn', in *The Cloud of Unknowyng and Related Treatises*. Analecta Cartusiana 3. Salzburg and Exeter, 1982.

Jacobus de Voragine. *Legenda Aurea*. Ed. Graesse, T. 3rd edn. Leipzig, 1890; rpt. Osnabrück, 1969.

Jerome. '*Epistula ad Paulinam or The Epistle of Seynt Ierome*, in MS. Bodley 959 Genesis-Baruch 3.20 in the Earlier Version of the Wycliffite Bible'. Ed. Lindberg, C. Stockholm, 1959, vol. 1.

John Bromyard (Johannes de Bromyard). *Distinctiones*. Bodleian MS. Bodl. 59. *Summa Predicantium*. Nuremberg, 1518.

Lorris, Guillaume de and Meun, Jean de. *Le Roman de la Rose*. Ed. Langlois, E. Paris: Didot and Champion, Société des anciens textes français, 1914–24, 5 vols.

———. *The Romance of the Rose*. Tr. Dahlberg, C. Hanover and London, 1986.

Love, Nicholas. *The Myrrour of the Blessed Life of Jesu Christ*. Ed. by a monk of Parkminster. London, 1926.

'Mundus et Infans'. *Three Late Medieval Morality Plays*. Ed. Lester, G.A. London, 1981, pp. 106–57.

Nicholas of Cusa. *De Docta Ignorantia testo Latino*. Ed. Rotta, P. Bari, 1913.

———. *Nicholas of Cusa: On Learned Ignorance*. Ed. and tr. Hopkins, J. Minneapolis, 1981.

Nicholas of Lyra. *Sacra bibla cum glossa ordinaria et expositione lyre litterali et morali*. 7 vols. Petri, J. and Froben, J., 1508.

The Pilgrimage of the Lyf of Manhode. Ed. Henry, A. EETS o.s. 288. London, 1985.

Pizan, Christine de. *The Book of the City of Ladies*. Tr. Richards, E.J. London, 1983.

The Pricke of Conscience (attrib. Rolle). Ed. Morris, R. New York, 1973, reprint of 1863.

'La Querelle de la Rose': Letters and Documents. Eds. Baird, J. and Kane, J. N. Carolina Studies in the Romance Languages and Literatures 119. Chapel Hill, 1978.

Richard of St Victor. *Benjamin Minor*. PL, 196.

———. 'The Benjamin Minor or the Twelve Patriarchs', in *Richard of St. Victor: The Twelve Patriarchs; The Mystical Ark; Book Three of the Trinity*. Tr. Zinn, G.A. Classics of Western Spirituality. London, 1979.

Robert of Basevorn. 'Forma Praedicandi', in *Artes Praedicandi: Contribution à l'histoire de la rhetorique au moyen âge*. Ed. Charland, Th.-M. Publications de l'institut d'études médiévales d'Ottawa. Paris and Ottawa, 1936, pp. 231–323.

———. 'Forma Praedicandi'. Tr. Krul, L., in *Three Medieval Rhetorical Arts*. Ed. Murphy, J.J. Berkeley, Los Angeles and London, 1971, pp. 114–215.

Rolle, R. *The English Writings of Richard Rolle*. Ed. Allen, H.E. Oxford, 1931.

———. *De Emendacione Vitae and De Incendio Amoris*. Tr. by Misyn R. in 1435, ed. Harvey R. EETS o.s. 106. London, 1896.

Ruysbroeck, Jan van. *The Seven Steps of the Ladder of Spiritual Love*. Tr. Sherwood Taylor, F. London, 1943.

Saint Erkenwald. Ed. Morse R. Cambridge and Totowa, New Jersey, 1975.

Trevisa, J. *'On the Properties of Things': Trevisa's Translation of Bartholomeus Anglicus 'De Proprietatibus Rerum'*. Ed. Seymour, M.C. 2 vols. Oxford, 1975.

Vincent of Beauvais. *Speculum Morale*. Douai, 1624; facsimile rpt. Graz, 1964.

Wyclif, J. 'De Officio Pastorali', in *Fourteenth Century Verse and Prose*, ed. Sisam, K. Oxford, 1982, pp. 117–19.

———. *Sermones*. Ed. Loserth, J. London, 2 vols. 1887–90.

Bibliography

Secondary Sources

Adams, R. 'Langland and the Liturgy Revisted', *Studies in Philology*, 73 (1976), 266–84.

————. 'Langland's Theology', in *A Companion to 'Piers Plowman'*. Ed. Alford, J. Berkeley, Los Angeles, London, 1988, pp. 87–114.

————. 'Piers' Pardon and Langland's Semi-Pelagianism', *Traditio* 31 (1983), 367–418.

Aers, D. 'Reflections on the "Allegory of the Theologians", Ideology and Piers Plowman', in *Medieval Literature, Criticism, Ideology and History*. Ed. Aers, D. Brighton, 1986, pp. 58–73.

————. Ed. *Medieval Literature, Criticism, Ideology and History*. Brighton, 1986.

Alford, J.A. 'The Idea of Reason in Piers Plowman', in *Medieval English Studies Presented to George Kane*. Ed. Kennedy, E.D., Waldron, R. and Wittig, J.S. Woodbridge, 1988, pp. 199–215.

————. 'Richard Rolle and Related Works', *Middle English: A Critical Guide to Major Authors and Genres*. Ed. Edwards, A.S.G. New Jersey, 1984, pp. 35–60.

————. 'The Role of the Quotations in Piers Plowman', *Speculum*, 52 (1977), 80–99.

————. Ed., *A Companion to 'Piers Plowman'*. Berkeley, Los Angeles, London, 1988.

Allen, J.B. 'Langland's Reading and Writing, Detractor and the Pardon Passus', *Speculum*, 59 (1984), 342–62.

Bakhtin, M. *Rabelais and His World*. Tr. Iswolski, H. Bloomington, Indiana, 1984.

Baldwin, A. *The Theme of Government in 'Piers Plowman'*. Piers Plowman Studies I. Woodbridge, 1981.

Baranski, Z. 'Dante's Biblical Linguistics', *Lectura Dantis* 5 (1989), 105–43.

Barr, H. 'The Use of Latin Quotations in *Piers Plowman* with special reference to Passus XVII of the B-Text', *Notes and Queries*, 33 (1986), 440–48.

Barthes, R. *The Pleasure of the Text*. Tr. Miller, R. New York, 1975.

————. 'Theory of the Text', *Untying the Text*. Ed. Young, R. London, 1981, pp. 31–47.

Beckwith, S. 'A Very Material Mysticism: The Medieval Mysticism of Margery Kempe', in *Medieval Literature, Criticism, Ideology and History*. Ed. Aers, D. Brighton, 1986, pp. 34–57.

Benjamin, W. *Illuminations*. Tr. Zoln, H., ed. Arendt, H. London, 1973.

Bishop, I. 'Relatives at the Court of Heaven: Contrasted Treatments of an Idea in Piers Plowman and Pearl', in *Medieval Literature and Antiquities: Studies in Honour of Basil Cottle*. Ed. Stokes, M. and Burton T.L., Woodbridge, 1987, pp. 111–18.

Bloomfield, M. *'Piers Plowman' as a Fourteenth-Century Apocalypse*, New Brunswick, 1961.

Bourquin, G. 'The Dynamics of the Signans in the Spiritual Quest', in *The Medieval Mystical Tradition in England*. Ed. Glasscoe, M. Exeter, 1982, pp. 182–98.

Burrow, J. 'The Action of Langland's Second Vision', *Essays in Criticism*, 15 (1965), 247–68.

———. 'The Alterity of Medieval Literature', *New Literary History*, 10 (1979), 385–90.

———. *Essays on Medieval Literature*. Oxford, 1984.

———. 'Fantasy and Language in *The Cloud of Unknowyng*', *Essays in Criticism*, 27 (1977), 283–298.

———. 'Words, Works and Will: Theme and Structure in *Piers Plowman*', in *Critical Approaches to 'Piers Plowman'*. Ed. Hussey, S.S. London, 1969, pp. 111–124.

Burton, T.L. 'Defining "Daftness" ', in *Medieval Literature and Antiquies: Studies in Honour of Basil Cottle*. Ed. Stokes, M. and Burton, T.L. Woodbridge, 1987, pp. 165–74.

Carruthers, M. *The Search for St. Truth: A Study in Meaning in 'Piers Plowman'*. Evanston, 1973.

Chambers, R.K. 'Long Will, Dante, and the Righteous Heathen', *Essays and Studies*, n.s. 9 (1954), 50–69.

Chenu, M-D. 'Auctor, Actor, Autor', *Archivum Latinitatis Medii Aevi. Bulletin du Cange* 3, Paris (1927), 81–86.

———. *La théologie comme science au XIIIe siècle*, Bibliothèque Thomiste XXIII, Paris, 1957.

Cixous, H. 'The Laugh of Medusa'. Tr. Cohen, K and Cohen, P., in *New French Feminisms*. Ed. Marks, E. and de Courtivron, I. Brighton, 1980, pp. 245–64.

Clopper, L.M. 'The Contemplative Matrix of *Piers Plowman* B', *Modern Language Quarterly*, March (1985), 3–28.

Coleman, J. *Medieval Readers and Writers: English Literature in History 1350–1400*. Ed. Williams, R. London, 1981.

———. *'Piers Plowman' and the Moderni*. Rome, 1981.

Colish, M. *The Mirror of Language: A Study in Medieval Theory of Knowledge*. New Haven and London, 1968.

Cook, J. 'Carnival and The Canterbury Tales: "only equals may laugh" (Herzen)', in *Medieval Literature, Criticism, Ideology and History*. Ed. Aers D. Brighton, 1986, pp. 169–90

Copeland, R. 'Rhetoric and Vernacular Tradition in the Middle Ages', *Studies in the Age of Chaucer* 9. (1987), pp. 41–75.

Curtius, E.R. *European Literature and the Latin Middle Ages*. Tr. Trask, W.R. London and Henley, 1953.

Davenport, W.A. 'Patterns in Middle English Dialogue' in *Medieval English Studies Presented to George Kane*. Ed. Kennedy, E.D., Waldron, R. and Wittig, J.S. Woodbridge, 1988, pp. 127–45.

Davidson, I. 'The Fool: his Social and Literary Perspective in the Later Middle Ages'. M.A. Dissertation. York, 1983/4.

Davlin, Str. M.C. ' "Kynde Knowyng" as a Major Theme in *Piers Plowman B.*' *Review of English Studies* n.s. 22:85 (1971), 1–19.

———. ' "Kynde Knowyng" as a Middle English Equivalent for Wisdom in *Piers Plowman*', *Medium Aevum* 50 (1981), 5–17.

D'Avray, D. 'The Transformation of the Medieval Sermon'. D.Phil. thesis Oxford, 1976.

———. *The Preaching of the Friars: Sermons diffused from Paris before 1300*. Oxford, 1985.

Delaney, S. ' "Mothers to Think Back Through": Who Are They? The Ambiguous Example of Christine de Pizan', in *Medieval Texts and Contemporary Readers*. Ed. Finke, L.A. and Shichtman, M.B. Ithaca and London, 1987, pp. 177–97.

de Man, P. 'The Epistemology of Metaphor'. *Critical Inquiry*, 5 (1978), 13–30.

———. *The Rhetoric of Romanticism*. New York, 1984.

de Wit, P. 'The Visual Experience of Fifteenth-Century Readers'. D.Phil thesis. Oxford, 1977.

Donaldson, E.T. *'Piers Plowman': The C-Text and its Poet*. Yale Studies in English, vol. 113. New Haven and London, 1949.

Doob, P. *Nebuchadnezzar's Children*. New Haven and London, 1974.

Dunning, Dom. T.P. 'Action and Contemplation in Piers Plowman', in *'Piers Plowman' Critical Approaches*. Ed. Hussey, S.S. London, 1969, pp. 213–220.

———. 'Langland and the Salvation of the Heathen', *Medium Aevum* 12 (1943), 45–54.

Evans, G.R. 'The Borrowed Meaning: Grammar, Logic and the Problem of Theological Language in Twelfth-Century Schools'. *The Downside Review*, 96 (1978), 165–75.

Ferster, J. 'Interpretation and Imitation in Chaucer's Franklyn's Tale', in *Medieval Literature, Criticism, Ideology and History*. Ed. Aers D. Brighton, 1986, pp. 148–68.

Finke, L.A. and Shichtman, M.B. eds. *Medieval Texts and Contemporary Readers*. Ithaca and London, 1987.

Fleming, J.V. *Reason and the Lover*. New Jersey, 1984.

Fletcher, D. *Praise of Folly*. Inaugural Lecture for Durham University. Durham, 1981.

Flower, R. *The Irish Tradition*. Oxford, 1947.

Foucault, M. *The History of Sexuality Volume One*. Tr. Hurly, R. Harmondsworth, 1979.

———. *Madness and Civilisation: A History of Insanity in the Age of Reason*. Tr. Howard, R. London, 1987.

———. 'The Order of Discourse', in *Untying the Text: A Post-Structuralist Reader*. Ed. Young, R. Boston and London, 1981, pp. 48–78.

Frank, R.W. 'The Pardon Scene in Piers Plowman'. *Speculum*, 26 (1951), 317–31.

Gadamer, H-G. 'The Historicity of Understanding as Hermeneutic Principle', *Heidegger and Modern Philosophy*. Ed. Murray, M. New Haven and London, 1978, pp. 161–84.

Gash, A. 'Carnival Against Lent: the Ambivalence of Medieval Drama', in *Medieval Literature, Criticism, Ideology and History*. Ed. Aers, D. Brighton, 1986, pp. 74–98.

Gellrich, J.M. *The Idea of the Book in the Middle Ages: Language Theory, Mythology and Fiction*. Ithaca and London, 1985.

Geremet, B. *The Margins of Society in Late Medieval Paris*. Tr. Birrell, J. Cambridge, 1987.

Gillespie, V. 'Mystic's foot: Rolle and Affectivity', *The Medieval Mystical Tradition in England*. Ed. Glasscoe M. Exeter, 1982, pp. 199–230.

Goldsmith, M. *The Figure of Piers Plowman: the Image on the Coin*, Piers Plowman Studies II. Woodbridge, 1981.

———. 'Wil's Pilgrimage in Piers Plowman B', in *Medieval Literature and Antiquities: Studies in Honour of Basil Cottle*. Ed. Stokes, M. and Burton, T.L. Woodbridge, 1987, pp. 119–32.

Godden, M. *The Development of 'Piers Plowman'*. London, 1992.

———. 'Plowmen and Hermits in Langland's *Piers Plowman*', *Review of English Studies*, n.s. 34 (1984), 129-63.

Gradon, P. 'Langland and the Ideology of Dissent', Gollancz Memorial Lecture. *Proceedings of the British Academy* 66, 1980, pp. 179–205.

Harwood, B.J. ' "Imaginative" in *Piers Plowman*', *Medium Aevum*, 44 (1975), 249–63.

Heffernan, T.J. 'Sermon Literature', in *Middle English Prose: A Critical Guide to Major Authors and Genres*. Ed. Edwards, A.S.G. New Jersey, 1984, pp. 177–208.

Heidegger, M. *On The Way to Language*. Tr. Hertz, P.D. London, 1971.

Howell, K. 'Two Aspects of Roger Bacon's Semiotic Theory in *De Signis*', *Semiotica*, 63, 1/2 (1987), 73–81.

Hurnard, N. *The King's Pardon for Homicide Before 1307*. Oxford, 1969.

Hussey, S.S. 'Langland, Hilton, and the Three Lives', *Review of English Studies* n.s. 8 (1956), 132–150.

———. Ed. *'Piers Plowman', Critical Approaches to 'Piers Plowman'*. London, 1969

Irvine, M. 'A Guide to the Sources of Medieval Theories of Interpretation, Signs and the Arts of Discourse: Aristotle to Ockham', *Semiotica*, 63 (1987), 89–108.

Jones, H.S.V. 'Imaginatif in Piers Plowman', *JEGP*, 13 (1914), 583–88.

Josipovici, G. *The World and the Book*. London, 1979.

Kane, G. 'The Text', in *A Companion to 'Piers Plowman'*. Ed. Alford, J. Berkeley, Los Angeles and London, 1988, pp. 175–20.

Kaske, R.E. 'The Character of Hunger in *Piers Plowman*', in *Medieval English Studies Presented to George Kane*. Ed. Kennedy, E.D., Waldron, R. and Wittig, J.S. Woodbridge, 1988, pp. 187–197.

Kaulbach, E.N. 'The *Vis Imaginativa Secundum Avicennum* and the Naturally Prophetic Powers of Ymaginatif in the B-Text of *Piers Plowman*'. *JEGP*, 86 (1987), 496–514.

Kennedy, E.D., Waldron, R. and Wittig, J.S. eds. *Medieval English Studies Presented to George Kane*. Woodbridge, 1988.

Kerby-Fulton, K. 'The Voice of Honest Indignation: A Study of Reformist Apocalypticism in Relation to *Piers Plowman*'. D.Phil. York, 1985.

Lawton, D. 'The Subject of *Piers Plowman*', in *Yearbook of Langland Studies*, 1 (1987), 1–30.

Leclercq, Dom. J. 'Le Magistère du Prédicateur au XIIe Siècle', *AHDLMA*, 21 (1946), 105–47.

Lees, R.A. *The Negative Language of the Dionysian School of Mystical Theology: An Approach to 'The Cloud of Unknowing'*, Analecta Cartusiana 107. Salzburg and Exeter, 1983.

Leonardi, C. 'Intellectuals and Hagiography in the Fourteenth Century', in *Intellectuals and Writers in Fourteenth-Century Europe: The J.A.W. Bennett Memorial Lectures*. Ed. Boitani, P. and Torti, A. Tübingen and Cambridge, 1986, pp. 7–21.

Lewis, E. 'Natural Law and Expediency in Medieval Political Theory', *Ethics*, 50 (1939–40), 144–63.

Lochre, K. 'The Book of Margery Kempe: The Marginal Woman's Quest for Literary Authority', *Journal for Medieval and Renaissance Studies*, 16 (1986), 33–55.

McKeon, R. 'Rhetoric in the Middle Ages', *Speculum*, 17 (1942), 1–29.

Maisonneuve, R. 'Margery Kempe and the Eastern and Western Tradition of the "Perfect Fool" ', *The Medieval Mystical Tradition in England*. Ed. Glasscoe, M. Exeter, 1982, pp. 1–17.

Mann, J. *Chaucer and Medieval Estates Satire*. Cambridge, 1973.

——. 'Eating and Drinking in Piers Plowman', *Essays and Studies*, n.s. 32 (1979), 26–43.

Marrone, S.P. 'Henry of Ghent and Duns Scotus on the Knowledge of Being', *Speculum*, 63 (1988), 22–57.

Middleton, A. 'The Audience and Public of *Piers Plowman*', in *Middle English Alliterative Poetry and its Background*. Ed. Lawton, D.A. Cambridge, 1982, pp. 100–23.

——. 'The Idea of Public Poetry in the Reign of Richard II', *Speculum*, 53 (1978), 94–114.

——. 'Two Infinities: Grammatical Metaphor in *Piers Plowman*', *ELH*, 39 (1972), 169–88.

———. 'The Passion of Seint Averoys [B.13.19]: "Deuynyng" and Divinity in the Banquet Scene', *Yearbook of Langland Studies*, 1 (1987), 31–40.

Minnis, A.J. 'Affection and Imagination in *The Cloud of Unknowyng* and Hilton's *Scale of Perfection*', *Traditio*, 39 (1983), 323–65.

———. 'Chaucer's Pardoner and the "Office of Preacher" ', in *Intellectuals and Writers in Fourteenth-Century Europe*. Ed. Boitani, P. and Torti, A. Tübingen and Cambridge, 1986, pp. 88–119.

———. 'Langland's Ymaginatif and Late Medieval Theories of Imagination', *Comparative Criticism*, 3 (1981), 71–103.

———. *Medieval Theories of Authorship*, 2nd edn. Aldershot, 1988.

Minnis, A.J. and Scott, A.B. eds. with the assistance of D. Wallace. *Medieval Literary Theory and Criticism: c.1100–c.1375: The Commentary Tradition*. Oxford, 1988.

Murphy, J.J. ed. *Three Medieval Rhetorical Arts*. Berkeley, Los Angeles and London, 1971.

———. *Rhetoric in the Middle Ages: A History of Rhetorical Theory*. Berkeley, Los Angeles and London, 1974.

Neale, R.A. 'The Fool and His Loaf', *Medium Aevum*, 54 (1985), 104–109.

Newhauser, R. 'Augustinian *Vitium Curiositatis* and its Reception', *St. Augustine and His Influence in the Middle Ages*. Ed. King, E.B. and Schaefer, J.T. Sewanee, 1989, pp. 39–124.

Oberman, H. 'Fourteenth-Century Religious Thought: A Premature Profile', *Speculum*, 53 (1978), 80–93.

———. *The Harvest of Medieval Theology: Gabriel Biel and Late Medieval Nominalism*. Cambridge, Mass., 1963.

Owst, G.R. *Literature and the Pulpit in Medieval England*, 2nd edn. Oxford, 1961.

Patterson, L. *Negotiating the Past: The Historical Understanding of Medieval Literature*. London and Wisconsin, 1987.

Peck, R.A. 'Chaucer and the Nominalist Questions', *Speculum*, 53 (1978), 745–60.

Peden, A.M. 'Macrobius and Medieval Dream Literature', *Medium Aevum*, 54 (1985), 59–73.

Phillips, J.C. 'Style and Meaning in Piers Plowman', D.Phil. thesis. York, 1985.

Pollock, F. 'The History of the Law of Nature: A Primary Study', *Journal of the Society of Comparative Legislature* 2, 1900, pp. 418–33.

Quirk, R. '*Vis Imaginativa*', *JEGP*, 53 (1953), 81–83.

Rand, E.K. 'The Classics in the Thirteenth Century', *Speculum*, 4 (1929), 249–69.

Rouse, R.H. and M.A. 'Biblical Distinctions in the Thirteenth Century', *AHDLMA*, 41 (1975), 27–37.

———. *Preachers, Florilegia and Sermons: Studies on the 'Manipulus Florum' of Thomas of Ireland*. Studies and Texts 47. Toronto, 1979.

Salter, E. 'Langland – Contexts of Piers Plowman', *Essays and Studies* n.s. 32, (1979), 19–26.

———. *English and International: Studies in the Literature, Art and Patronage of Medieval England*. Ed. Pearsall, D. and Zeeman, N. Cambridge, 1988.

Scase, W. *'Piers Plowman' and the New Anticlericalism*, Cambridge Studies in Medieval Literature 4. Cambridge, 1989.

Schless, H.H. 'Fourteenth-Century *Imitatio* and *Piers Plowman*', in *Intellectuals and Writers in Fourteenth-Century Europe*. Ed. Boitani, P. and Torti, A. Tübingen and Woodbridge, 1984, pp. 164–77.

Schmidt, A.V.C. *The Clerkly Maker: Langland's Poetic Art*, Piers Plowman Studies IV. Woodbridge, 1987.

———. 'The Inner Dreams in Piers Plowman', *Medium Aevum*, 55 (1986), 24–40.

Shoaf, R.A. ' "Speche Þat Spire is of Grace": A Note on *Piers Plowman* B.9.104', *Yearbook of Langland Studies*, 1 (1987), 128–33.

Simpson, J. 'From Reason to Affective Knowledge: Modes of Thought and Poetic Expression in *Piers Plowman*', *Medium Aevum*, 55 (1986), 1–23.

———. *'Piers Plowman': An Introduction to the B-Text*. London, 1990.

———. 'The Role of *Scientia* in *Piers Plowman*', in *Middle English Religious and Ethical Literature; Essays in Honour of G.H. Russell*. Ed. Kratzmann, G. and Simpson, J. Woodbridge, 1986, pp. 49–55.

———. 'Spiritual and Earthly Nobility in *Piers Plowman*', *Neuphilologische Mitteilungen* 86 (1985), 467-81.

———. 'The Transformation of Meaning: A Figure of Thought in *Piers Plowman*', *Review of English Studies* n.s. 37 (1986), 161-83.

Smalley, B. *Studies in Medieval Thought and Learning from Abelard to Wyclif*. London, 1981.

———. *The Study of the Bible in the Middle Ages*. Oxford, 1952.

Spearing, A.C. *Criticism and Medieval Poetry*. London, 1964.

———. Ed. *Readings in Medieval Poetry*. Cambridge, 1987.

Steele, F.J. 'Definitions and Depictions of the Active Life in Middle English Religious Literature of the Thirteenth to Fifteenth Centuries, Including Special Reference to *Piers Plowman*', D.Phil. Oxford, 1979.

Steiner, G. *After Babel*. Oxford, 1975.

———. *Language and Silence: Essays on Language, Literature, and the Inhuman*. New York, 1977.

———. *Real Presences: Is There Anything In What We Say?* London, 1989.

Stokes, M. *Justice and Mercy in 'Piers Plowman'. A Reading of the B-Text Visio*. London, 1984.

Swanson, R.N. 'Langland and the Priest's Title', *Notes and Queries*, 33 (1986), 438–40.

Szittya, P.R. *The Antifraternal Tradition in Medieval Literature*. Princeton, 1986.

Taylor, R. *The Political Prophecy in England*. New York, 1911.

Todorov, T. *An Introduction to Poetics*. Tr. Howard, R. Brighton, 1981.

Torrell, J-P. *Théorie de la prophétie et philosophie de la connaissance aux environs de 1230: La Contribution d'Hughes de Saint-Cher*, Spicilegium Sacrum Louvaniense 40. Louvain, 1977.

Turville-Petre, T. *The Alliterative Revival*. Woodbridge, 1977.

Vance, E. 'Mervelous Signs: Poetics, Sign Theory and Politics in Chaucer's Troilus', *New Literary History*, 10 (1979), 293–337.

Welsford, E. *The Fool, His Social and Literary History*. London, 1938.

Wenzel, S. 'Chaucer and the Language of Contemporary Preaching', *Studies in Philology*, 73 (1976), 138–54.

White, H. 'Langland's Ymaginatif, Kynde Wit and the *Benjamin Major*', *Medium Aevum*, 55 (1986), 241–48.

Wirtjes, H. '*Piers Plowman* B.XVIII.371: Right ripe must', in *Medieval Literature and Antiquities: Studies in Honour of Basil Cottle*. Ed. Stokes, M. and Burton, T.L. Woodbridge, 1987, pp. 133–44.

Wittig, J.S. '*Piers Plowman* B Passus IX–XII: Elements in the Design of the Inward Journey', *Traditio*, 28 (1972), 211–80.

Young, R. ed. *Untying the Text: A Post-Structuralist Reader*. Boston and London, 1981.

Index